Mary Jones, Diane Fellowes-Freeman and David Sang

Cambridge Checkpoint
Science

Coursebook

7

CAMBRIDGE
UNIVERSITY PRESS

University Printing House, Cambridge CB2 8BS, United Kingdom

One Liberty Plaza, 20th Floor, New York, NY 10006, USA

477 Williamstown Road, Port Melbourne, VIC 3207, Australia

4843/24, 2nd Floor, Ansari Road, Daryaganj, Delhi – 110002, India

79 Anson Road, #06–04/06, Singapore 079906

Cambridge University Press is part of the University of Cambridge.

It furthers the University's mission by disseminating knowledge in the pursuit of education, learning and research at the highest international levels of excellence.

Information on this title: education.cambridge.org

© Cambridge University Press 2012

This publication is in copyright. Subject to statutory exception and to the provisions of relevant collective licensing agreements, no reproduction of any part may take place without the written permission of Cambridge University Press.

First published 2012
20

Printed in Malaysia by Vivar Printing

A catalogue record for this publication is available from the British Library

ISBN 978-1-107-61333-1 Paperback

Cambridge University Press has no responsibility for the persistence or accuracy of URLs for external or third-party internet websites referred to in this publication, and does not guarantee that any content on such websites is, or will remain, accurate or appropriate.

NOTICE TO TEACHERS

References to Activities contained in these resources are provided 'as is' and information provided is on the understanding that teachers and technicians shall undertake a thorough and appropriate risk assessment before undertaking any of the Activities listed. Cambridge University Press makes no warranties, representations or claims of any kind concerning the Activities. To the extent permitted by law, Cambridge University Press will not be liable for any loss, injury, claim, liability or damage of any kind resulting from the use of the Activities.

Introduction

Welcome to your Cambridge Secondary 1 Science course!

This book covers the first year, Stage 7, of the Cambridge Secondary 1 Science curriculum. At the end of the year, your teacher may ask you to take a test called a Progression Test. This book will help you to learn how to be a good scientist, and to do well in the test.

The main areas of science

The book is divided into three main sections, each one dealing with one of three main areas of science. These are:

Biology – the study of living organisms

Chemistry – the study of the substances from which the Earth and the rest of the Universe are made

Physics – the study of the nature and properties of matter, energy and forces.

There are no sharp dividing lines between these three branches of science. You will find many overlaps between them.

Learning to be a scientist

During your course, you will learn a lot of facts and information. You will also begin to learn to think like a scientist.

Scientists collect information and do experiments to try to find out how things work. You will learn how to plan an experiment to try to find out the answer to a question. You will learn how to record your results, and how to use them to make a conclusion.

When you see this symbol **SE**, it means that the task will help you to develop your scientific enquiry skills.

Using your knowledge

It's important to learn facts and scientific ideas as you go through your science course. But it is just as important to be able to **use** these facts and ideas.

When you see this symbol **A+I**, it means that you are being asked to use your knowledge to work out an answer. You will have to think hard to find the answer for yourself, using the science that you have learnt. (A+I stands for Applications and Implications.)

Contents

Introduction   3

Biology

Unit 1 Plants and humans as organisms
1.1	Plant organs	6
1.2	Human organ systems	8
1.3	The human skeleton	10
1.4	Joints	12
1.5	Muscles	14
1.6	Studying the human body	16
	End of unit questions	18

Unit 2 Cells and organisms
2.1	Characteristics of living organisms	20
2.2	Micro-organisms	22
2.3	Micro-organisms and decay	24
2.4	Micro-organisms and food	26
2.5	Micro-organisms and disease	28
2.6	Plant cells	30
2.7	Animal cells	32
2.8	Cells, tissues and organs	34
	End of unit questions	36

Unit 3 Living things in their environment
3.1	Adaptations	38
3.2	Food chains	40
3.3	Humans and food chains	42
3.4	Pollution	44
3.5	Ozone depletion	46
3.6	Conservation	48
3.7	Energy resources	50
	End of unit questions	52

Unit 4 Variation and classification
4.1	What is a species?	54
4.2	Variation in a species	56
4.3	Investigating variation	58
4.4	Classifying plants	60
4.5	Classifying vertebrates	62
4.6	Classifying invertebrates	64
	End of unit questions	66

Chemistry

Unit 5 States of matter
5.1	States of matter	68
5.2	Particle theory	70
5.3	Changing state	72
5.4	Explaining changes of state	75
	End of unit questions	78

Unit 6 Material properties
6.1	Metals	80
6.2	Non-metals	82
6.3	Comparing metals and non-metals	84
6.4	Everyday materials and their properties	86
	End of unit questions	88

Unit 7 Material changes
7.1	Acids and alkalis	90
7.2	Is it an acid or an alkali?	92
7.3	The pH scale	94
7.4	Neutralisation	96
7.5	Neutralisation in action	98
7.6	Investigating acids and alkalis	100
	End of unit questions	102

Unit 8 The Earth
8.1	Rocks, minerals and soils	104
8.2	Soil	106
8.3	Igneous rocks	108
8.4	Sedimentary rocks	110
8.5	Metamorphic rocks	112
8.6	Weathering	114
8.7	Moving rocks	116
8.8	Fossils	118
8.9	The fossil record	120
8.10	The structure and age of the Earth	122
8.11	The geological timescale	124
	End of unit questions	126

Contents

Physics

Unit 9 Forces and motion

9.1	Seeing forces	128
9.2	Forces big and small	131
9.3	Weight – the pull of gravity	134
9.4	Friction – an important force	136
9.5	Air resistance	138
9.6	Patterns of falling	140
	End of unit questions	142

Unit 10 Energy

10.1	Using energy	144
10.2	Chemical stores of energy	146
10.3	More energy stores	148
10.4	Thermal energy	150
10.5	Kinetic energy	152
10.6	Energy on the move	154
10.7	Energy changing form	156
10.8	Energy is conserved	158
	End of unit questions	160

Unit 11 The Earth and beyond

11.1	Day and night	162
11.2	The starry skies	164
11.3	The moving planets	166
11.4	Seeing stars and planets	168
11.5	The Moon and its phases	170
11.6	A revolution in astronomy	172
11.7	400 years of astronomy	174
11.8	Journey into space	176
	End of unit questions	178

Reference

Laboratory apparatus	180
Units	181
How to measure a length	181
How to measure a temperature	182
How to measure a volume of liquid	182
How to construct a results table	183
How to draw a line graph	184
Glossary and index	185
Acknowledgements	191

1.1 Plant organs

This map shows where plants cover the surface of the Earth. The map was made using information collected by a space satellite.

- ■ rainforest
- ■ grassland and forest
- ■ desert
- □ ice

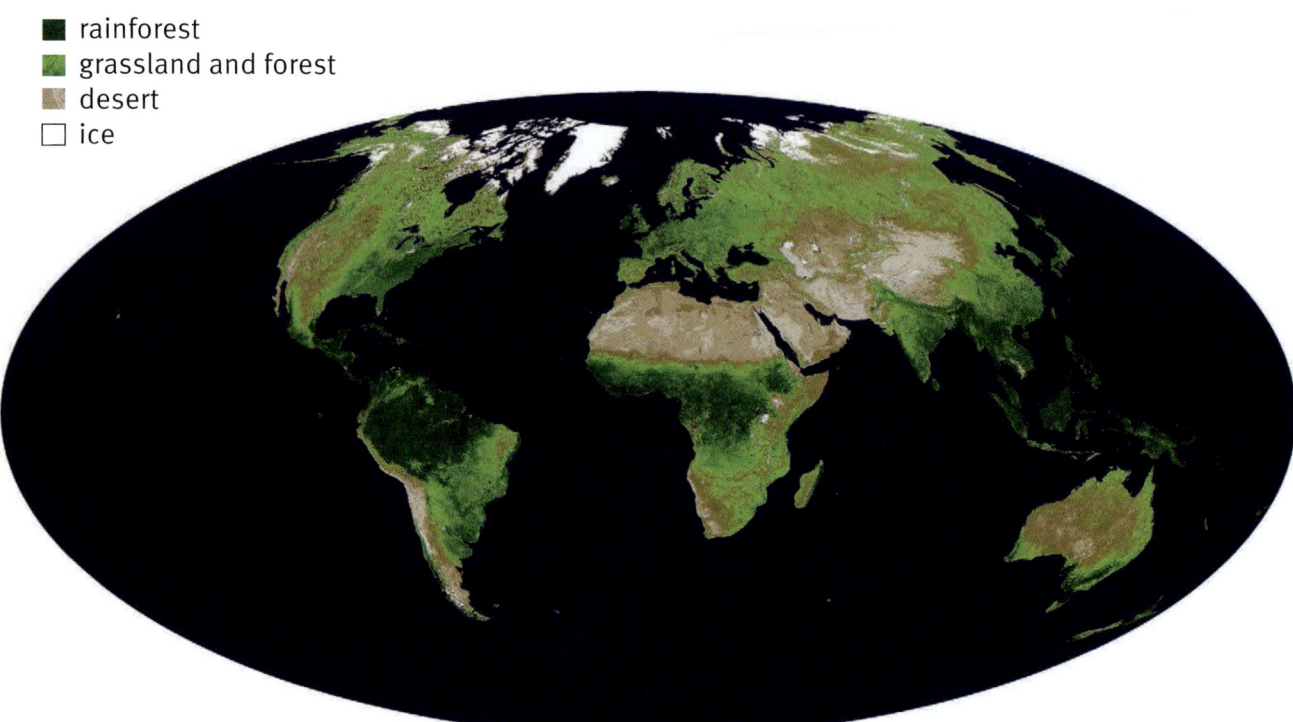

Most plants are green. This is because they contain a green pigment (colouring) called **chlorophyll**. Chlorophyll absorbs (takes in) energy from sunlight.

Plants use this energy to make food. All the food that is eaten by animals was originally made by plants.

Plants give out oxygen during the daytime. The oxygen in the air, which almost all living things need to stay alive, was all made by plants.

Questions

1 Look at the map. Explain why some parts of the map are shown in dark green, and some parts are light green.
2 There are very few plants in the brown parts of the map. Suggest why there are not many plants in these places.
3 Find the place where you live on the map.
   a What does the map tell you about the plants that cover the part of the world where you live?
   b Do you agree with the information on the map about your part of the world? Explain your answer.
4 Animals can only live on Earth because there are plants on Earth. Explain why.

1 Plants and humans as organisms

1.1 Plant organs

The structure of a plant

A plant is a living thing. Another word for a living thing is an **organism**.

The parts of an organism are called **organs**. The diagram shows some of the organs in a flowering plant.

Flowers are reproductive organs. They produce seeds, which can grow into new plants.

Leaves are the food factories of the plant. They absorb energy from sunlight, and use it to make food.

The stem holds the leaves and flowers above the ground.

The roots hold the plant firmly in the soil. They absorb water and minerals from the soil.

Questions

A+I 5 Why do you think roots branch out into the soil? You may be able to think of two reasons.

A+I 6 Suggest why many leaves are very broad and thin.

Activity 1.1
Pressing a plant

Your teacher will help you to find a complete, small plant.

1 Wash the roots of your plant carefully. Try to get rid of all the soil, but don't damage the roots.
2 Carefully place the plant on a sheet of newspaper. Spread it out so that all of its parts are as flat as you can make them.
3 Put another sheet of newspaper over the top of your plant. Put a heavy weight on it to press the plant flat.
4 Leave your plant for at least a week to dry out.
5 Put your plant into your notebook and stick it down with some strips of sticky tape. Label the different organs, and write down what each of them does.

Summary
- Roots hold a plant in the ground and absorb water and minerals.
- Leaves absorb sunlight and make food.
- Flowers are reproductive organs.
- The stem holds the leaves and flowers above the ground.

1 Plants and humans as organisms

1.2 Human organ systems

We have seen that the different parts of plants are called **organs**. Animals also have organs.

For example, an eye is an organ. The heart is an organ, and so is the brain.

The organs in a human work together in teams. A group of organs that work together is called an **organ system**.

The digestive system

When you eat or drink, food goes into your digestive system. This is a long tube that runs all the way through the body. Food usually takes between one and three days to travel from one end of the tube to the other.

Most of the food is broken down into tiny particles inside the digestive system. The breaking down is called **digestion**. The tiny particles move out of the digestive system, through its walls. They move into the blood. The blood carries them to every part of the body.

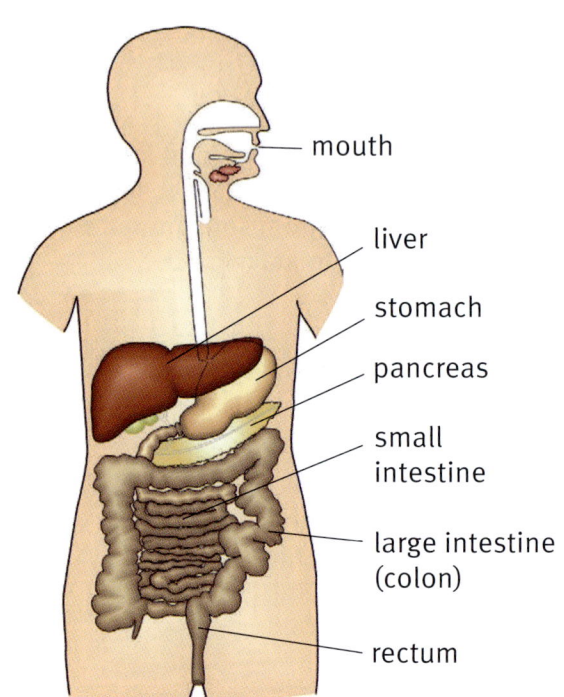

Questions

1. Look at the diagram of the digestive system. Write down, in order, the organs that food passes through as it moves through the digestive system.
2. Some of the food you eat is **not** broken down into tiny particles in the digestive system. Suggest what happens to the food that is not broken down.

The circulatory system

The circulatory system transports substances all over the body. It is made up of tubes called **blood vessels**. These tubes contain blood. The blood is pumped around the circulatory system by the heart.

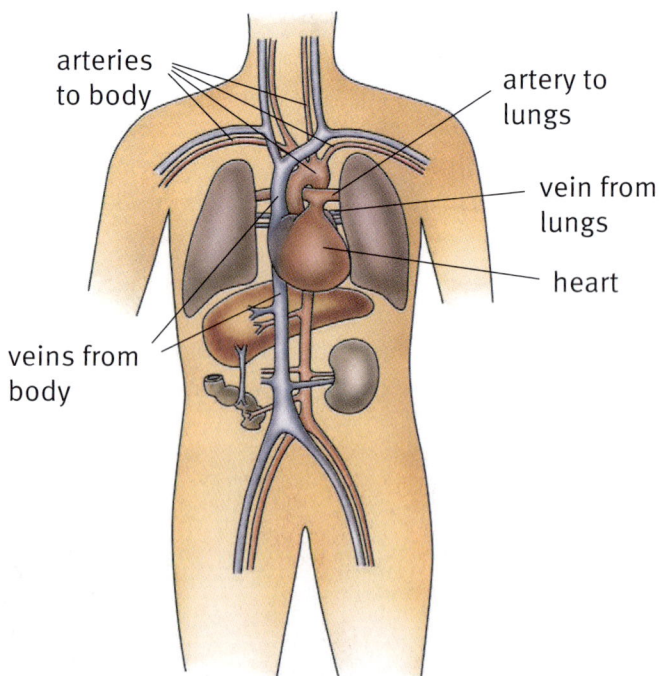

1 Plants and humans as organisms

1.2 Human organ systems

The nervous system

The nervous system helps different parts of the body to communicate with one another. Signals travel along **nerves** from the brain and spinal cord to all the other body organs.

Sense organs are also part of the nervous system. For example, your eyes sense light. Signals travel from your eyes to your brain.

The respiratory system

The respiratory system is where oxygen enters your body and carbon dioxide leaves it. All of your cells need oxygen, so that they can **respire**. This is how they get their energy. When cells respire, they make carbon dioxide, which is a waste product.

Air moves down a series of tubes, until it is deep inside the lungs. This is where oxygen moves into your blood. Carbon dioxide moves out of the blood and into the lungs. The air containing this carbon dioxide moves out of the lungs when you breathe out.

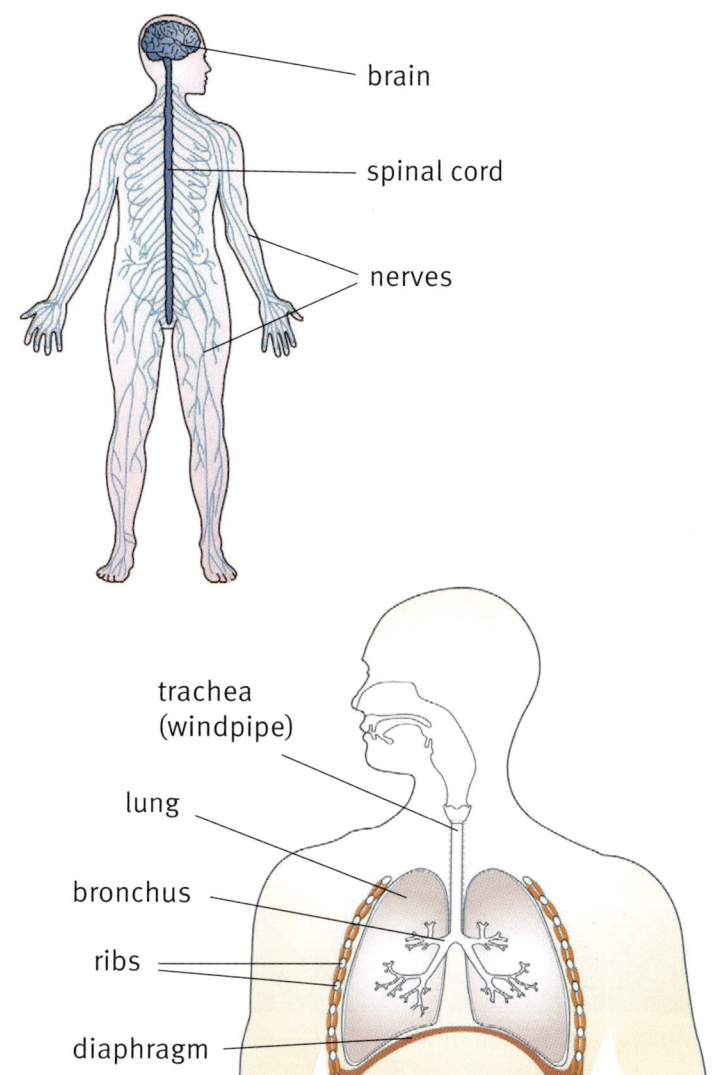

Questions

3. Explain how nerves help the different organs in the body to work together.
4. Why do all cells in the body need oxygen?
5. Describe the function of the lungs.

Summary
- The digestive system breaks down food so that it can be absorbed into the blood.
- The circulatory system transports substances all over the body.
- The nervous system allows all the parts of the body to communicate.
- The respiratory system helps oxygen to enter the body and carbon dioxide to leave it.

1 Plants and humans as organisms

1.3 The human skeleton

Your skeleton supports your body and helps it to move. It also protects some of the soft organs inside you.

The diagram shows the main bones in the skeleton.

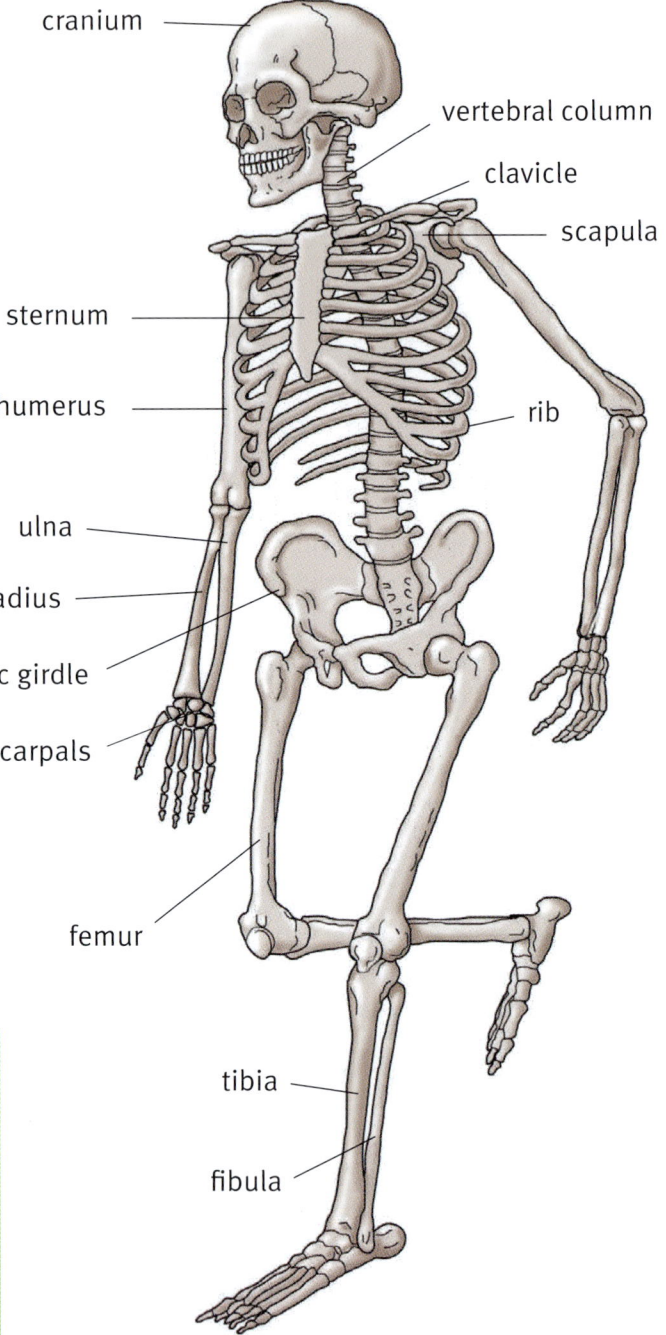

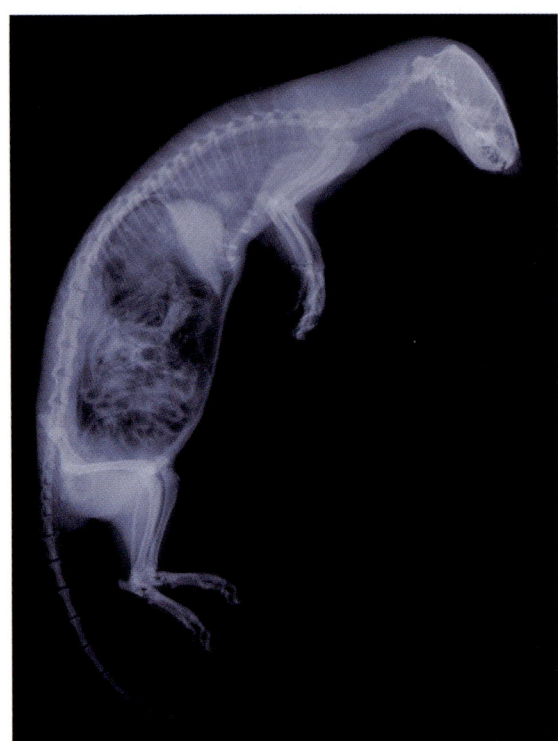

This is an X-ray of a mink.

Questions

1. List **three** functions of the skeleton.
2. Look at the diagram of the skeleton. How are the bones in the arms and legs similar?
3. How many ribs does a person have? (Remember that there are the same number on both sides of the body.)
4. As well as supporting the body, some bones protect other organs. Name the bones that protect: brain, heart and lungs.
5. Look at the X-ray of a mink. Do you think a mink has the same bones as a human? What evidence do you have for your answer?

1 Plants and humans as organisms

1.3 The human skeleton

Activity 1.3
Do long bones break more easily than short bones?

In this experiment, you will use drinking straws instead of real bones.

You will measure the force needed to make the straw bend, rather than break.

The diagram shows how you will find the force needed to bend the straw. You will use a forcemeter. You can find out how to use a forcemeter on page **131**.

It's easiest to do this in pairs. One of you pulls the forcemeter. The other one notes the reading on the forcemeter when the straw collapses.

1. Copy the results table, ready to fill in as you do your experiment.
2. Collect two identical straws. Keep one full length. Cut one in half. Cut one of the halves into half again.
3. Measure the length of a full-length straw, in cm. Fill in your measurement in the first row of your results table.
4. Find the force needed to make a full-length straw bend. Write your result in your results table.
5. Now repeat steps 3 and 4 with the half-length straw and the one-quarter-length straw.

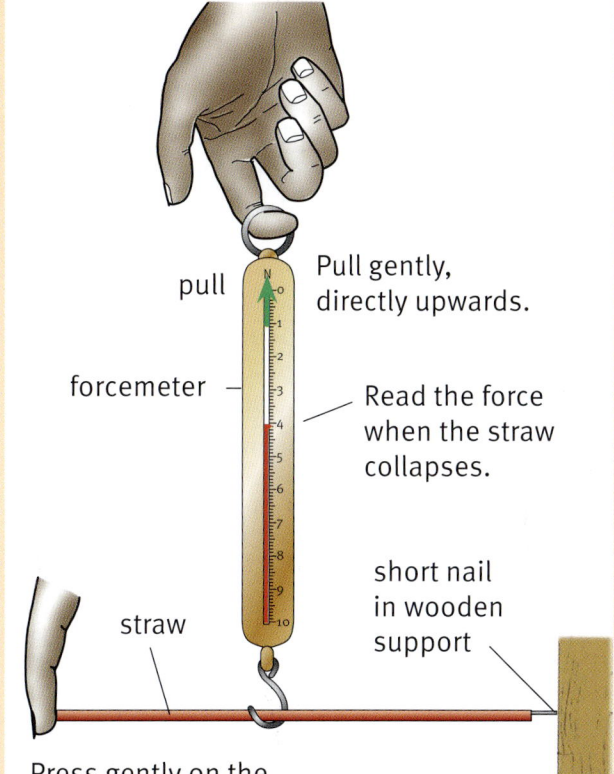

Questions
A1 To make this experiment a fair test, you kept everything the same except the length of the straws. Write down **three** things that you kept the same.
A2 What conclusion can you make from your results?

Length of straw / cm	Force needed to bend the straw / N

Summary
- The skeleton supports the body.
- The cranium protects the brain. The ribs and sternum protect the lungs and heart.

1 Plants and humans as organisms

1.4 Joints

Fixed and moveable joints

A **joint** is a place where two bones meet. We have two main types of joints in our bodies:

- fixed joints
- moveable joints.

The skull has fixed joints in the cranium. The cranium is made up of several bones firmly joined together. This helps the cranium to protect the brain.

The jawbone is joined to the rest of the skull by a moveable joint. This allows the jaw to move up and down and from side to side when you chew, talk or yawn.

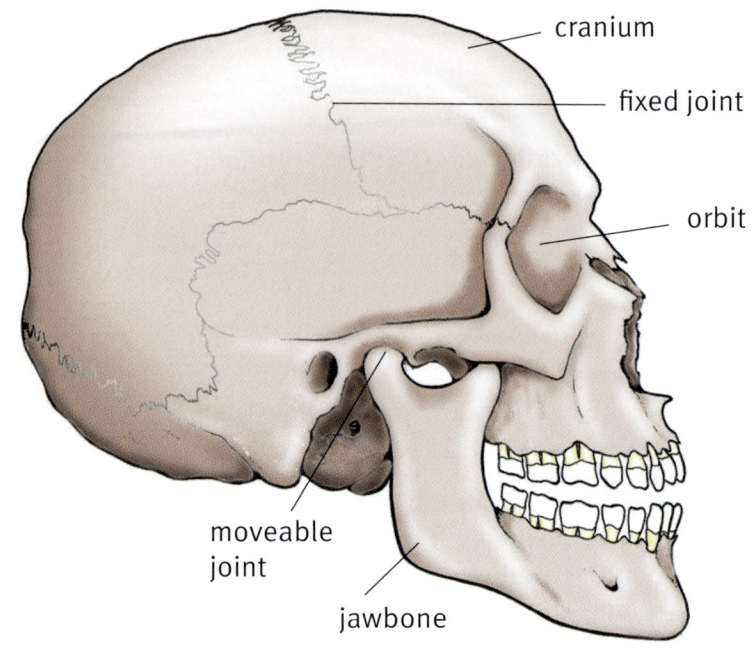

The skull contains both fixed joints and moveable joints.

Hinge joints and ball-and-socket joints

Your shoulder joint can move in almost all directions. You can swing your arm round in a complete circle.

This is because the shoulder joint is a **ball-and-socket joint**. A ball on one bone fits into a socket on the other.

Your elbow joint is a **hinge joint**. It can move in only one direction. It moves like a door on a hinge.

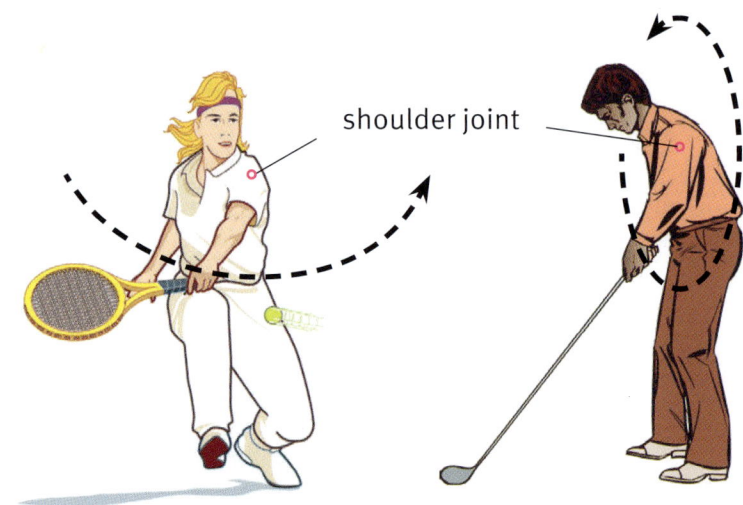

The shoulder is a ball-and-socket joint.

Questions

1. State **one** place in the body where you have a fixed joint. Why is it useful to have a fixed joint in this place?
2. Name the bones that form the ball-and-socket joint in your shoulder.
3. Name the bones that form the hinge joint at your elbow.

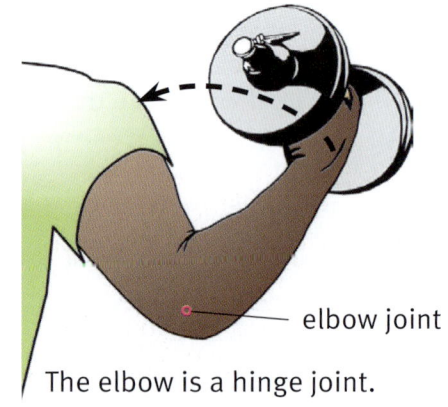

The elbow is a hinge joint.

1 Plants and humans as organisms

1.4 Joints

Structure of a moveable joint

The diagram shows what the elbow joint would look like if you could cut through it.

It is important that joints can move easily.

When two surfaces move against each other, a force called **friction** tries to stop them. You can read more about friction on page **136**.

To reduce friction:

- the ends of the bones are covered with a very smooth, slippery material called **cartilage**
- a thick, slippery fluid called **synovial fluid** fills the spaces between the two bones.

The synovial fluid helps to **lubricate** the joint, like oil in the moving parts of an engine or bicycle.

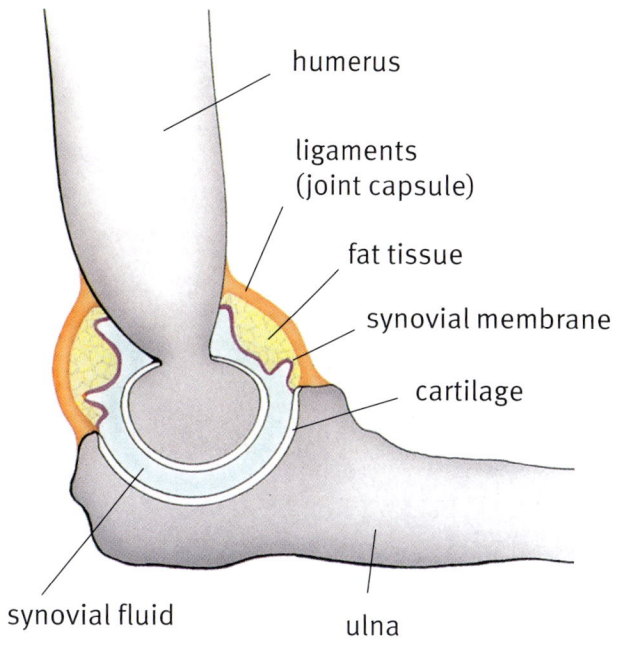

Questions

4 Suggest why it is important to reduce friction at moveable joints.
5 Describe where cartilage is found at the elbow joint. Why is the cartilage there?
6 What is the function of synovial fluid?
7 Look at the diagram of the elbow joint. Suggest how the two bones are held together at the elbow joint.

Activity 1.4
Which kind of joint?

Try moving each of these joints in your body, and decide whether each one is:

a fixed joint   **a hinge joint**   **a ball-and-socket joint**

a a finger joint, b the knee joint, c a toe joint, d the hip joint

Summary
- A joint is a place where two bones meet.
- The bones at a fixed joint cannot move. The bones at a hinge joint or ball-and-socket joint can move.
- Cartilage and synovial fluid reduce friction at moveable joints.

1 Plants and humans as organisms

1.5 Muscles

Muscles are organs that help us to move.

The diagram shows the two main muscles in the upper arm.

The muscles are attached to the bones by **tendons**. Tendons are very strong, and they do not stretch.

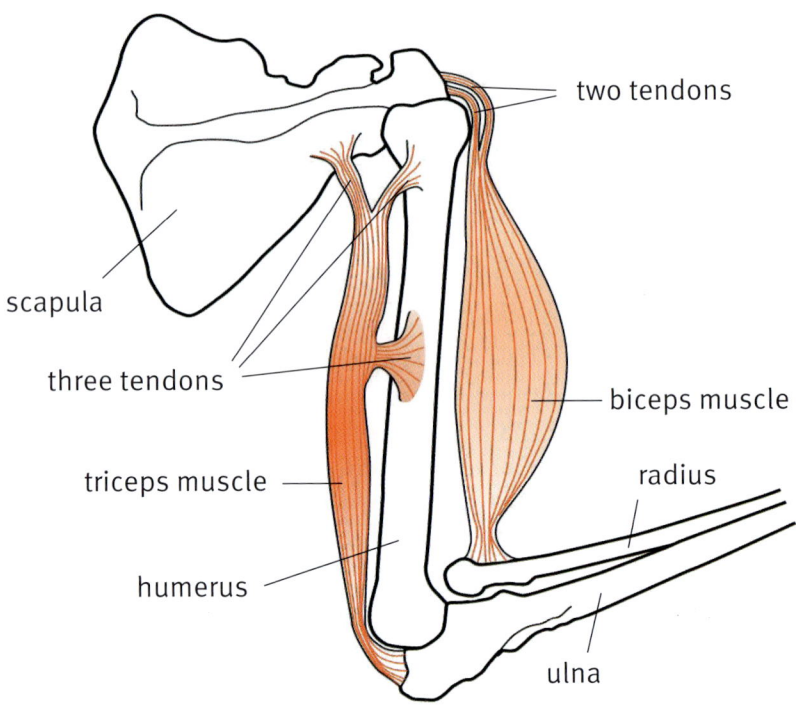

Questions

1. Name the bones that the biceps muscle is attached to.
2. Name the bones that the triceps muscle is attached to.
3. 'Bi' means 'two'. 'Tri' means three. Look carefully at the diagram, and suggest why the biceps and triceps are given their names.

How muscles work

Muscles can get shorter. This is called **contraction**. When muscles contract, they produce a pulling force.

Look at the diagram of the muscles in the arm. When the biceps muscle contracts, it pulls on the radius and scapula.

The pulling force is transmitted to these bones through the strong tendons.

The radius is pulled upwards, towards the scapula. The arm bends.

You can see the biceps muscle bulging when it makes the arm bend.

Questions

4. Predict what will happen if the biceps stops contracting, and the triceps contracts.
5. Explain why it is important that tendons do not stretch.

1 Plants and humans as organisms

1.5 Muscles

Antagonistic muscles

Muscles can contract and make themselves shorter. However, muscles cannot make themselves get longer.

When a muscle is not contracting, we say that it is **relaxed**.

A relaxed muscle does not do anything by itself. But if a force pulls on it, the force can make the relaxed muscle get longer.

The top diagram shows what happens when the biceps muscle contracts and the triceps muscle relaxes.

The contracting biceps muscle makes the arm bend at the elbow joint. It also pulls the relaxed triceps muscle and makes it longer.

The next diagram shows how the arm can be made straight again. To do this, the triceps muscle contracts, and the biceps muscle relaxes.

You can see that the biceps and triceps work as a team. When one of them contracts, the other one relaxes. When one of them contracts, it pulls the bones in one direction, and when the other contracts, it pulls the bones in the opposite direction.

A pair of muscles that work together like this are called **antagonistic muscles**.

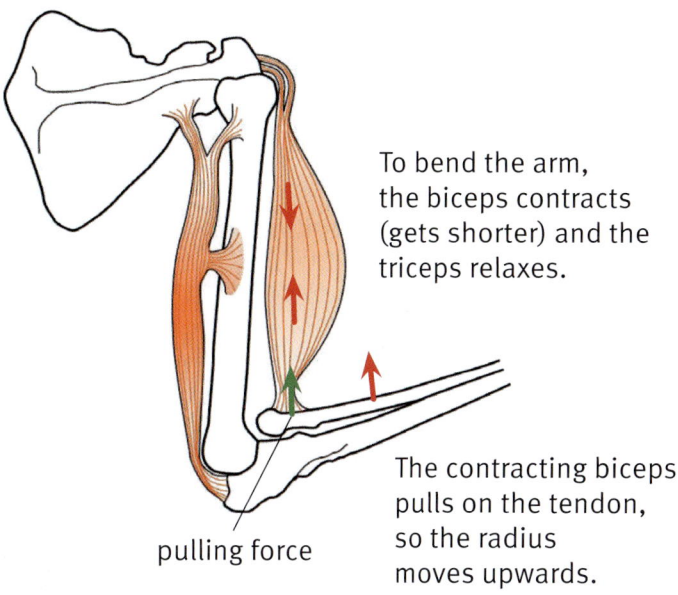

To bend the arm, the biceps contracts (gets shorter) and the triceps relaxes.

pulling force

The contracting biceps pulls on the tendon, so the radius moves upwards.

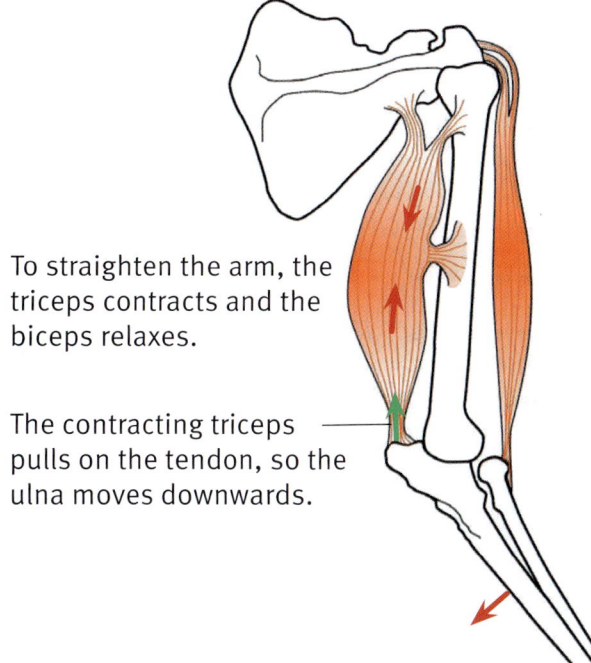

To straighten the arm, the triceps contracts and the biceps relaxes.

The contracting triceps pulls on the tendon, so the ulna moves downwards.

Question

6 Explain why the biceps muscle alone cannot make the arm straighten.

Summary
- Muscles produce a pulling force when they contract. They can only pull. They cannot push.
- Muscles are joined to bones by tendons.
- Antagonistic muscles are a pair of muscles working together, pulling in opposite directions.

1 Plants and humans as organisms

1.6 Studying the human body

There is still a lot that we do not know about the human body and how it works.

Many different scientists study the human body, to find out some of the things that we do not understand yet.

Here are some examples of what different kinds of scientists do.

Anatomists

An anatomist studies the structure of the body. Most anatomists work in universities.

Anatomists can study living bodies using X-rays, CAT scans and MRI scans. These techniques allow them to see inside the body, without having to cut it open.

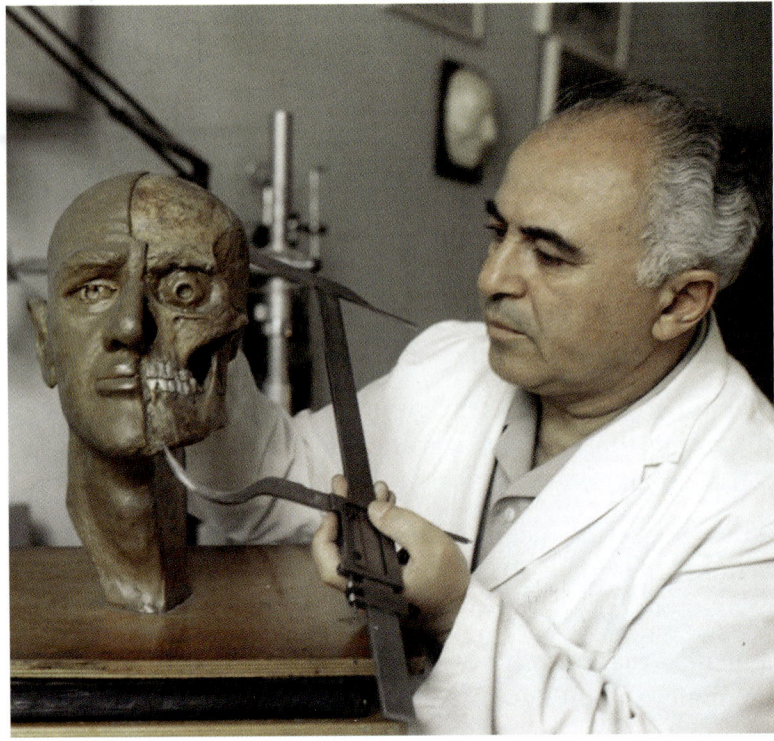

This anatomist is studying the structure of a model of the head.

Physiologists

Physiologists study the way that the body works. There are many different kinds of physiologists. Here are two examples.

A **sports physiologist** studies what happens to the body when we exercise. Some sports physiologists work in universities. Some sports physiologists work with professional sportswomen and sportsmen. For example, they may study how a person's diet and their training programme affects their heart or lungs.

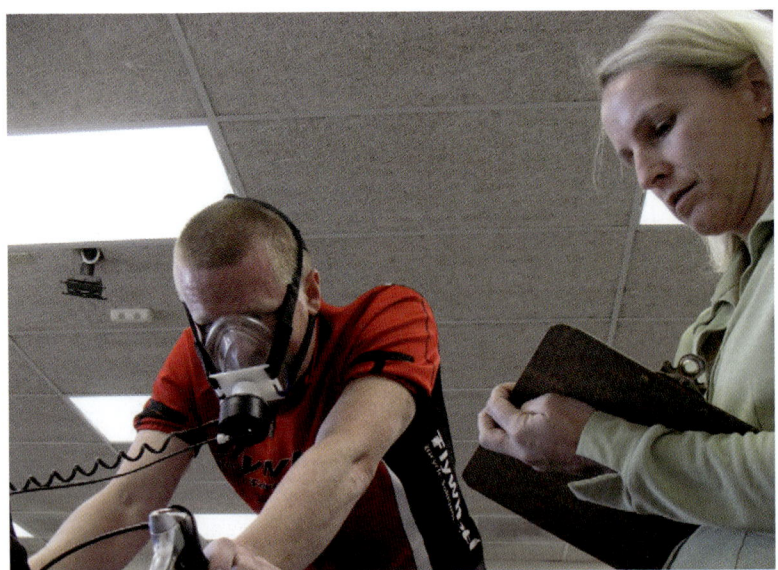

The sports physiologist is studying the effect of exercise on the athlete's body.

1.6 Studying the human body

A **neuroscientist** is a physiologist who studies how the brain and the rest of the nervous system work. They do research into many different kinds of questions, such as how we learn, or how the brain sends signals to other parts of the body.

Questions

1. Which **three** letters come at the end of the name of each kind of scientist named on these pages?
2. Explain the difference between an anatomist and a physiologist.
3. Suggest how a sports physiologist could help a professional athlete to improve their performance.

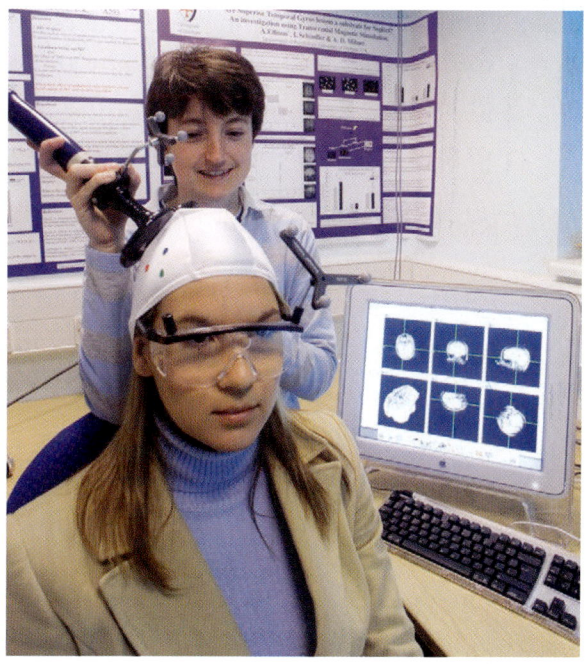

The neuroscientist is mapping activity in the brain of the woman at the front. The woman is wearing glasses that track where she is looking. The monitor shows her brain activity.

Activity 1.6
Researching the work of scientists

Find out about how one kind of scientist studies the human body.

You can choose from one of these:

nutritionist   **psychologist**   **osteologist**   **geneticist**

If you want to research a kind of scientist that is not listed here, check with your teacher first.

Your teacher will tell you what resources you can use.

Write **three** sentences summarising what you have found out.

Summary
- There is still a lot that we do not know about the human body and how it works.
- Many different kinds of scientists do research into the human body, to find out things that we do not yet know or understand.

1 Plants and humans as organisms

Unit 1 End of unit questions

1.1 Copy and complete these sentences using words from the list.
You may use each word once, more than once or not at all.

air	flowers	food	ground	leaves	organs
organ systems		reproduction		roots	water

Roots, leaves, stems and flowers are found in plants. Roots absorb

.... and help to hold the plant in the ....

Leaves are where the plant makes its .... Flowers are for

.... The stem holds the .... and

.... above the ground. [6]

1.2 The diagram shows an organ system in a person.

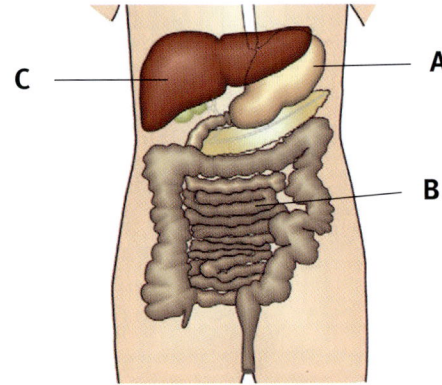

- **a** Name this organ system. [1]
- **b** Name the organs labelled **A**, **B** and **C**. [3]
- **c** What is the function of this organ system? Choose from these answers:
  - providing energy for the body by respiration
  - breaking down food into small particles that can be absorbed
  - transporting food to every part of the body
  - helping different parts of the body to communicate with each other. [1]

1.3 Plant stems can bend. This helps to stop them breaking when strong sideways forces act on them, such as a strong wind.

Anji did an experiment to compare how much stems from different plants bend when the same force is applied to them.

She cut pieces of stem from three different plants, **P**, **Q** and **R**. She chose stems that all had the same diameter.

1 Plants and humans as organisms

1 End of unit questions

The diagram shows how Anji tested the stems.

a What should Anji keep the same in her experiment? Choose **two** answers from the list:

- the length of each stem
- the width of the card
- the weights hung on each stem.

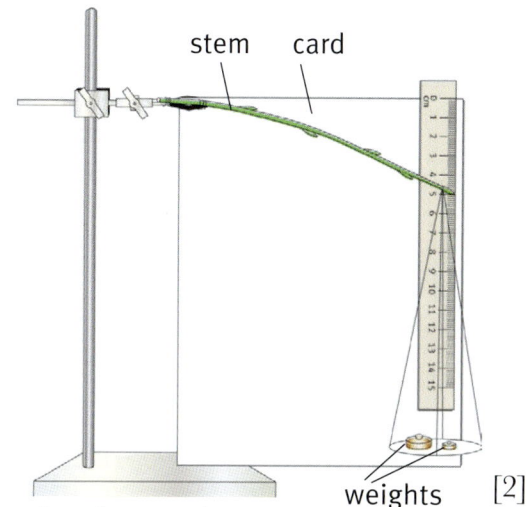

[2]

b The diagrams show the readings for the distance of each stem tip from the top of the card. Write down the readings for each of stems **P**, **Q** and **R**. Give your answers in cm.

[3]

P 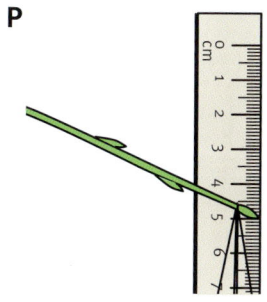   Q 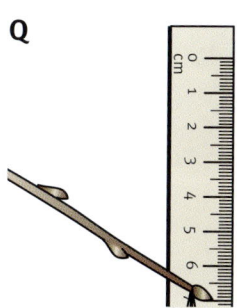   R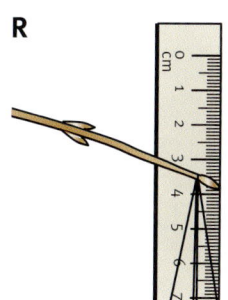

c Anji recorded her results in a results table.

Copy the results table, and complete it by writing in:

- a suitable heading for the first column
- the unit for the second column
- the readings for each stem (your answers to **b**).

....	Distance of tip of stem from the top of the card / ....
P	
Q	
R	

[3]

d What conclusion can Anji make from her experiment? Choose **one** from the list.

- Thick stems bend less than thin stems.
- Plant **P** has stems that bend less than Plant **Q**.
- The more a stem bends, the taller the plant can grow.
- The stronger the force, the more a stem bends.

[1]

1 Plants and humans as organisms

2.1 Characteristics of living organisms

How do you know when something is alive? If it is a person, you can check to see if they are breathing, or if they have a heart beat.

But plants don't breathe or have hearts, and they are alive.

Living organisms have a set of seven characteristics that make them different from non-living things.

Nutrition Plants feed by photosynthesis. Bears eat meat.

Growth All living organisms grow.

Movement Living organisms can move.

Sensitivity Living organisms are sensitive to changes going on around them.

Excretion Living organisms get rid of waste materials, such as carbon dioxide.

Reproduction Living organisms can produce young.

Respiration Food is broken down inside cells to provide energy.

2 Cells and organisms

2.1 Characteristics of living organisms

Activity 2.1
Living, non-living and dead

To do this activity, you need to be outside. You could search in a place in your school grounds, or near your home.

Draw a table with three columns. Write these headings at the top of the columns.

- Is alive now
- Was once alive, but is now dead
- Has never been alive

Look carefully around you, and find at least 20 different things. Decide which category each of them belongs to. List each object in the correct column in your table.

Questions

A+I

1 Living things don't show all of the seven characteristics all of the time.
   a Which characteristics are you showing at this moment? Explain your answer.
   b Which characteristics is this plant showing?

Flowers produce seeds for reproduction.

A+I

2 Some cars have sensors that detect things around them, to help the driver to park or to turn the lights on automatically when it gets dark.
   a How is a car similar to a living organism?
   b What makes a car different from a living organism?

Cars can move. They use fuel and produce exhaust gases.

Summary
- Living organisms have a set of seven characteristics – growth, movement, reproduction, excretion, sensitivity, nutrition and respiration.
- Non-living things may have some of these characteristics, but not all seven of them.

2 Cells and organisms

2.2 Micro-organisms

What is a micro-organism?

A micro-organism is a living organism so small that we can only see it when we use a microscope.

Micro-organisms are made of cells, like all living organisms. Most micro-organisms are made of only one cell. (You can find out more about cells on pages **30** to **33**.)

There are several groups of micro-organisms.

- **Bacteria**
  Bacteria are found everywhere. (Bacteria is a plural word. The singular of bacteria is bacterium.) The bacteria in the photograph live in the soil. Their cells are much smaller than human cells. You could line up one thousand of these bacteria, end to end, between two of the millimetre marks on your ruler.
- **Microscopic fungi**
  Many fungi, including mushrooms and toadstools, are large. However, there are also some microscopic ones. Yeast, for example, is a single-celled microscopic fungus.
- **Single-celled algae and protozoa**
  If you are able to look at some pond water under a microscope, you will see many tiny living organisms in the water. Some of them are tiny plant-like organisms, called algae. Some of them are one-celled animals, called protozoa.

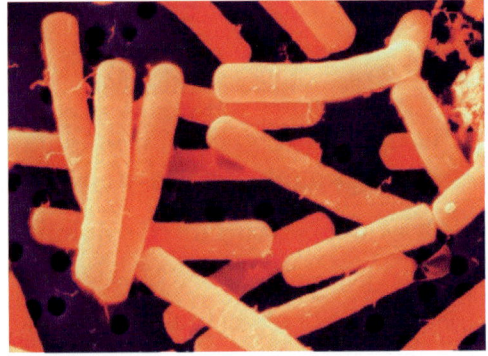

Each of these orange cylinders is a bacterium. Each bacterium is made of only one cell.

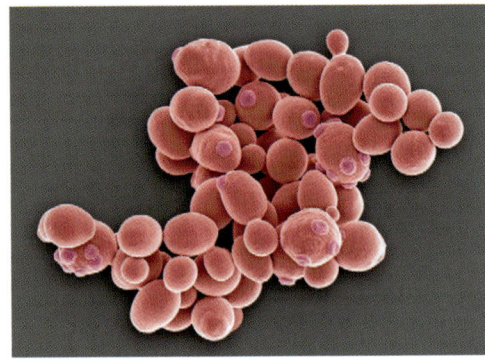

This is a group of yeast cells seen through a microscope. If you look carefully, you can see little buds growing out of some of the cells. This is how yeast reproduces.

Questions

1. Bacterial cells are much smaller than human cells. Yeast cells are about the same size as human cells. Use this information to work out which photograph above – the one of bacteria, or the one of yeast – has been magnified the most.

2. The photograph on the right shows some pond water, under a microscope. Suggest how you can tell which micro-organisms are algae, and which ones are protozoa.

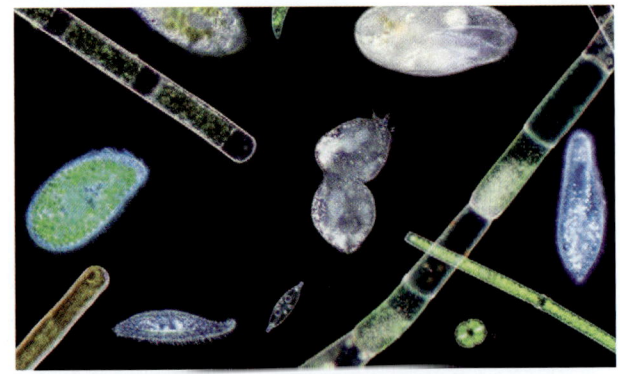

Can you spot the protozoan that is reproducing?

2.2 Micro-organisms

Activity 2.2
Growing micro-organisms from the air

Individual micro-organisms are too small to see. But if we can get a whole colony of them to grow, we can see the colony with the naked eye.

1. Your teacher will give you a small, transparent dish called a Petri dish. The dish contains agar jelly.
   The dish and the jelly are **sterile**. 'Sterile' means that any living organisms on them have been killed.
2. Take the lid off the dish. Leave the dish open for about 5 or 10 minutes, to allow micro-organisms from the air to get onto the jelly, but don't breathe or talk over it.
3. Put the lid back on the dish. Use sticky tape to fasten the lid onto the dish.
4. Tip the dish upside down. This is so that any condensation does not make puddles on the jelly and drown the micro-organisms.
5. Leave the dish in a safe place for a few days. Do not, at any stage, take the lid off the dish.
6. After a few days, you will see blobs growing on the surface of the jelly. Each blob is a colony that began as a single micro-organism.

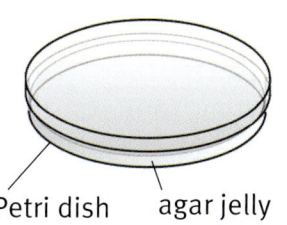

Petri dish   agar jelly

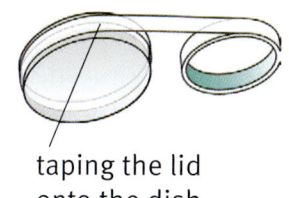

taping the lid onto the dish

Questions

A1 The agar jelly contains **nutrients** for the micro-organisms to use. Can you suggest what the word 'nutrients' means?

A2 Suggest why the Petri dish and agar jelly needed to be sterile.

A3 Suggest why it is important not to open the dish after you've sealed it with sticky tape.

A4 Make a large drawing of the colonies of micro-organisms that grew on the surface of the jelly. You may have some colonies of bacteria and some of fungi. If so, label one of each kind.

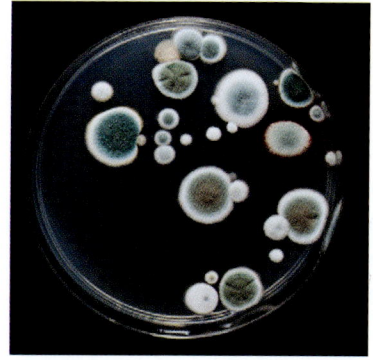

These are all colonies of fungi. Bacteria usually make colonies with smoother edges.

Summary
- Micro-organisms are living organisms that are too small to see with the naked eye.
- All bacteria are micro-organisms, and so are some fungi.

2.3 Micro-organisms and decay

Micro-organisms are everywhere. They live in the air, in the soil, in water, on our skin and inside our bodies. One teaspoon of soil may contain one thousand million bacteria.

Decay

Micro-organisms are growing on this apple. They have changed the apple, and have made it go bad.

Apples come from plants. A substance that has been made from living organisms is called **organic matter**.

Micro-organisms can break down organic matter. They make it **decay**. This is a nuisance to us if they make our food decay.

But most of the time, decay by micro-organisms is useful. Micro-organisms break down dead bodies and animal waste. They return the nutrients in this organic matter to the soil. Plants can use the nutrients to help them to grow.

The spots on the apple are colonies of fungi.

Questions

1 Which of these things are organic matter?

bread   **water**   **leather**
pebble   **wood**   **fruit**

2 Which ones can be broken down by micro-organisms?
3 Describe one way in which decay by micro-organisms is a nuisance.
4 Describe one way in which decay by micro-organisms is useful.

Slowing down decay

Most micro-organisms grow fastest when they have:

- a warm temperature
- plenty of water
- plenty of oxygen.

We can use this information to find ways of slowing down the rate at which food decays.

Micro-organisms grow slowly when they are cold.

We can slow down the growth of micro-organisms by keeping food in a refrigerator. We can keep the food longer without it decaying.

2 Cells and organisms

2.3 Micro-organisms and decay

Activity 2.3
Investigating how temperature affects decay

1. Put two similar pieces of bread onto two paper plates.
2. Moisten both pieces of bread with water. Take care not to get them too wet.
3. Leave the bread open to the air for about 30 minutes. Then cover both plates with a plastic bag or cling film.
4. Put one plate in a warm place. Put the other plate in a refrigerator.
5. Record the appearance of each piece of bread each day, for three or four days.

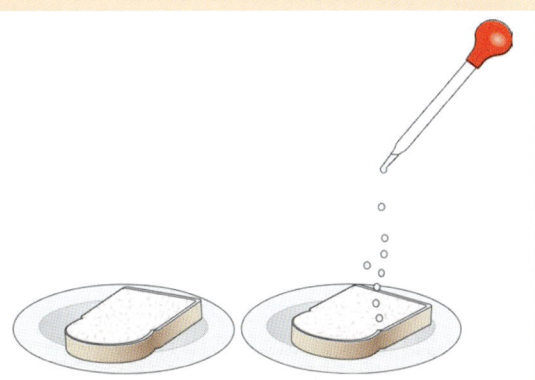

Questions

A1 Compare the results for the bread in the warm place, and the bread in the refrigerator.

A2 Did other people in your class get similar results? If they were not the same, suggest what might have caused the differences.

A3 What conclusion can you make from the results of your investigation?

A4 Plan an experiment that you could do to investigate how moisture affects the rate of decay of a piece of bread.
Think carefully about the variables you will change, the variables you will control (keep the same), and the variables you will observe or measure.

Questions

5. The soil in a tropical rain forest is always warm and wet. The soil in a woodland in northern Europe is often cold and sometimes dry.
In which of these places would you expect dead leaves from the trees to decay more quickly? Explain your answer.

6. The photograph shows some vacuum-packed food. There is no air inside the pack. Explain why this helps the food to keep fresh for a long time.

Summary

- Micro-organisms cause organic matter to decay.
- Micro-organisms cause decay fastest when it is warm and damp, and when they have plenty of oxygen.

2 Cells and organisms

2.4 Micro-organisms and food

Making cheese and yoghurt

Micro-organisms can feed on the same things that humans eat. Sometimes, we like the changes that micro-organisms make in our food. For example, some special kinds of bacteria change milk into yoghurt or cheese.

These bacteria feed on sugar in the milk. They change the sugar into a weak acid, called lactic acid. Lactic acid gives yoghurt its sharp taste.

Questions

1. We can measure how acidic something is by measuring its pH. The lower the pH, the more acidic it is. The pH of milk is often about 6.7. The pH of yoghurt is about 4.5. Explain what causes this change in pH, as milk is changed to yoghurt.
2. Suggest why the worker in the cheese factory is wearing an apron and head-covering.

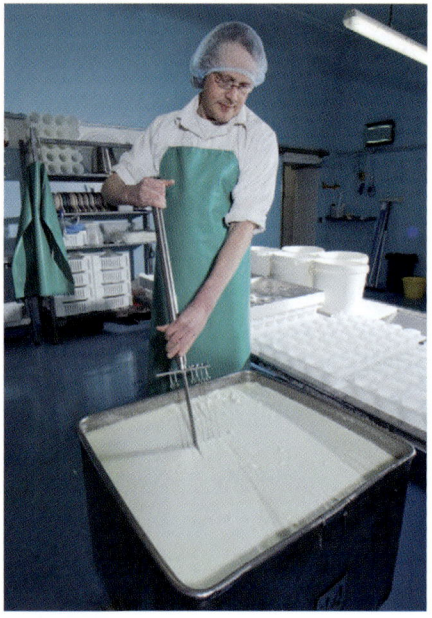

Bacteria in the milk are beginning to turn it into cheese in this cheese-making factory.

Activity 2.4A
Making yoghurt

If you are doing this activity in a laboratory, you must not taste your yoghurt. **You should never eat anything in a laboratory**.

1. Collect some 'live' yoghurt. This is yoghurt that still has living yoghurt-making bacteria in it.
2. Put some milk into a sterile container. Add a small amount of live yoghurt. Mix gently, using a sterile glass rod.
3. Cover the container with cling film. Leave it in a warm place for at least two hours.

Questions

A1 Explain why it is important to use a sterile container for making yoghurt.
A2 Suggest why it is a good idea to leave the milk in a warm place.
A3 Describe any changes that you can see in the milk.

2 Cells and organisms

2.4 Micro-organisms and food

Making bread

We use yeast to make some kinds of bread. The yeast feeds on nutrients in the flour. When the yeast respires, it makes carbon dioxide gas. The gas makes bubbles in the dough, which makes the dough rise.

Bread dough is kneaded to mix the yeast into the flour and to make the dough stretchy.

Questions

3 After bread dough has been kneaded, it is left in a warm place for a while, to allow the dough to rise. Explain why it takes time for the dough to rise.
4 Suggest what happens to the yeast in the bread dough, when the bread is baked.

Activity 2.4B
How does yeast affect bread dough?

You are going to make some bread dough with yeast, and some bread dough without yeast.

1 Collect about 75 g of bread flour. Mix it with about 50 cm^3 of yeast and sugar solution. Use your hands to knead the mixture into a ball of stretchy dough.
2 Now make another ball of dough in just the same way, but using sugar solution instead of the yeast–sugar mixture.
3 Gently push each ball of dough into a measuring cylinder. Record the volume of each ball of dough.
4 Leave the dough in a warm place. If you can, leave it for at least one hour. Then record the new volume of the dough.

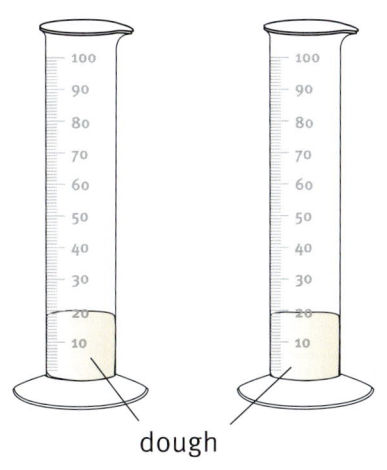

Questions

A4 What can you conclude from your results?
A5 Suggest an explanation for your results.

Summary
- Some kinds of bacteria change milk into yoghurt or cheese. They do this by changing sugar in the milk to lactic acid.
- Yeast is used for making bread. The yeast respires, producing carbon dioxide gas that makes the bread dough rise.

2.5 Micro-organisms and disease

Most micro-organisms are harmless. Many of them are useful to us.

However, there are some micro-organisms that can make people ill. If they get inside your body, they reproduce there. They produce harmful substances called **toxins**. The toxins can damage your cells, and can make you feel ill.

Diseases that are caused by micro-organisms are called **infectious diseases**. This means that they can be passed from one person to another. This happens when the micro-organisms from one person's body move to another person.

The micro-organisms that cause colds can be passed from one person to another through the air.

Some examples of harmful micro-organisms

One kind of bacterium causes a disease called **tuberculosis**, or **TB** for short. TB bacteria grow inside cells in the lungs. Over time, this makes the person very weak and they may die. Drugs called **antibiotics** can be used to kill bacteria that are causing disease.

Malaria is a disease caused by a protozoan. The protozoa live in the blood. The protozoa are passed from one person to another by mosquitoes. Sometimes the malaria protozoa infect the brain, which is very dangerous.

Influenza (flu) and colds are caused by a **virus**. A virus is even smaller than a bacterium. Viruses are so small that you can only see them using a special kind of microscope, called an electron microscope.

Viruses do not show any of the characteristics of living things, until they get inside a living cell. Then they force the cell to copy the virus, making many new viruses that burst out of the cell and infect other cells.

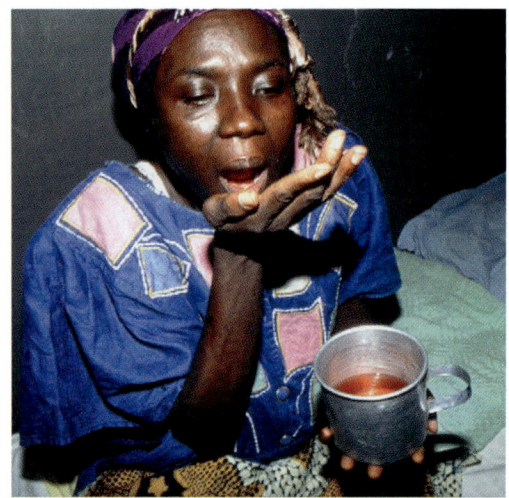

A woman with tuberculosis taking antibiotics.

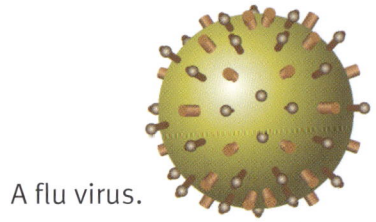

A flu virus.

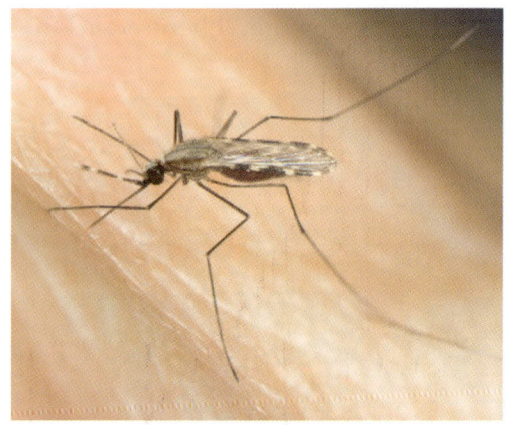

When a mosquito bites a person, malaria protozoa may pass from the mosquito into the person's blood.

2 Cells and organisms

2.5 Micro-organisms and disease

> **Questions**
> 1. Describe **two** ways in which an infectious disease can be passed from one person to another.
> 2. Explain why antibiotics cannot cure a cold.
> 3. Anna said that mosquitoes cause malaria. Why is she wrong?
> 4. Do you think that viruses are living organisms? Explain your answer.

Louis Pasteur

Louis Pasteur was born in France in 1822. At that time, no-one knew that micro-organisms could cause disease.

Pasteur was asked to investigate a disease that was killing silkworms. Silkworms are caterpillars that make silk. Pasteur did experiments that showed that the disease passed from one silkworm to another through the air, or when people handled the silkworms.

Pasteur had already discovered that microscopic organisms were involved in making wine from grapes. He thought that perhaps other microscopic organisms were making the silkworms ill.

Pasteur's work gave ideas to other scientists. By the 1870s, people had begun to use **antiseptics** to prevent infections. (An antiseptic is a substance used to kill micro-organisms outside the body.) But it was many more years before all biologists and doctors really believed that micro-organisms caused infectious diseases.

Louis Pasteur working in his laboratory.

> **Summary**
> - Infectious diseases are caused by micro-organisms.
> - Some kinds of bacteria, viruses and protozoa can cause diseases.
> - Antibiotics can be used to cure diseases caused by bacteria.
> - Louis Pasteur was the first person to obtain evidence that infectious diseases are caused by micro-organisms.

2.6 Plant cells

All living things are made of tiny structures called **cells**. Most cells are too small to be seen with the naked eye. You can see cells using a microscope.

These cells are from a moss plant.

The structure of a plant cell

Plant cells are often larger than animal cells, so it is easier to see them under a microscope.

The drawing shows a cell from a leaf.

Cell wall All plant cells have a cell wall. The cell wall is strong and quite stiff. It holds the plant cell in shape. Plant cell walls are made of a material called **cellulose**.

Cell membrane All cells have a cell membrane. The cell membrane is very thin and flexible. It controls what enters and leaves the cell.

Cytoplasm All cells have cytoplasm. It is a jelly-like substance. Chemical reactions happen inside the jelly. These reactions keep the cell alive.

Nucleus Plant cells have a nucleus. The nucleus contains **chromosomes**. It controls the activities of the cell.

Large vacuole Many plant cells have a large vacuole. It is a fluid-filled space in the cell. It contains a sugary solution called **cell sap**.

Chloroplast Plant cells that are in the sunlight often contain chloroplasts. This is where plants make their food. Chloroplasts look green because they contain a green substance called **chlorophyll**.

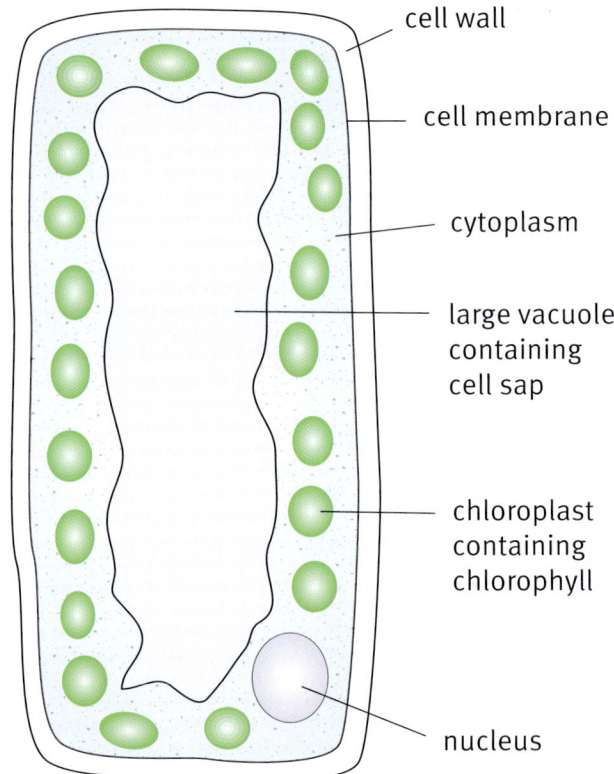

Questions

1. What are the green circles in the photograph of the moss plant cells? What makes them green?
2. Describe **four** differences between a cell wall and a cell membrane.

2.6 Plant cells

Activity 2.6
Looking at plant cells

1. Collect a small piece of onion. Cut out a piece about 1 cm square.
2. Put a small drop of water onto a clean microscope slide.
3. Very carefully peel the thin layer from the inside of your piece of onion.
4. Gently push the layer into the drop of water on the slide. Spread it out as flat as you can.
5. Collect a very thin piece of glass called a cover slip. (Take care – cover slips break very easily!) Gently lower the cover slip onto your piece of onion on the slide. Try not to get too many air bubbles under the cover slip.
6. Swivel the objective lenses on the microscope until the smallest one is over the hole in the stage. Put the slide onto the stage of the microscope, with the piece of onion over the hole.
7. Looking from the side, turn the focusing knob until the lens is close to the slide. Be very careful not to hit the slide, or it may break.
8. Look down the eyepiece. Slowly turn the focusing knob to move the lens away from the slide. Stop when the piece of onion comes into focus.
9. Make a drawing of some of the cells that you can see.

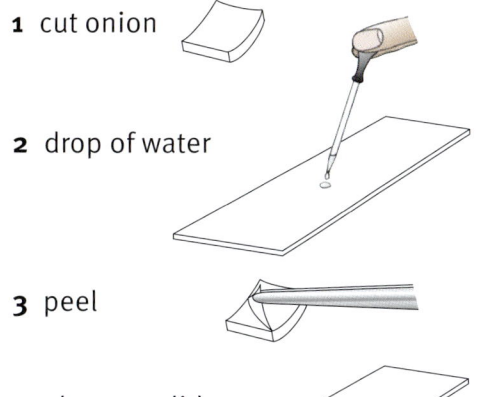

1. cut onion
2. drop of water
3. peel
4. place on slide

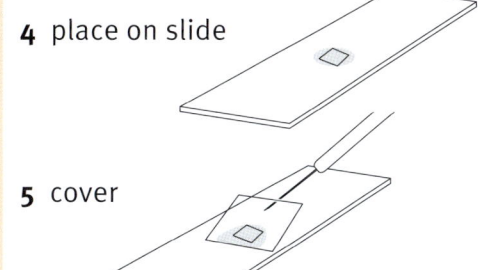

5. cover

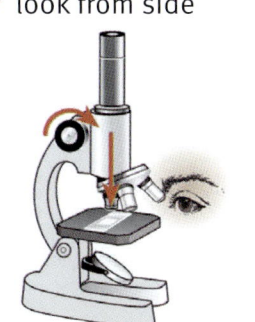 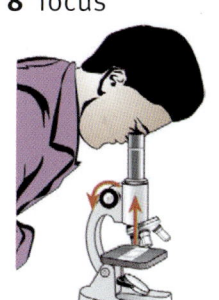

7. look from side
8. focus

Questions

A1 Suggest why the cells in the piece of onion did not look green.
A2 Describe any difficulties you had with this activity. How did you solve them?

Summary
- All living organisms are made of cells.
- All plant cells contain a cell wall, cell membrane, cytoplasm, nucleus and vacuole.
- Plant cells in the light may also contain chloroplasts.

2.7 Animal cells

All animals are made of cells. No-one knows exactly how many cells there are in the human body, but one estimate is about 100 trillion. That is 100 000 000 000 000 cells.

Like plant cells, animal cells have a cell membrane, cytoplasm and a nucleus.

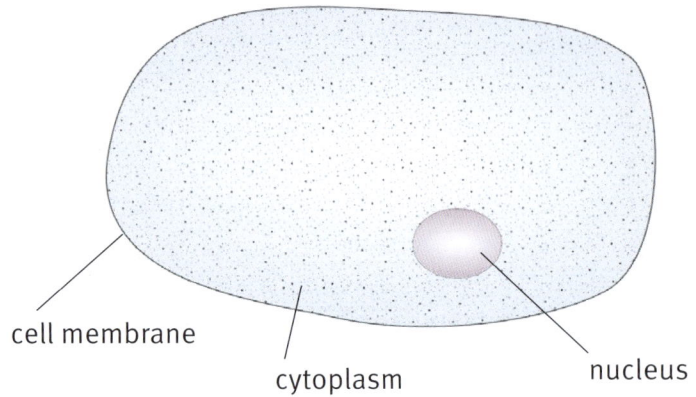

cell membrane
cytoplasm
nucleus

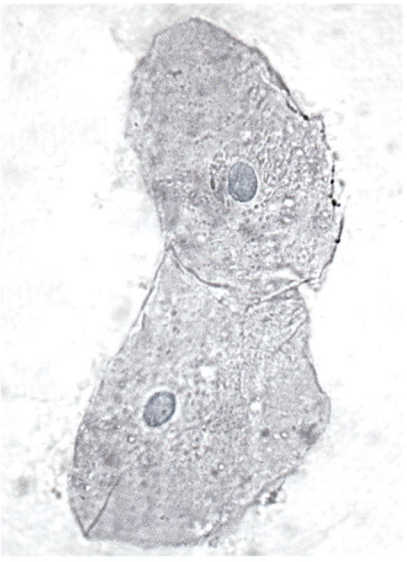

These cells came from the inside of a person's mouth. They have been coloured with a blue dye.

Questions

1. Name the part of an animal cell that matches each of these descriptions.
   a This part controls the activities of the cell.
   b This is a jelly-like substance where chemical reactions take place.
   c This controls what enters and leaves the cell.
2. Name **three** structures that are found in plant cells, but not in animal cells.
3. Name the part of the cells in the photograph that has absorbed the largest amount of the blue dye.

Protozoa

Protozoa are organisms made of a single cell, like an animal cell. Amoebae are protozoa that crawl around on the surfaces of mud and leaves in ponds. They feed by flowing around organisms even smaller than themselves. They digest the organisms inside their cell.

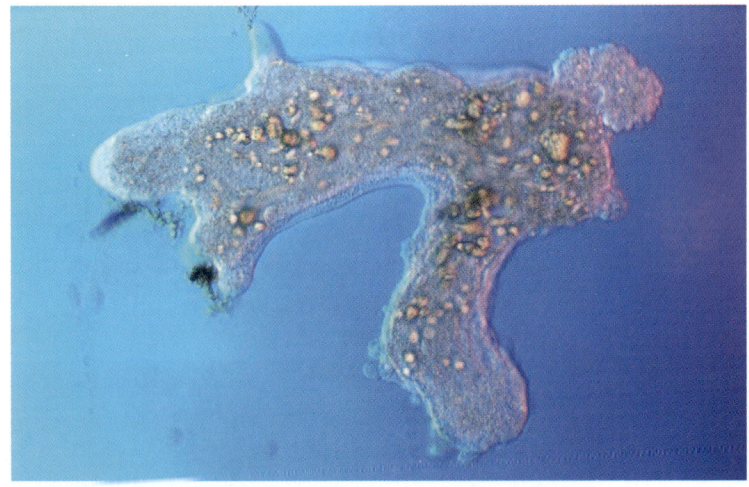

The brownish blobs inside this amoeba are tiny organisms that it has eaten. The amoeba moves by pushing out parts of its cell in the direction it wants to travel.

2 Cells and organisms

2.7 Animal cells

Questions

4 If an amoeba had a cell like a plant cell, it would not be able to move or feed in the way that it does. Explain why.

5 Give an example of a disease that is caused by a protozoan. (You'll need to think back to some earlier work you have done.)

Activity 2.7
Looking at animal cells

Your teacher will explain where you can obtain animal cells. For example, you may be able to take some from the inside of an animal's windpipe, obtained from a butcher.

1 Smear a little material that contains cells onto the centre of a microscope slide. You won't be able to see any cells yet, because they are much too small.

2 Use a dropper pipette to add a drop of methylene blue dye to the cells. The dye will stain the cells, making it easier to see them.

3 Carefully lower a cover slip over the drop of dye.

4 Put the smallest lens of the microscope over the stage. Put the slide on the stage. Looking from the side, turn the focusing knob until the lens is very close to the slide.

5 Look down the eyepiece. Slowly turn the focusing knob to move the lens upwards. Stop when you can see the cells.

6 Swivel the lenses until the next biggest one is over the stage. Look down the eyepiece. You should be able to see a more magnified view of the cells.

7 Make a drawing of one or two of the cells that you can see. Label your drawing.

2 Add dye.

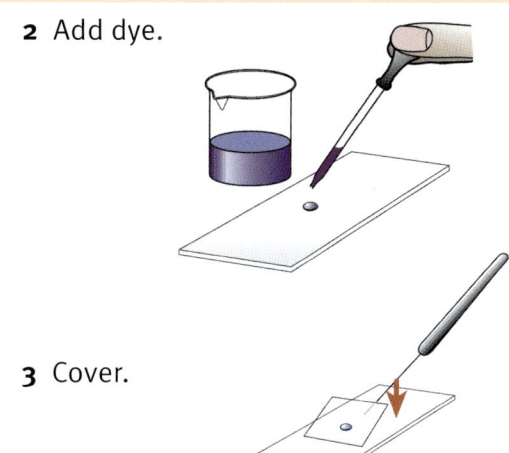

3 Cover.

4 Select low power.

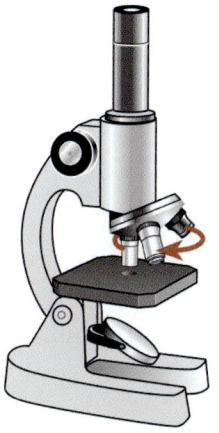

Summary
- Animal cells have a cell membrane, cytoplasm and nucleus.
- Animal cells do not have a cell wall, chloroplasts or a large vacuole containing cell sap.

2 Cells and organisms

2.8 Cells, tissues and organs

A bacterium or a protozoan has only one cell. The cell has to do all the activities that are needed to keep the organism alive.

But animals and plants are made of many cells. Different cells can take on different tasks. Each cell is **specialised** to carry out a particular function.

Cells with different functions have different structures. The cell is **adapted** to carry out its function really well.

Some specialised animal cells

Red blood cells
These carry oxygen around the body. The cells are very small, so they can squeeze through even the tiniest blood vessels. Their cytoplasm contains a red substance called **haemoglobin**, which carries oxygen. They do not have a nucleus. This makes more room for haemoglobin.

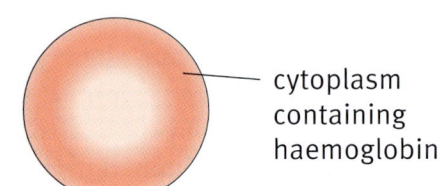

Nerve cells
These transfer messages from one part of the body to another. They have little strands of cytoplasm that collect electrical signals from other nerve cells. Electrical signals flow quickly along the long strand.

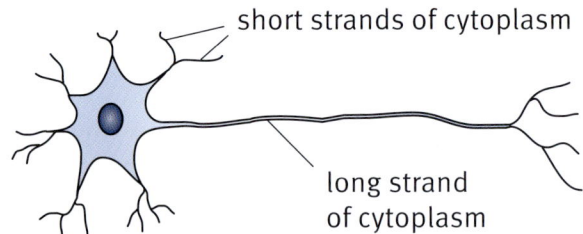

> **Questions**
> 1 List **two** structures in a red blood cell that are found in all animal cells.
> 2 What is haemoglobin?
> 3 List **three** structures in a nerve cell that are found in all animal cells.
> 4 How does the structure of a nerve cell help it carry out its function?

A specialised plant cell

Root hair cells grow from the surface layer of a root. They absorb (soak up) water from the soil. They have a long, thin extension that allows water to move easily from the soil into the cell.

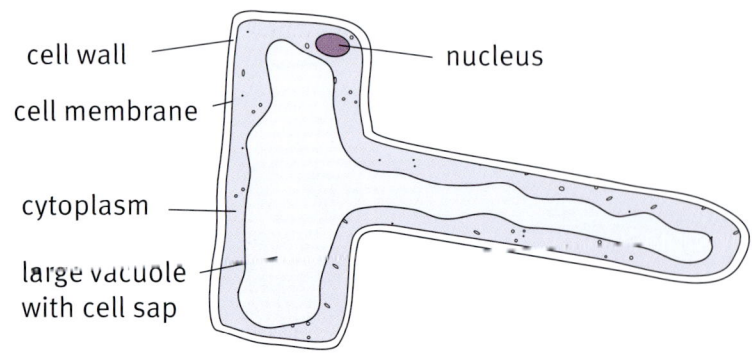

The root hairs in the photograph are growing from the roots of a poppy plant.

2.8 Cells, tissues and organs

> **Questions**
>
> 5 Explain how a root hair cell is adapted for its function.
> 6 Suggest why root hair cells do not contain chloroplasts.
> 7 Water moves through several parts of the root hair cell as it goes from the soil into the vacuole of the cell. List these parts, in order.

Tissues

There are many different kinds of cells in an animal or a plant. Usually, lots of cells of one kind group together.

A group of cells that are adapted to carry out a particular function is called a **tissue**.

Each organ in an animal or plant usually contains several different kinds of tissues.

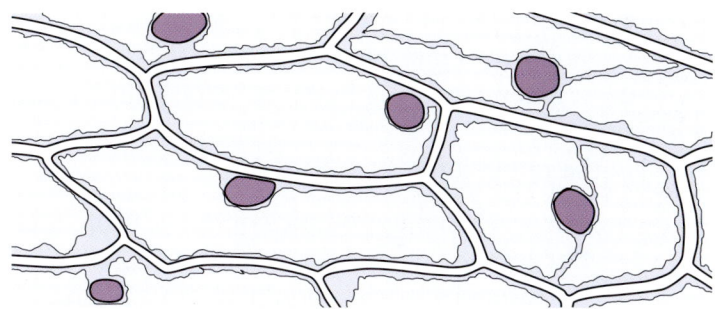

This is part of a tissue from inside an onion. This tissue covers the surface of layers inside the onion.

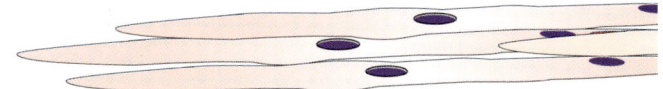

This is muscle tissue. Muscle tissue is made up of cells that are adapted to be able to contract.

> **Question**
>
> 8 Copy and complete these sentences, using the words in the list.
>
> **organism   tissue   organ   organ system**
>
> A group of similar cells is called a ....
> An .... is a structure made up of many different tissues.
> An .... is a group of organs that carry out a particular function.
> An .... is a living thing. It may contain many different organ systems, organs and tissues.

> **Summary**
> - Different kinds of cells are adapted to carry out different functions.
> - The structure of red blood cells helps them to transport oxygen. The structure of nerve cells helps them to transmit electrical signals. The structure of root hair cells helps them to absorb water.
> - A tissue is a group of similar cells, carrying out a particular function.
> - Tissues group together to form organs.

Unit 2 End of unit questions

2.1 Write the word that matches each description. Choose words from the list below.

cell membrane   cell wall   cytoplasm   chloroplast
chlorophyll   nucleus   tissue   vacuole

- **a** a jelly-like substance in which chemical reactions take place [1]
- **b** the part of a cell that contains chromosomes, and that controls the activities of the cell [1]
- **c** a strong outer covering, found around plant cells but not animal cells [1]
- **d** a thin, flexible covering, found around all cells, that controls what enters and leaves the cell [1]
- **e** a green colouring found in some plant cells [1]

2.2 Latha made some yoghurt.

- She washed out a plastic container using boiling water.
- She let the pot cool down, and then put some fresh milk into the container.
- She added a small spoonful of live yoghurt.
- She covered the container with cling film.
- She put the container in the refrigerator.

- **a** Explain why it was a good idea to wash the container with boiling water. [1]
- **b** Suggest what was in the live yoghurt that would help to turn Latha's fresh milk into yoghurt. [1]
- **c** It took a long time for Latha's milk to turn into yoghurt.
  What could she have done to make it happen faster?
  Explain your answer. [2]
- **d** Latha measured the pH of the milk before she put it into the pot.
  She measured it again after it had been in the pot for four days.
  Suggest how the pH changed. Choose from:

  became higher   became lower   stayed the same

  Explain your answer. [2]

2 Cells and organisms

2 End of unit questions

2.3 Janzi investigated how temperature affects the rate at which bread dough rises.

- He made some bread dough using flour, yeast, sugar and water.
- He divided the dough into three equal pieces, **A**, **B** and **C**.
- He put each piece of bread dough into a measuring cylinder.
- The volume of each piece of dough was 20 cm³.
- Janzi put each measuring cylinder into a place at a different temperature.
- After one hour, he measured the volume of each piece of dough again.

The diagram shows the three measuring cylinders.

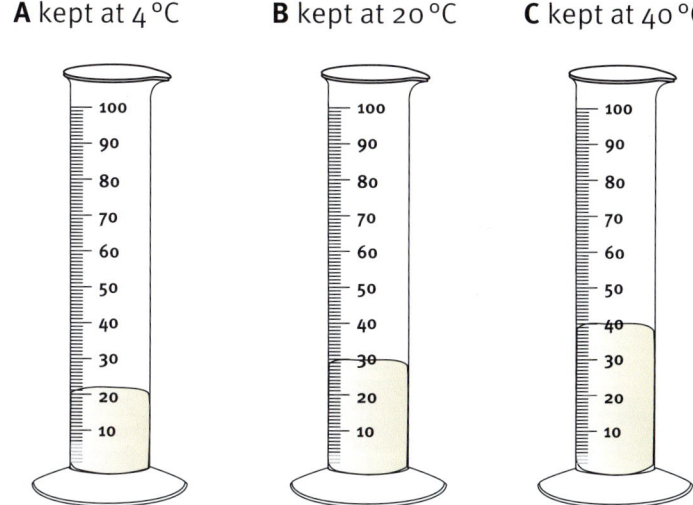

a Copy the results chart. Then complete the headings by writing in the units for each column.

Dough	Temperature /	Volume at start /	Volume after one hour /	Increase in volume / ....
A	4	20		
B		20		
C		20		

[2]

b Complete the **Temperature** column in the results chart. [1]
c Look carefully at the diagrams of the measuring cylinders. Complete the **Volume after one hour** column in the results chart. [3]
d Complete the **Increase in volume** column in the results chart. [1]
e Write down a conclusion that Janzi could make from his results. [1]
f Explain what makes bread dough rise. [3]

3.1 Adaptations

Fish can live in water, but they cannot live on land.

Earthworms can live in soil, but they cannot live in trees.

Giraffes can live on the African savannah, but they cannot live in the Arctic.

Fish cannot live on land.

> **Questions**
> 1 Suggest why a fish cannot live on land.
> 2 Explain why a person cannot live under water.
> 3 Suggest why giraffes cannot live in the Arctic.

The place where an organism lives is called its **habitat**. Each kind of living organism has **adaptations** that help it to live in a particular habitat. Adaptations are special features that help it to live there.

Fish have adaptations that help them to live in water.

The tail helps the fish to move forward through the water.

Fins help the fish to stay balanced.

Gills absorb dissolved oxygen from the water.

The lateral line senses movement in the water around the fish.

The body is streamlined, reducing friction as the fish moves forward.

Fennec foxes have adaptations that help them to live in the hot desert and hunt at night.

Thick fur keeps the fox warm on cold nights.

Sandy coloured fur camouflages the fox.

Large ears lose heat easily, helping to keep the fox cool on hot days. The large ears also help the fox to hear tiny noises, so it can find prey in the dark.

Eyes are adapted to see when there is very little light.

Strong front legs help the fox to make burrows where it rests in the daytime. Thick fur on the soles of the feet stops them burning on the hot sand.

3 Living things in their environment

3.1 Adaptations

Cacti have adaptations that help them to live in the desert, where there is not much water.

The thick stem stores water.

Spines stop thirsty animals eating the cactus to get water.

Long roots can find water deep under the soil.

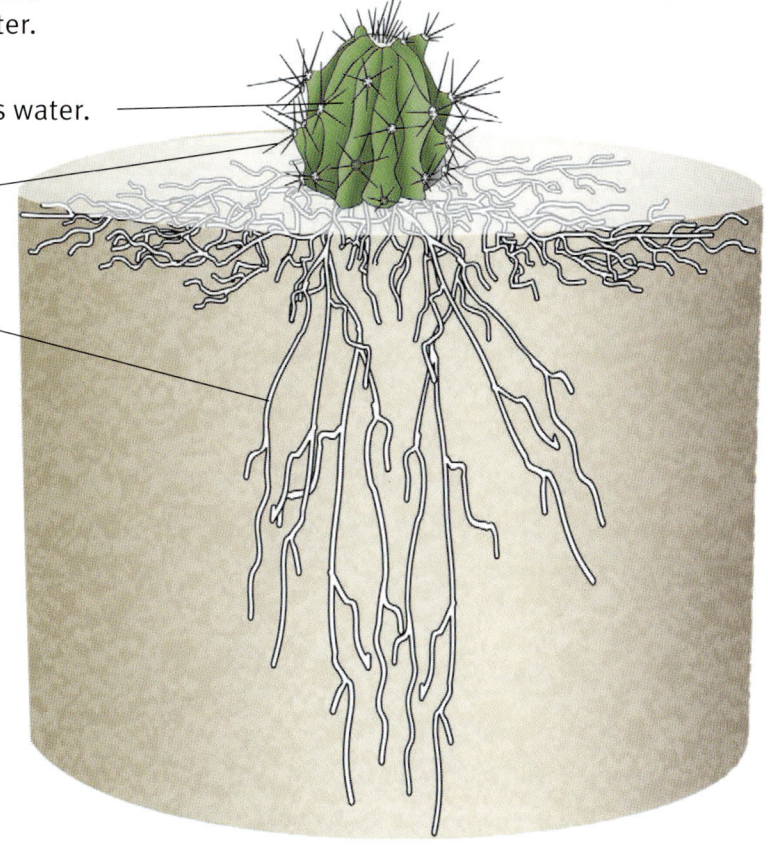

Question

4 How is the eagle adapted to live and hunt in the air?

Activity 3.1
Researching adaptations

1. Choose an animal or plant that lives in your country.
2. Find out about the habitat where the animal or plant lives. Describe the habitat.
3. Make a large drawing of the animal or plant. (If you have a camera, you might be able to take a photograph of it instead.)
4. Use labels to explain some of the features of the animal or plant that help it to live in its particular environment.

Summary
- The place where an organism lives is called its habitat.
- Organisms have special adaptations that help them to live in their habitat.

3 Living things in their environment

3.2 Food chains

Amal had chicken and rice for lunch. It gave him lots of energy. The food that we eat gives us energy.

But how did the energy get into the food?

The energy in our food began in the Sun. Energy from the Sun reaches the Earth in sunlight.

Plants use energy from sunlight to make food. Some of the energy from the sunlight goes into the food that the plant stores inside its roots, stems and leaves.

When an animal eats the plant, it eats the plant's food stores. This is how the animal gets energy.

We can show how the energy passed from the Sun into the rice, and then into Amal's body, by drawing a **food chain**.

The arrows in the food chain show the energy passing from one thing to another.

sunlight   rice   human

Questions

A+I 1. The chicken that Amal ate for lunch ate wheat. Wheat is a plant. Draw a food chain showing how the energy passed from the Sun to Amal when he ate the chicken.

A+I 2. Draw a food chain showing how energy from the Sun passed into you when you ate one of the things that you had for breakfast or lunch.

A+I 3. The snake in the photograph is eating a bird's egg. The bird ate insects. The insects ate plants. Draw a food chain showing how energy from the Sun passes into the snake when it eats the egg.

3 Living things in their environment

3.2 Food chains

Producers and consumers

The first organism in a food chain is always a plant. Plants use energy from sunlight to produce food. They are called **producers**.

Animals cannot make food using sunlight. They have to eat ready-made food. They consume (eat) plants or other animals. They are called **consumers**.

grass → cricket → spider → small bird → hawk

Questions

4 Look at the drawing of the food chain that ends in a hawk.
  a Which organism is the producer in this food chain?
  b Which organisms are consumers in this food chain?
  c What do the arrows in the food chain show?

A+I

5 The lions in the photograph have killed a zebra.
  a How are the lions adapted to live in their environment?
  b List **three** characteristics of living organisms that the lions are showing.
  c Draw a food chain linking some of the organisms in the photograph.
  d Name **two** different producers that you can see in the photograph.

Summary
- A food chain shows how energy passes from one organism to another, when it makes or eats food.
- Food chains begin with plants, which use energy from sunlight to make food.
- Plants are producers, because they produce food.
- Animals are consumers, because they consume food that was originally made by plants.

3 Living things in their environment

3.3 Humans and food chains

Hunter-gatherers

Long ago, humans found all their food in the wild.

They hunted and killed animals. They gathered and ate berries, seeds, leaves and roots from plants that grew where they lived. The hunters had to work hard to find and kill prey. They did not kill very many animals.

They were careful not to gather too many plants. They always left some to grow, so that there would still be food for them in the future.

This painting was made on a rock near Tassili N'Ajjer in Algeria, about 6000 years ago. It shows a man and his dog hunting with a bow and arrow.

Questions

1. Prehistoric hunters killed and ate mammoths. Mammoths ate grass. Draw a food chain to show how prehistoric hunters got energy from mammoths.
2. Explain why prehistoric hunters did not wipe out (destroy) the populations of animals and plants that they used for food.

Farmers

Today, most of the food that we eat comes from farms and gardens. Farmers need land to grow their crops and keep animals. When farming began, trees and plants that grew naturally were cut down and killed. Farmers planted crops on the cleared land.

This forest in Zambia is being cleared to provide land for growing wheat.

How farming affects food chains

When land is cleared to grow crops or to keep animals, most of the plants and animals that used to live there can no longer survive. Their habitat and their food supply is destroyed.

The trees and plants at the beginnings of food chains are killed. Most of the animals further along the food chains have nothing to eat. They die, or they move to other places where they can find food.

But some animals can eat the crops that the farmer grows. They may have even more food to eat than before the land was cleared.

This leaf hopper eats rice leaves. Very large numbers of them can live in rice fields, because they have so much food.

Questions

3. Write a list of **three** crops that are grown in the area where you live.
4. Write a list of **three** animals that are kept for food where you live.
5. Describe **one** way in which farming has a negative effect on a food chain.
6. Describe **one** way in which farming has a positive effect on a food chain.

3.3 Humans and food chains

Human activities and food chains

Any human activity that affects the living organisms around us also affect food chains. Here are two examples.

Fishing

When we take fish from the sea, we are taking away food that another animal could eat. If we take too many fish, then there may not be enough food for these animals, and they may die out.

For example, numbers of puffins in some parts of Scotland have decreased. Puffins eat fish called sand eels. Humans catch a lot of sand eels. Perhaps the puffins cannot find enough food.

A puffin.

Introducing new species

Possums were introduced from Australia into New Zealand to be bred for their fur. Many escaped, and now there are 30 million of them. Possums eat young growth on trees. The trees in New Zealand do not have adaptations to protect them from possums. The possums eat so much that there is not enough food for the native animals and birds. They also eat the eggs and young of the native birds.

A possum.

Activity 3.3
Researching human effects on a food chain

Find out about one way in which human activities in your country have affected a food chain. You may be able to use books and the internet for your research. Try to find out:

- what humans have done, and why
- which animals or plants have been affected by the human activity
- how this has affected a food chain.

You could write an account of what you have found, or make a poster.

Summary
- **Humans clear land to grow crops. This destroys habitats and harms food chains.**
- **Some wild animals can live in the crops that farmers grow.**
- **Fishing and the introduction of new species can harm food chains.**

3 Living things in their environment

3.4 Pollution

The number of humans living on the Earth is growing. We affect our **environment** in many different ways. Some of these effects are harmful to other living things.

For example, we add things to the environment that should not be there. Some of these things harm living organisms. Adding harmful things to the environment is called **pollution**.

The more people there are in the world, the more we pollute the environment.

Water pollution

Some human activities add harmful things to water. This is called water pollution.

Waste from toilets and streets contains harmful bacteria and viruses that can make people ill. It also contains other substances that can harm water plants and animals.

In most countries, sewage is collected in pipes. The pipes carry the sewage to a place where it is treated to make it safe. Treated sewage does not pollute the environment.

Few animals or plants can live in this polluted water.

Air pollution

Some human activities add harmful gases to the air. This is called air pollution.

Burning fuels such as coal, oil and petrol (gasoline) produces **carbon dioxide**. Too much carbon dioxide in the atmosphere stops heat escaping from the Earth. This makes the Earth get warmer.

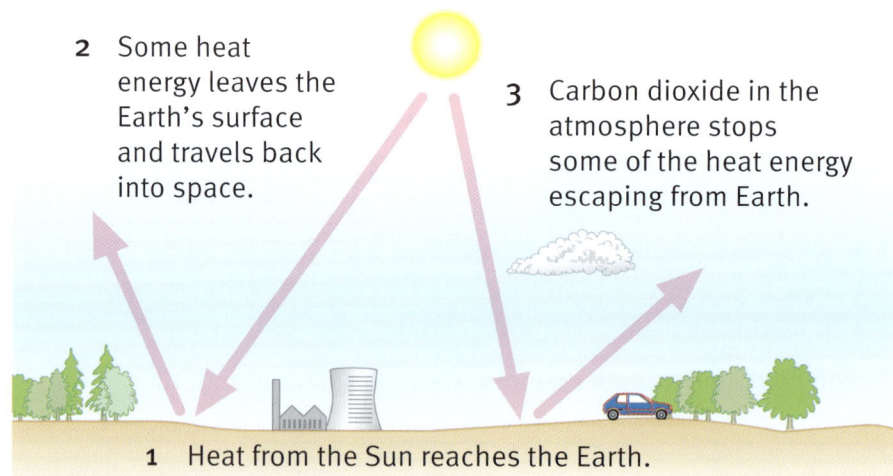

2 Some heat energy leaves the Earth's surface and travels back into space.

3 Carbon dioxide in the atmosphere stops some of the heat energy escaping from Earth.

1 Heat from the Sun reaches the Earth.

Some kinds of coal contain a lot of sulfur. When they burn, they produce a harmful gas called **sulfur dioxide**. Sulfur dioxide dissolves in rainwater and produces **acid rain**. Acid rain harms trees, and animals that live in lakes and rivers.

44 3 Living things in their environment

3.4 Pollution

Questions

1. If the Earth gets warmer, some of the ice at the North Pole and South Pole will melt. Predict how this will affect sea level.
2. Trees use carbon dioxide to make their food. Explain how cutting down trees and burning them will affect the amount of carbon dioxide in the atmosphere.

Destroying forests and burning trees causes air pollution.

Activity 3.4
How does acid rain affect bean seedlings?

1. Take two small dishes or pots with drainage holes. Partly fill them with soil or compost.
2. Plant five mung bean seeds in each pot.
3. Water one pot with ordinary water. Water the other pot with water to which some dilute sulfuric acid has been added.
4. Keep both pots in a warm place. Check them every day. Give them ordinary water or acidified water whenever the soil starts to dry out. Make sure each pot gets the same quantity of water.
5. Record your results. You can do this in a table, or you can draw diagrams to show the differences between the seedlings in the two pots.

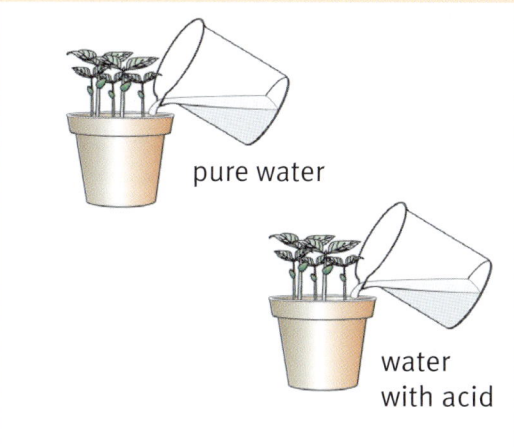

Questions

3. What causes acid rain?
4. In many countries, sulfur is removed from coal before the coal is burnt.
   a. Explain how this reduces air pollution.
   b. Will this completely prevent air pollution from the burning coal? Explain your answer.

Summary
- **Pollution means adding harmful things to the environment.**
- **Untreated sewage causes water pollution.**
- **Burning fossil fuels causes air pollution.**

3 Living things in their environment

3.5 Ozone depletion

Ozone is a gas. There is a layer of ozone high up in the atmosphere. The ozone layer is about 25 kilometres above the ground.

The Sun emits (sends out) **ultraviolet light**. These ultraviolet rays can cause skin cancer and eye damage in humans. They can also damage plants.

The ozone layer protects organisms on the Earth from harmful ultraviolet radiation. Ozone absorbs ultraviolet rays from the Sun. The ozone layer reduces the quantity of ultraviolet radiation that reaches the ground.

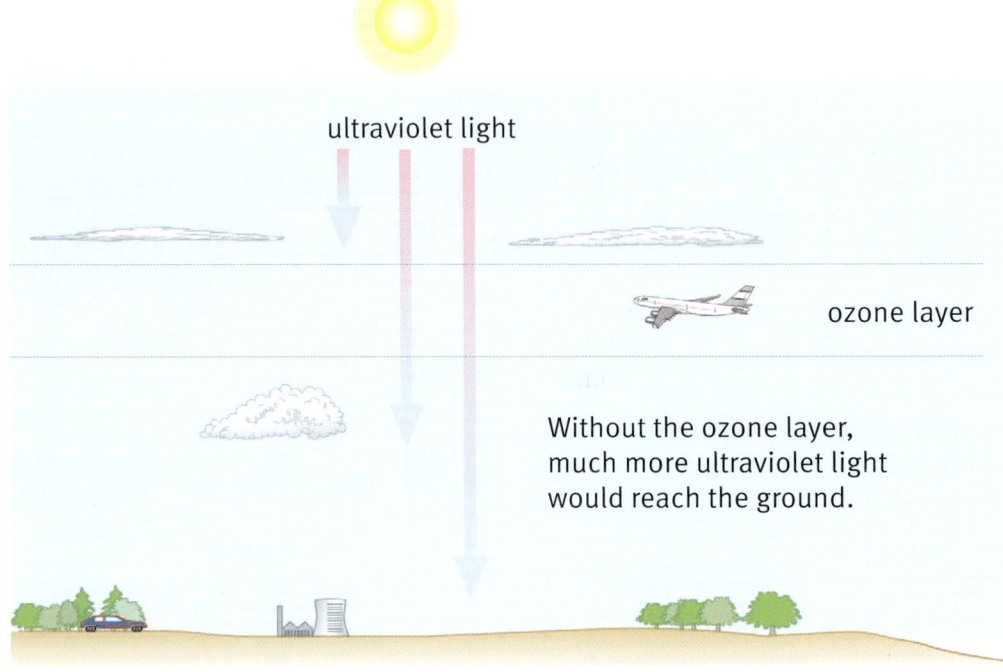

Questions

1. Where is the ozone layer?
2. Describe how ultraviolet rays can harm a person.
3. How does the ozone layer protect us?

The 'hole' in the ozone layer

In 1985, scientists discovered that there was less ozone than there should be over the Antarctic, especially in the Antarctic spring. They called this the **ozone hole**.

The ozone hole isn't really a hole. It is just an area where there is less ozone than normal.

Satellites, such as NASA's Aurora satellite, measure how much ozone there is in the atmosphere. Each year, the ozone hole has been getting larger. It has also been lasting for longer in the year.

Protecting your skin and eyes from the sun is very important, especially if you have a pale skin.

3 Living things in their environment

3.5 Ozone depletion

> **Question**
>
> 4 Look at the images showing the ozone hole.
>   a Describe how the ozone layer over the Antarctic changed between 1981 and 1999.
>   b Suggest why people living in Australia, southern Chile and southern Argentina are more worried about the ozone hole than people living near the equator.

September 1981

What causes the ozone hole?

Gases called CFCs caused the problems with the ozone layer. (CFC is short for chloro-fluorocarbon.)

CFCs are man-made. They were invented in the 1920s. They were used in air-conditioners, refrigerators and aerosol cans. No-one knew that they were harmful.

CFCs rise up high into the atmosphere. They react with ozone and break it down. This happens especially when it is cold, and when sunlight shines onto the CFCs and ozone.

CFCs last for a very long time. Scientists think that the CFCs in the atmosphere will stay there for about one hundred years.

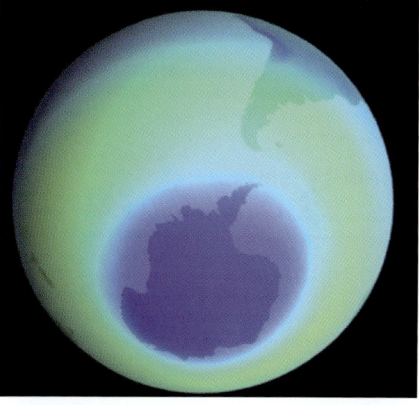
September 1987

Today, CFCs are banned. The ozone layer will eventually recover, but it will take a long time.

> **Questions**
>
> 5 What are CFCs?
> 6 Explain how CFCs harm the ozone layer.
> 7 Use the information about CFCs to explain why the hole in the ozone layer appears:
>   • over the Antarctic, and not over the equator
>   • in the Antarctic spring, not in the Antarctic winter.
> 8 Explain why it will take a very long time for the ozone hole to disappear, even though CFCs have now been banned.

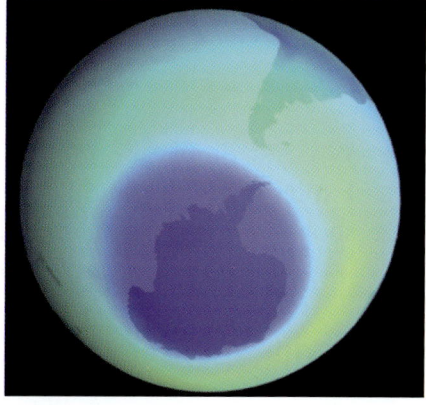
September 1999

less ozone

more ozone

Summary
- Ozone is a gas found in a layer high up in the atmosphere.
- The ozone layer protects us from ultraviolet radiation.
- CFCs have damaged the ozone layer over the Antarctic.
- CFCs are now banned and the ozone layer is recovering.

3.6 Conservation

We share the Earth with millions of other organisms. If we are not careful, many of our activities make it difficult for them to survive.

There are many things that we can do to make sure that other species (kinds) of organisms have suitable habitats to live in.

Taking care of the environment, and helping other species to survive, is called **conservation**.

Reducing pollution

It's very important to try not to pollute the environment. For example:

- we have stopped using CFCs – this will allow the ozone layer to recover.
- we should try to burn less fuel, so that less carbon dioxide is added to the atmosphere
- we can bury rubbish in carefully constructed landfill sites – as the rubbish rots, it produces a gas called methane, which can be collected and used as fuel.

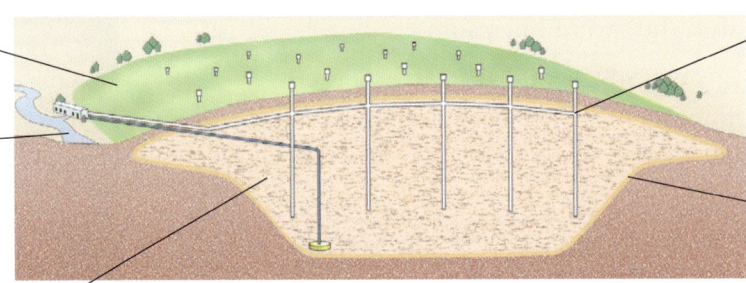

Soil and grass cover the rubbish.

Water is pumped out and treated, so that it is safe to release into the environment.

Waste is compacted so it takes up less space.

Pipes allow methane to be collected and used as fuel.

Waterproof liner prevents pollutants escaping into the soil.

Questions

1. What is conservation?
2. Explain how the landfill site shown in the diagram helps wildlife to survive.

Preserving habitats

We must try not to destroy the habitats of plants and animals. Each species has adaptations that help it to live in a particular habitat. If we destroy the habitat, for example by cutting down trees, then some species may not have a suitable place to live. They may become extinct.

This forest is in Chile. Many of the trees are very old. If they are cut down, many animals and plants will lose their habitat.

3.6 Conservation

We can make nature reserves and other protected areas, where people are not allowed to do any harm to the environment or to the animals and plants that live there.

These sand gazelles live on the island of Sir Bani Yas, Abu Dhabi. The island is a nature reserve where thousands of animals and plants are conserved.

Activity 3.6
A school nature reserve

Nature reserves do not have to be big. Perhaps there is a small nature reserve in your school grounds. If not, perhaps you could make one.

- If your school has a nature reserve, make a map or drawing of it. Annotate your map or drawing to explain how the nature reserve helps plants and animals to live there.
- If your school does not have a nature reserve, think of a place where there could be one. It does not have to be big – even a tiny area could be a place for animals and plants to live in peace. Make a map or drawing explaining how you think this place could look if it became a nature reserve.

A pond can be a good nature reserve.

Questions

3 Describe **two** reasons why we should try not to cut down forests. (If you can only think of one reason, look back to pages **44–45**.)
4 Think of a habitat near to your school, or where you live, that is under threat from human activities.
  a Describe the habitat.
  b Explain why it is under threat.
  c Suggest what could be done to protect the habitat.

Summary
- Conservation means looking after the environment so that animals and plants can live there.
- Reducing pollution and preserving habitats are important ways of looking after the environment.

3 Living things in their environment

3.7 Energy resources

People use a lot of energy each day.

- Our bodies use energy for moving around, for thinking, for growing and for keeping warm. All of this energy comes from the food that we eat.

- Vehicles use energy for moving. They get their energy from fuels. Cars use petrol (gasoline). Trucks use diesel. Aeroplanes use kerosene.

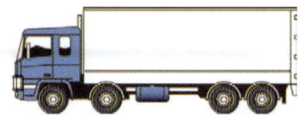

- Many things in the home use energy to make them work. Most of these use energy from electricity. The electricity is made in power stations. Many power stations use coal or gas to make the electricity.

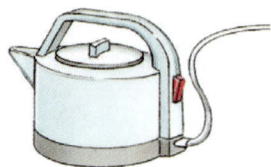

Fossil fuels

Coal, oil and natural gas are **fossil fuels**. We get these fuels from deep under the Earth's surface.

Fossil fuels formed millions of years ago. They were produced when plants and microscopic organisms died in swamps and bogs. Their bodies did not decay. Instead, they turned into coal, oil or gas.

Today, only tiny quantities of new fossil fuels are forming. We are using them up quickly. One day, we will run out of fossil fuels.

Fossil fuels are **non-renewable** energy resources. Non-renewable means that, when we use them, they are not being made again.

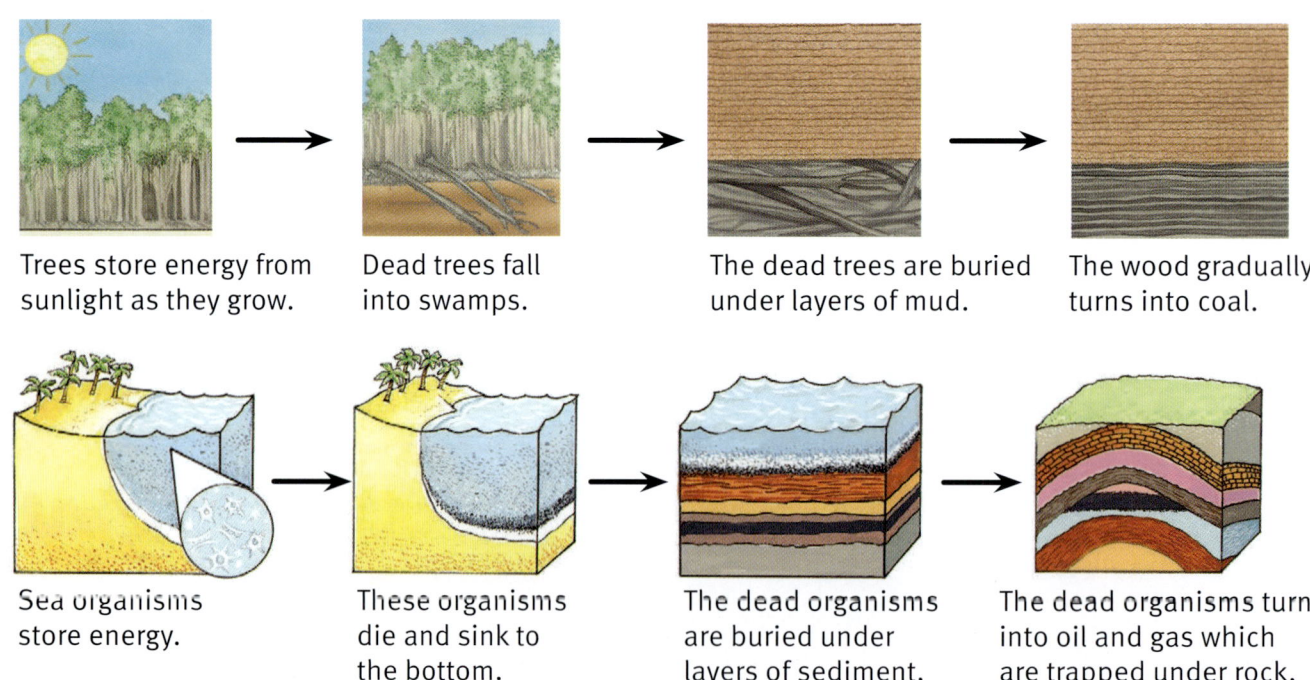

Trees store energy from sunlight as they grow. → Dead trees fall into swamps. → The dead trees are buried under layers of mud. → The wood gradually turns into coal.

Sea organisms store energy. → These organisms die and sink to the bottom. → The dead organisms are buried under layers of sediment. → The dead organisms turn into oil and gas which are trapped under rock.

3.7 Energy resources

Questions

1. Name **one** example of a non-renewable energy resource.
2. Look around you. What things are using energy at this moment? What is the energy being used for?
3. Suggest **two** reasons why we should try to use less fossil fuel. (If you can only think of one reason, look back to pages **44–45**.)

Renewable energy resources

There are some energy resources that will not run out. They are called **renewable** energy resources.

Wind is always blowing somewhere on Earth. The energy in wind can be used to turn turbines. This can make electricity.

Plants absorb energy from sunlight to help them to grow. We can burn wood or other plant material to get some of this energy from them.

Energy from the Sun reaches Earth as heat and light. These can be used to heat water or make electricity.

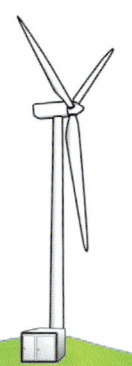

The wind makes the turbine turn. This drives a generator, which produces electricity.

Energy is transferred to trees by sunlight. Trees are stores of chemical energy.

Solar cells in the solar panel transform energy in sunlight to electrical energy.

Questions

4. Suggest **one** reason why some people do not want wind turbines near their house.
5. Suggest **one** advantage and **one** disadvantage of using wood, rather than electricity, for cooking food.
6. Suggest **one** advantage and **one** disadvantage of using energy from the Sun, rather than petrol (gasoline), for running a car.

Summary
- A non-renewable energy resource is one that we are using up faster than it is being formed. It will eventually run out.
- Fossil fuels are non-renewable.
- A renewable energy resource is one that will not run out.
- Wind, plants and energy in sunlight are renewable energy resources.

Unit 3 End of unit questions

3.1 The diagram shows a food chain.

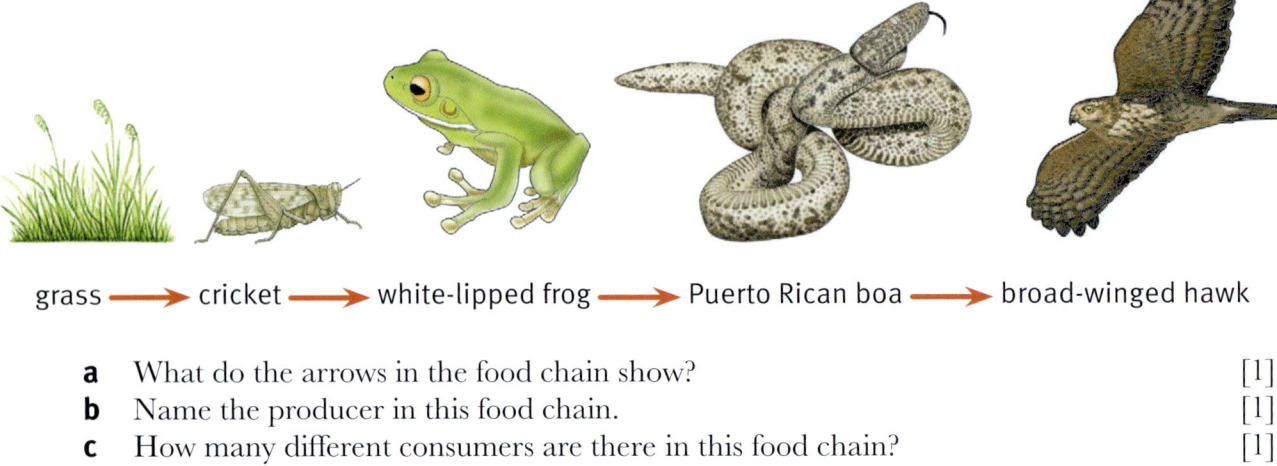

grass → cricket → white-lipped frog → Puerto Rican boa → broad-winged hawk

    a What do the arrows in the food chain show? [1]
    b Name the producer in this food chain. [1]
    c How many different consumers are there in this food chain? [1]
    d The frog lives in trees. Using features that you can see in the drawing, explain **two** ways in which the frog is adapted to avoid being eaten by snakes. [4]

3.2 Nuts are seeds. When we eat nuts, we get energy from them.
Debbie wanted to find out if cashew nuts contain more energy than pecan nuts.

- Debbie measured 20 cm³ of water into a test tube.
- She measured the temperature of the water.
- She speared a cashew nut on a long needle, and then held it in a flame until it began to burn.
- She held the nut under the water until the nut had completely burnt.
- Then she measured the new temperature of the water.

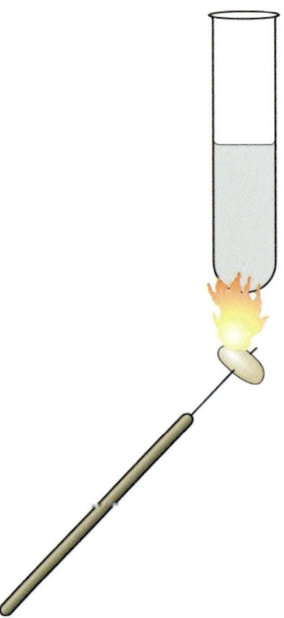

3 Living things in their environment

3 End of unit questions

a Which apparatus should Debbie use to measure 20 cm³ of water? Choose from the list.

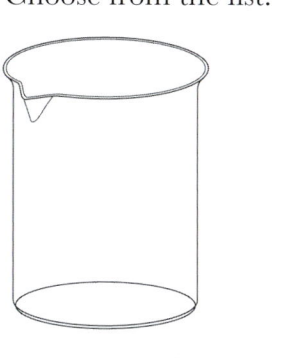

beaker   measuring cylinder   test tube   ruler   [1]

b The diagrams show the thermometer readings at the start, and after the nut had finished burning.

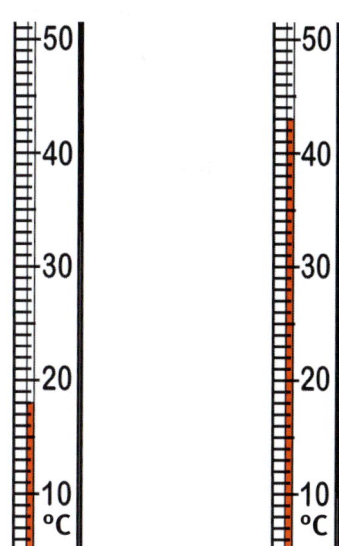

Write down:
- the temperature of the water at the start
- the temperature of the water after the nut had finished burning
- the change in the temperature. [4]

c Debbie repeated her experiment using a pecan nut.
State **three** things that Debbie should keep the same when she repeated her experiment. [3]

d Explain how Debbie could use her results to decide whether a cashew nut or a pecan nut contains more energy. [2]

3.3 The ozone layer is high above the Earth's surface.
  a What is ozone? [1]
  b Explain how the ozone layer protects humans and other organisms on Earth. [2]
  c The ozone layer over the Antarctic has got thinner. This is called the 'ozone hole'. Explain what has made this happen. [2]

3 Living things in their environment

4.1 What is a species?

Scientists group living organisms into different kinds, called **species**.

A species is a group of organisms that all share the same characteristics.

> **Questions**
>
> 1. What similarities can you see between the two species of ground squirrels in the photographs?
> 2. What differences can you see between the two species of ground squirrels?

These are Cape ground squirrels.

Species and breeding

Organisms that belong to the same species can breed with each other. When they have offspring, the offspring belong to the same species as their parents.

Organisms that belong to different species cannot usually breed with each other.

But very occasionally two organisms from different species do breed with each other. This might happen in a zoo, where two animals from different species are put into the same enclosure. Their offspring are **hybrids** of the two species.

For example, a male lion and a female tiger in a zoo will sometimes breed together, if they don't have a member of their own species to breed with. The young animals that are produced are called ligers.

Ligers, like all hybrids between two different species, cannot have offspring. They are **infertile**.

This is a Columbian ground squirrel.

This liger was born in a zoo in China. She is a hybrid between a lion and a tiger.

> **Questions**
>
> 3. Copy and complete these sentences.
>   A species is a group of organisms with the same ....
>   Organisms from the same species can .... with each other.
> 4. Explain why lions and tigers belong to different species, even though they can sometimes breed together.

4 Variation and classification

4.1 What is a species?

Activity 4.1
Comparing species

Your teacher will give you some samples of two similar species of organisms.

1 Write down **five** similarities between the two species.
2 Write down **five** differences between the two species. You could do this in a table to make your answer clearer.
3 Suggest what a scientist would need to do to be sure that these two organisms really do belong to different species.

Naming species

The names of the same species can be very different in different countries. For example, in English-speaking countries, a killer whale is also known as an orca or a blackfish (though it isn't really a fish at all). Each language in the world also has a different name for the same species.

A killer whale has the Latin name *Orcinus orca*.

In 1735, a Swedish scientist called Carl Linnaeus decided to give every species a two-word Latin name. Linnaeus's naming system meant that every scientist could use the same name for the same species.

We still use Linnaeus's system today. The Latin names of species are written in italics. For example, the Latin name of our species is *Homo sapiens*. 'Sapiens' means 'thinking', so our Latin name means 'thinking humans'.

Summary
- A species is a group of organisms that have the same characteristics, and that can breed with one another to produce fertile offspring.
- Each species has a two-word Latin name.

4 Variation and classification

4.2 Variation in a species

We have seen that organisms that share the same characteristics, and that can breed with one another, are classified in the same species.

But the members of a species are not all exactly the same. There are always differences between individuals. Differences between individual members of a species are called **variation**.

Domestic dogs all belong to the same species.

These are ox-eye daisy flowers.

Questions

A+I
1   a   Make a list of **five** kinds of variation that you can see between the dogs in the photograph above.
    b   Suggest why scientists classify all domestic dogs in the same species, even though the different breeds of dog show so much variation.

A+I
2   The flowers in the picture above all come from the same species of daisy plant.
    a   What characteristics do all of the flowers share?
    b   Make a list of ways in which these flowers show variation.

Activity 4.2
Variation in humans

SE
All humans belong to the same species. But none of us is identical with any other human. Even identical twins have small differences.

Choose four or five features that vary among the members of your class. Choose at least one feature that you have to measure.

Then construct a results table like this. Change the headings to match the features that you have chosen. Draw enough rows so that you can record your results for at least eight people.

Person	Hair colour	Eye colour	Shoe size	Height / cm

Collect your results and complete your results table.

4.2 Variation in a species

Frequency diagrams

If we count up the number of individuals with each version of a variable feature, we can display the results as a **frequency diagram**.

A species of plant called kidney vetch has flowers that show variation in colour.

A student counted the number of plants with each colour of flower growing in a small area of a field.

red   pink   orange   yellow   cream

She recorded her results like this:

Colour	Red	Pink	Orange	Yellow	Cream
Tally	⋕⋕	II	III	⋕⋕ IIII	III
Number	5	2	3	9	3

For each plant that she found, she put a stroke / in the correct column of the Tally row.

When she had recorded the flower colour of each plant, she added up all the tally strokes and wrote the number in the last row.

Then she used her results to draw a frequency diagram, like the one on the right.

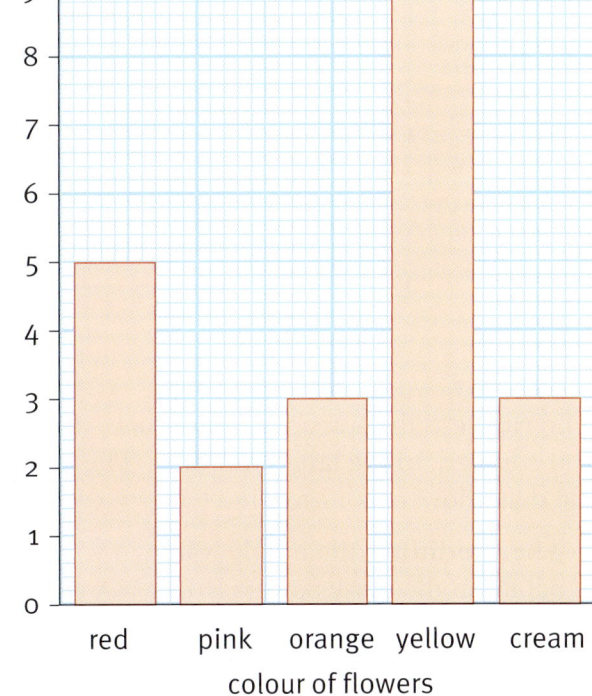

Questions

3 How many plants did the student find?
4 Which was the most common flower colour?
5 The student recorded her results in a results table, and then in a frequency diagram. Which of these do you think shows the results more clearly? Explain your answer.

Summary
- **Differences between organisms belonging to the same species are called variation.**
- **We can show the pattern of variation in a group of organisms using a frequency diagram.**

4 Variation and classification

4.3 Investigating variation

Often, the variation in a species involves differences that we can count or measure. We have seen that we can use frequency diagrams to make it easy to see any patterns in this variation.

We can also use the results that we collect to find some useful information about the variation.

For example, imagine that you have counted the numbers of petals on ten daisy flowers. These were your results:

18, 21, 19, 20, 20, 17, 19, 18, 17, 20.

You could draw a frequency diagram like this.

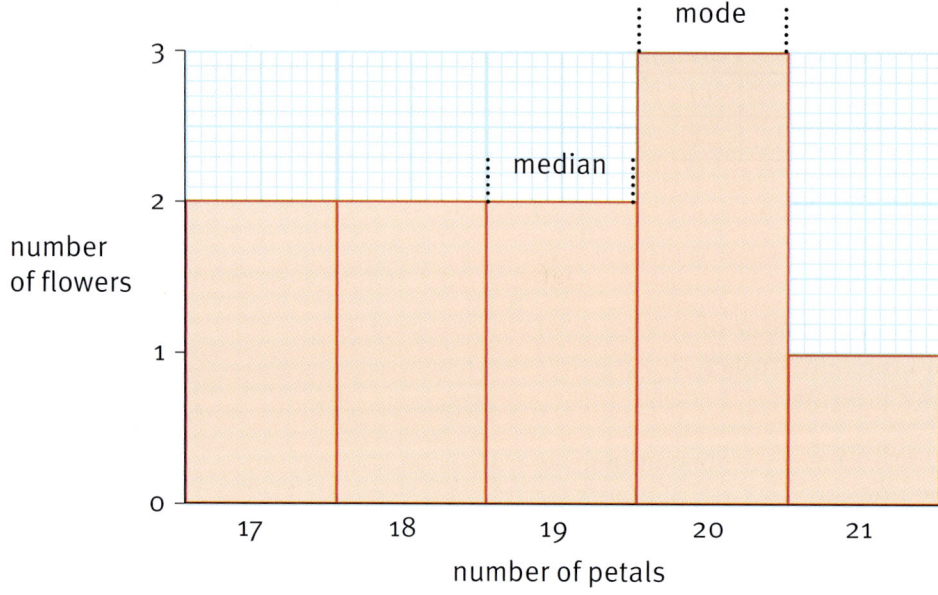

The **range** is the spread of the values – from the smallest number of petals you counted, to the largest number. The range for the number of petals on the daisy flowers is 17 to 21.

- The **median** is the middle value in your results. The median number of petals on the daisy flowers is 19.
- The **mode** is the most common value. The mode for the number of petals on the daisy flowers is 20.
- The **mean** number of petals is often called the 'average'. To find the mean, add up all the individual values and divide by the number of results. For the daisy petals, the total number is:

    18 + 21 + 19 + 20 + 20 + 17 + 19 + 18 + 17 + 20 = 189

So the mean is:

    189 ÷ 10 = 18.9

4.3 Investigating variation

Activity 4.3
Investigating variation in leaves

Some trees have leaves that are divided up into several leaflets.

You are going to investigate the variation in the number of leaflets in a leaf.

1. Collect at least 20 leaves from one species of tree. Your teacher will suggest suitable trees for you to collect them from.
2. Count the numbers of leaflets on each leaf, and write them down in a list, like this:

    11, 15, 12, 11, 13 ... and so on.

3. When you have counted and recorded the number of leaflets for each leaf, you can calculate the mean number of leaflets per leaf.
    To calculate the mean:
    - add up the total number of leaflets
    - divide that number by the number of leaves that you used.
4. Next, draw and complete a results table like this. You will need to adapt the numbers in the first row so that the results table works for the range of numbers for your leaves.
5. Now you are ready to draw a frequency diagram of your results. Use the frequency diagram opposite to help you.

leaflet

Number of leaflets	11	12	13	14	15
Tally					
Number of leaves					

Questions

A1 What is the overall range of the number of leaflets on a leaf?
A2 What is the median for the number of leaflets in your leaves?
A3 What is the mode in your results?
A4 Describe any patterns that you can see in your results.

Summary
- To calculate the mean of a set of results, add them all up and divide by the number of results.
- We can show the range and pattern of variation in a characteristic using a frequency diagram.
- The range is the spread of numbers, from the smallest to the largest.
- The median is the middle value.
- The mode is the most common value.

4.4 Classifying plants

Living organisms are classified into groups. Carl Linnaeus was one of the first people to classify living organisms. We have seen that he grouped them into species.

We can also classify organisms into much larger groups. For example, we classify all the organisms that have green leaves and can photosynthesise as **plants**. Organisms that can move around and eat other organisms as food are **animals**. The plant group and the animal group are called **kingdoms**.

> **Question**
>
> 1 Describe how the cells of an organism belonging to the plant kingdom differ from the cells of an organism belonging to the animal kingdom.

The plant kingdom contains several million different species of plants. These are classified into four major groups.

Mosses

Mosses are very small plants. Most of them live in damp, shady places. They do not produce flowers. They produce **spores** for reproduction. They have thin leaves that dry out easily.

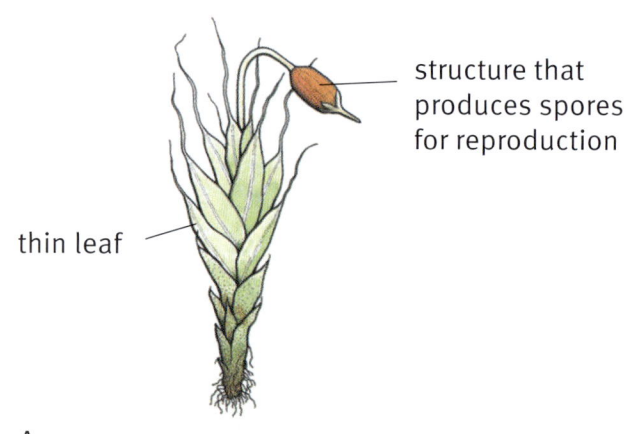

A moss.

Ferns

Ferns also like to grow in shady places, but they are much bigger than mosses. Some of them grow so big that they are called tree ferns.

Ferns have leaves called **fronds**. Like mosses, they don't produce flowers. They reproduce using spores. The spores grow on the backs of their fronds.

A fern.

4 Variation and classification

4.4 Classifying plants

Conifers

Most conifers grow into large trees. They often have tough, narrow leaves called **needles**. They don't have proper flowers. They reproduce using **seeds**. The seeds are produced inside **cones**.

Part of a pine tree.

Flowering plants

These plants reproduce using seeds that are produced inside flowers. There is a diagram of a flowering plant on page **7**.

This is a strawberry plant. The flowers develop into strawberry fruits containing seeds.

> **Question**
>
> 2 Divide a page in your notebook into four spaces, one for each of the four major groups of plants. Write bullet points inside each space, to summarise the characteristics of each group. You could also include a drawing of a plant from each group.

Summary
- Plants are divided into four major groups – mosses, ferns, conifers and flowering plants.

4 Variation and classification

4.5 Classifying vertebrates

Vertebrates are animals with backbones. They are classified into five groups called **classes**.

Fish

Fish are vertebrates with fins. Their skin is covered with scales. They breathe using **gills**. They lay eggs in the water.

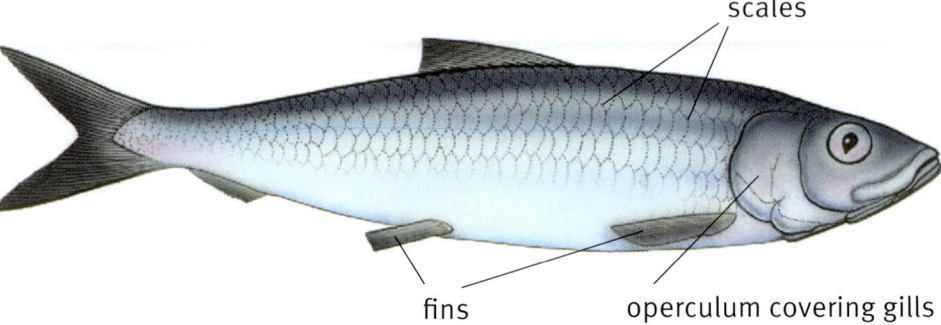

A sardine.

Amphibians

Amphibians include frogs, toads, newts and salamanders. The adults live on land and breathe using lungs. They have four **limbs**. They lay eggs in water. The young are called tadpoles, and develop in water where they breathe using gills. Amphibians have smooth skin without scales.

A tree frog.

Reptiles

Reptiles are vertebrates with scaly skins. Most of them have four legs, although snakes have lost their legs. Some reptiles live on land, but some – such as crocodiles – live in water. Reptiles reproduce by laying eggs on land. The dinosaurs were reptiles.

A boa.

4 Variation and classification

4.5 Classifying vertebrates

Birds
Birds are vertebrates with wings, feathers and a beak. They lay eggs on land.

A European robin.

Mammals
This is the group that humans belong to. Mammals are vertebrates with hair. Mammals give birth to live young, which are fed on milk from the mother.

A wolf.

Questions

1. Divide a page in your notebook into five spaces, one for each of the five major groups of vertebrates. Write bullet points inside each space, to summarise the characteristics of each group. You could also include a drawing of an animal from each group.
2. Decide which group of vertebrates each of these animals belongs to. (You may need to look some of them up if you don't know anything about them.) Give a reason for each of your decisions.

   tiger   ostrich   toad   whale
   lizard   sea turtle   mud skipper

Summary
- Vertebrates are animals with backbones.
- Vertebrates are classified into five classes – fish, amphibians, reptiles, birds and mammals.

4.6 Classifying invertebrates

Invertebrates are animals without backbones. There are many different groups of invertebrates. Only a few of them are described here.

Molluscs

Molluscs are animals with a soft body. They have a muscular foot which they use to move around. Some molluscs have shells. Slugs, snails and octopuses are molluscs.

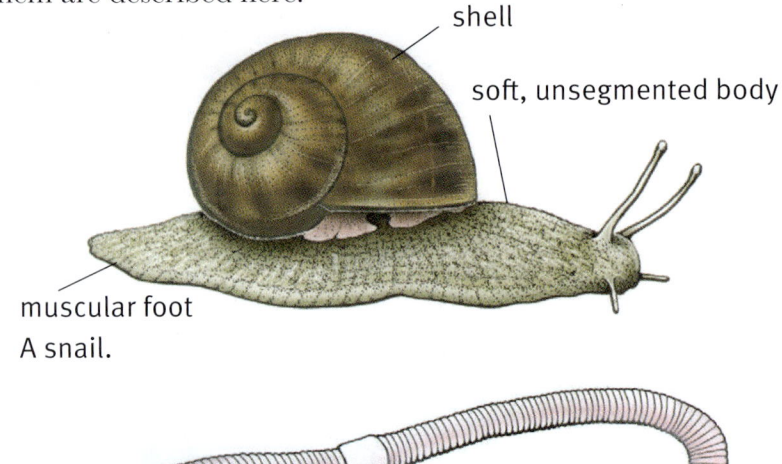

A snail.

Annelids

Annelids are worms with bodies divided up into rings (**segments**). They do not have legs but they do have tiny bristles called chaetae. Earthworms are annelids.

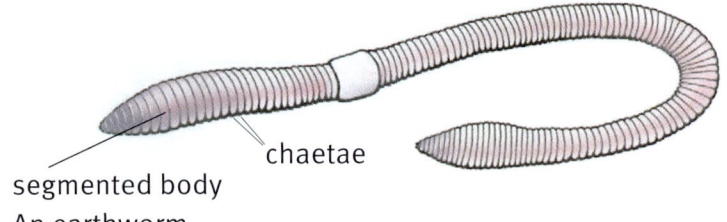

An earthworm.

Arthropods

Arthropods are invertebrates with jointed legs. Their bodies are divided into segments. Arthropods have a skeleton on the outside of their bodies, called an **exoskeleton**.

Arthropods are the most common kinds of animals on Earth. There are several different groups of arthropods.

Insects

Insects are arthropods with six jointed legs. Their bodies are divided into three parts – a head, thorax and abdomen. Each of these parts is made up of several segments. Most insects have two pairs of wings attached to their thorax. The legs are also attached to the thorax. They have one pair of **antennae** on their head.

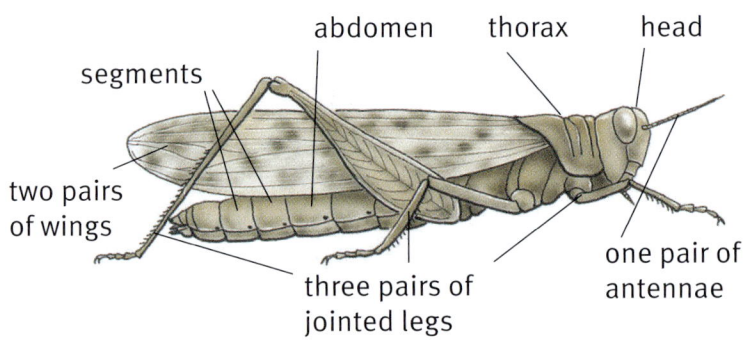

A locust.

Arachnids

Arachnids are arthropods with eight jointed legs. They do not have wings or antennae. Spiders and scorpions are arthropods.

A spider.

4 Variation and classification

4.6 Classifying invertebrates

Crustaceans

Crustaceans are arthropods with an especially tough exoskeleton. They have more than four pairs of jointed legs. They have two pairs of antennae. Lobsters, water fleas and woodlice are crustaceans.

Myriapods

Myriapods are arthropods with many pairs of jointed legs. They have one pair of antennae. Millipedes and centipedes are myriapods.

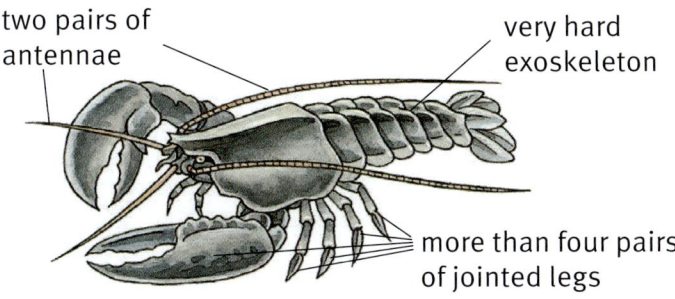

A lobster.

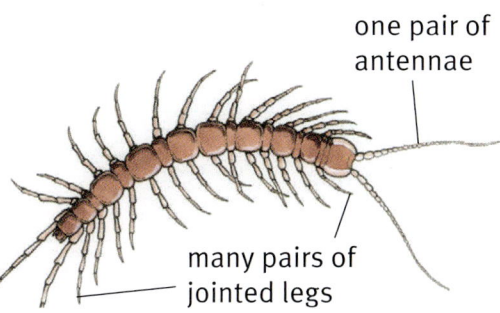

A centipede.

Question

1. Divide a page in your notebook into three spaces, one for each of the groups of invertebrates described in this Topic. The third space needs to be much bigger than the first two and divided into four smaller spaces. Write bullet points inside each space, to summarise the characteristics of each group. You could also include a drawing of an animal from each group.

Activity 4.6
Finding and classifying invertebrates

Go outside and hunt for invertebrates. Your teacher will suggest some good places to look.

If you have a camera, you could take pictures of the invertebrates that you find. If not, make simple drawings of them.

- Decide which group each invertebrate belongs to. (You might find some that don't belong to any of the groups described here. If so, ask your teacher for help.) Explain the reasons for your decision.
- Describe the habitat in which each animal lives.

Summary
- Invertebrates are animals without backbones.
- Some important invertebrate groups are the molluscs, annelids and arthropods.
- Arthropods are divided into four main groups: insects, arachnids, crustaceans and myriapods.

Unit 4 End of unit questions

4.1 Takafumi investigated variation in bean pods.
He picked 20 bean pods, all from the same species of bean plant. He counted the number of beans in each pod. These are the results that he wrote down.

7, 3, 8, 6, 3, 4, 7, 5, 5, 8, 6, 4, 6, 7, 5, 5, 6, 5, 4, 8

  a Calculate the mean (average) number of beans in a pod. Show how you worked out your answer. [2]

  b Copy this results table. Use Takafumi's results to complete it.

Number of beans in a pod						
Tally						
Number of pods						

[2]

  c Copy these axes onto a large piece of graph paper. Then complete a frequency diagram to show Takafumi's results.

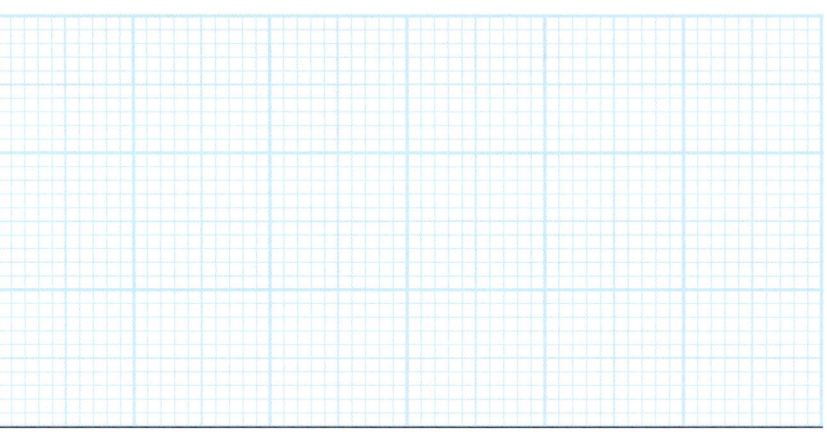

number of pods

number of beans in a pod

  Add a suitable scale on each axis. [2]
  Draw touching bars to show the results. [2]

4.2 The drawing shows a small animal that lives in water, magnified.

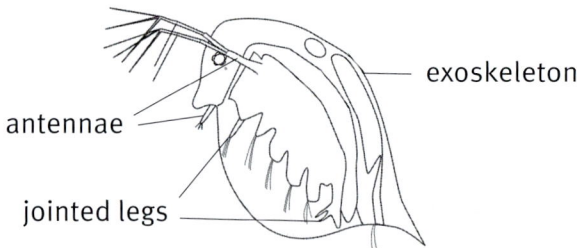

Which **three** of these groups of organisms does this animal belong to?

animals   arthropods   insects   vertebrates
crustaceans   myriapods   amphibians [3]

4 Variation and classification

4 End of unit questions

4.3 A scientist studies birds in New Zealand. The photographs show two kinds of parakeets that live there.

 Yellow-crowned parakeet, *Cyanoramphus auriceps*.

 Red-crowned parakeet, *Cyanoramphus novaezelandiae*.

a Explain why scientists give Latin names to birds and other organisms. [2]

The scientist wanted to find out if these two kinds of parakeet belong to different species.
She searched in suitable habitats for nesting pairs of parakeets.
She never found a yellow-crowned parakeet that had paired up with a red-crowned parakeet.

b Explain the meaning of each of these terms:
- species [2]
- habitat. [1]

c The scientist concluded that the yellow-crowned parakeet and red-crowned parakeet did belong to two different species.
What evidence did she have for making this conclusion? [1]

d Suggest what the scientist should do to be even more certain that her conclusion is correct. Choose from:
- looking at stuffed specimens of parakeets in a museum
- checking more pairs of parakeets in the wild
- looking at other species of parakeets. [1]

4.4 The photographs show parts of three plants.

 plant A (underside)

 plant B

 plant C

Copy and complete the table.

Plant	Major group to which it belongs	Reasons
A		
B		
C		

[6]

5.1 States of matter

Everything you can see and feel is called **matter.** Bricks, air and water are all examples of matter.

Scientists sort matter into three groups. These groups are called **solid, liquid** and **gas**. These three groups are called **states of matter**.

Solids, liquids and gases behave in different ways. The ways they behave are called their **properties**.

Solids

Solids keep the same shape. They take up the same amount of space. They keep the same **volume.** They cannot be squashed (**compressed**) or poured.

fruit   book   bricks   shoe

Liquids

Liquids take the shape of the container they are in. Liquids can be poured and can move through gaps. They cannot be squashed. Liquids take up the same amount of space. They keep the same volume.

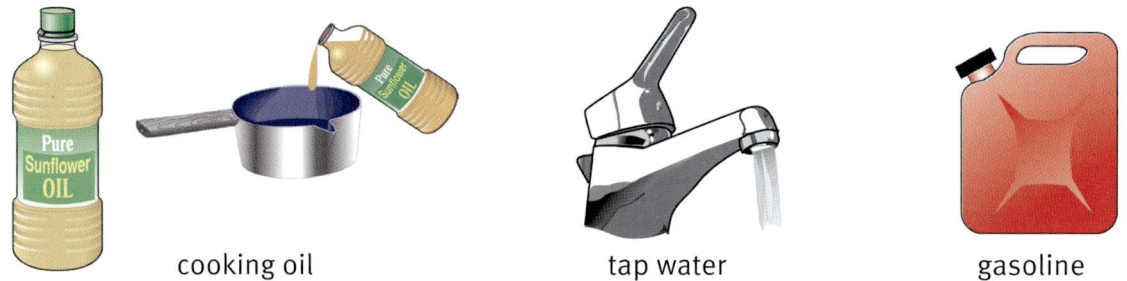

cooking oil   tap water   gasoline

Gases

Gases move to fill any closed container they are in. Gases flow like liquids. They are very easy to squash. The volume of a gas can change. Gases weigh very little. You often cannot see or feel gases, but you can sometimes smell them, and you can feel moving air on your face.

wind   air inside balloons   smells from food

5.1 States of matter

Properties of solids, liquids and gases

The pictures show some of the properties of solids, liquids and gases.

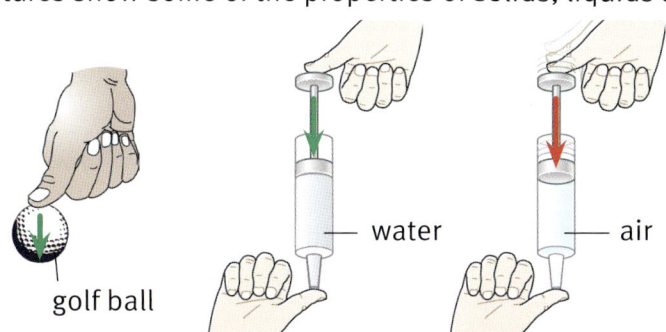

golf ball — water — air

dry ice in beaker

water in watering can

Questions
1. What are the three states of matter?
2. Which state of matter can be squashed easily?
3. Which state of matter cannot be poured?

Activity 5.1
Solid, liquid or gas?

Copy the table and complete it using objects around you. Discuss your reasons for each decision with your group.

Substance	Solid, liquid or gas	I know this because ...
water	liquid	I can pour it.

Scientists look at what matter does

Scientists try to explain what they see. Here are some examples of how matter behaves that scientists have tried to explain.

- You can smell food cooking in another room.
- Some substances get bigger when you heat them.
- Liquids such as water change to a gas when you heat them.
- Substances change from liquid to solid if you cool them.

The ideas that scientists have are called **theories**. The best theory to explain how matter behaves uses the idea of **particles**. This theory says that all matter is made up of tiny particles arranged in different ways.

Summary
- Solids, liquids and gases are the three states of matter.
- Each state of matter has different properties.
- Matter is made up of tiny particles.

5.2 Particle theory

All matter is made up of tiny particles. These particles are much too small to see. These particles are arranged differently in solids, liquids and gases.

Solids

In solids the particles are arranged in a fixed pattern. The particles are held together strongly and are tightly packed. This is why solids have a fixed shape.

The particles in a solid can **vibrate** but they stay in the same place.

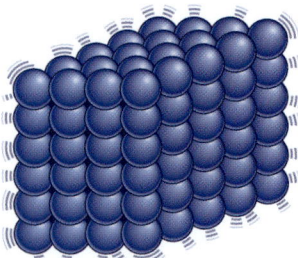

In solids the particles are packed together and can vibrate. They stay in place.

Liquids

In liquids the particles touch each other. The particles are held together weakly. The particles can move past one another but they remain touching one another. Liquids can change shape.

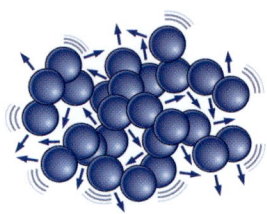

In liquids the particles touch each other, can move and can change places.

Gases

In gases the particles do not touch each other. They are a long way apart. The particles can spread out by themselves. The particles can spread out to fill up the space they are in. Gases can change shape.

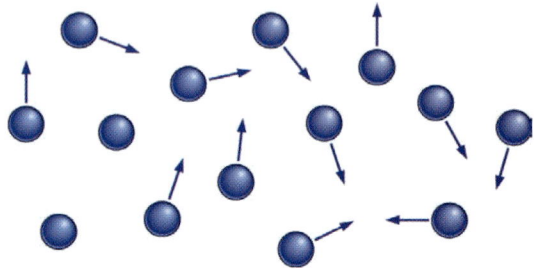

In gases the particles are far apart and can move about freely.

Questions

1. List the properties of solids.
2. Name a property of liquids that they do **not** share with solids.
3. Name a property of gases that they share with liquids.
4. Name a property of gases that they do **not** share with solids or liquids.

Activity 5.2
Modelling the particles in solids, liquids and gases

1. As a group, arrange yourselves in a pattern as if you are the particles in a solid.
2. Arrange yourselves as if you are the particles in a liquid.
3. Arrange yourselves as if you are the particles in a gas.
4. Write down the ways you had to organise yourselves to behave as the particle theory suggests.

5.2 Particle theory

Explaining the properties

Matter can only flow if the particles can move past each other.

Matter can only change volume if the particles in it can spread out or move closer together.

Solids
The particles in a solid are already very close together. This makes it difficult for the volume of a solid to be made smaller. Solids have a fixed shape because the particles are held together by attractive forces. These forces stop the particles from moving around. The particles can only vibrate. This means that a solid cannot flow.

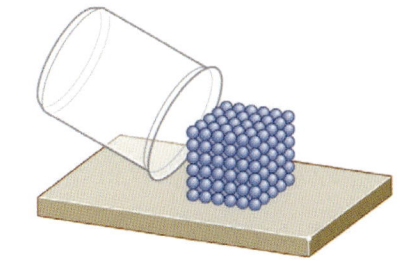
Solids cannot flow.

Liquids
The volume of a liquid cannot be changed. The particles are very close together and cannot be squashed. The particles can move past each other. The attractive forces between the particles are weak enough to allow them to move but strong enough to hold them together.

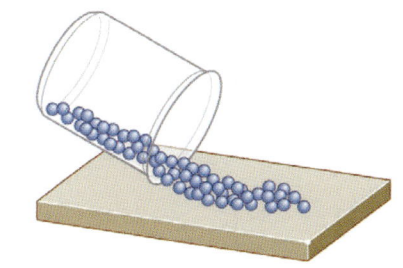
Liquids can flow.

Gases
Particles in a gas are a long way apart so they can move quickly in all directions. The particles can move easily because there are no attractive forces between them. This means that a gas has no fixed shape or volume.

When you squash a gas, the particles move closer together and the gas takes up less space.

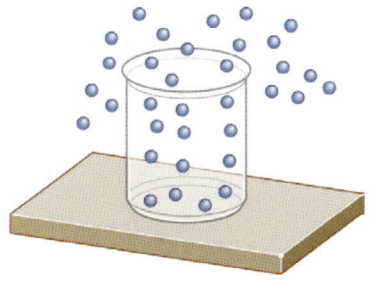
Gases can flow and spread out.

Summary
- In a solid the particles are packed in a fixed pattern, with strong forces between them. The particles can only vibrate.
- In a liquid the particles are packed together with weaker forces so the particles can move past each other.
- In a gas the particles are a long way apart and they can move freely.

5 States of matter

5.3 Changing state

If you leave ice in a warm place it **melts** and becomes liquid water.

A puddle of water will gradually disappear as it changes to **water vapour**, an invisible gas. This is called **evaporation**. Warmer water evaporates more quickly.

If you heat water until its temperature reaches 100 °C, it will **boil**. Now all of the water changes rapidly to **steam**. 100 °C is the boiling point of water.

If the water vapour or steam touches something cold, it **condenses** and changes back into liquid water. This is called **condensation.**

If you place liquid water in the freezer, it **freezes** and becomes ice.

These changes are known as **changes of state**.

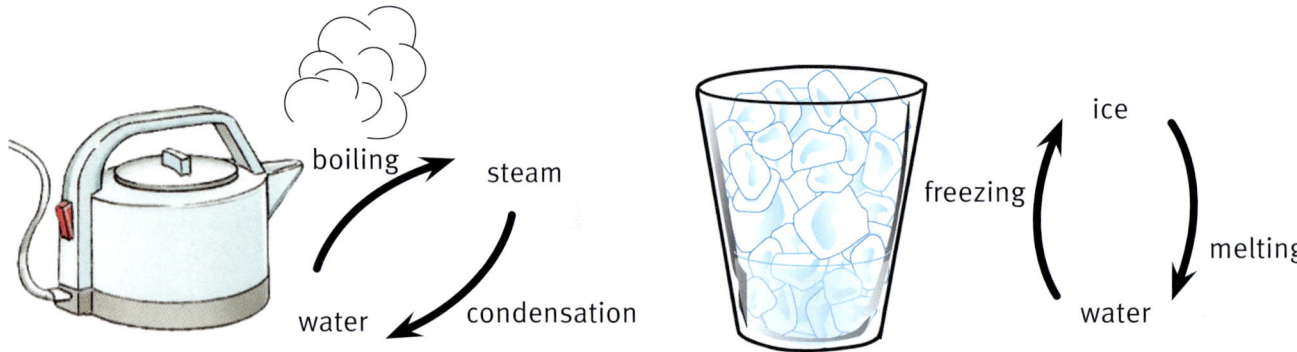

Measuring

Measuring volume

When you measure the volume of a liquid you use a **measuring cylinder.** The liquid forms a curve at the top. This is called the **meniscus.** You measure the volume from the bottom of the meniscus. To do this, you must put your eye level with the meniscus.

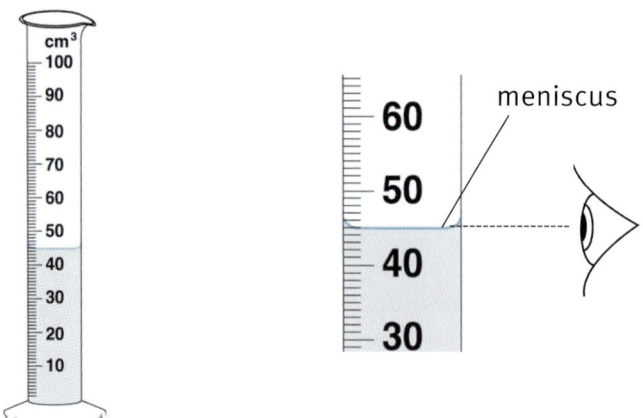

Measuring the volume of water in a measuring cylinder.

5.3 Changing state

Measuring temperature

When you measure temperature, you use a **thermometer**. The liquid inside the thermometer expands as it gets hotter. You read the temperature from the scale. Place your eye level with the top of the liquid in the thermometer.

Questions

1. What is the volume of water in each measuring cylinder?

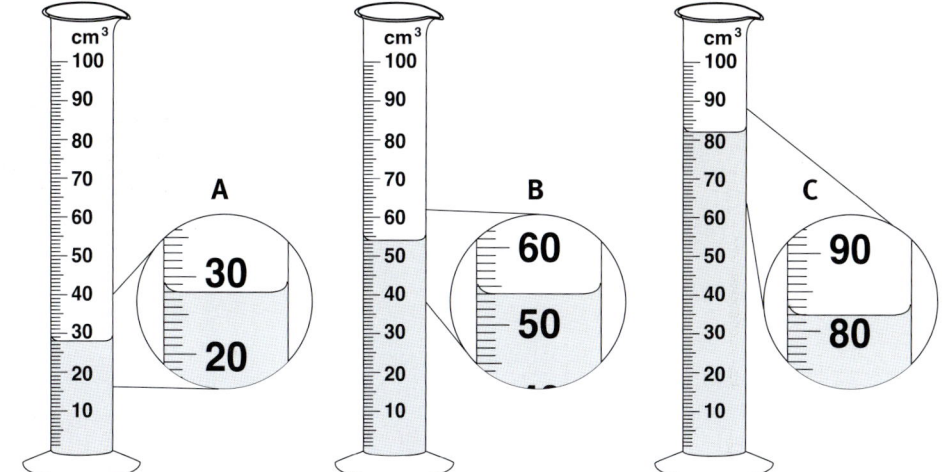

2. What are the temperatures shown on the thermometers?

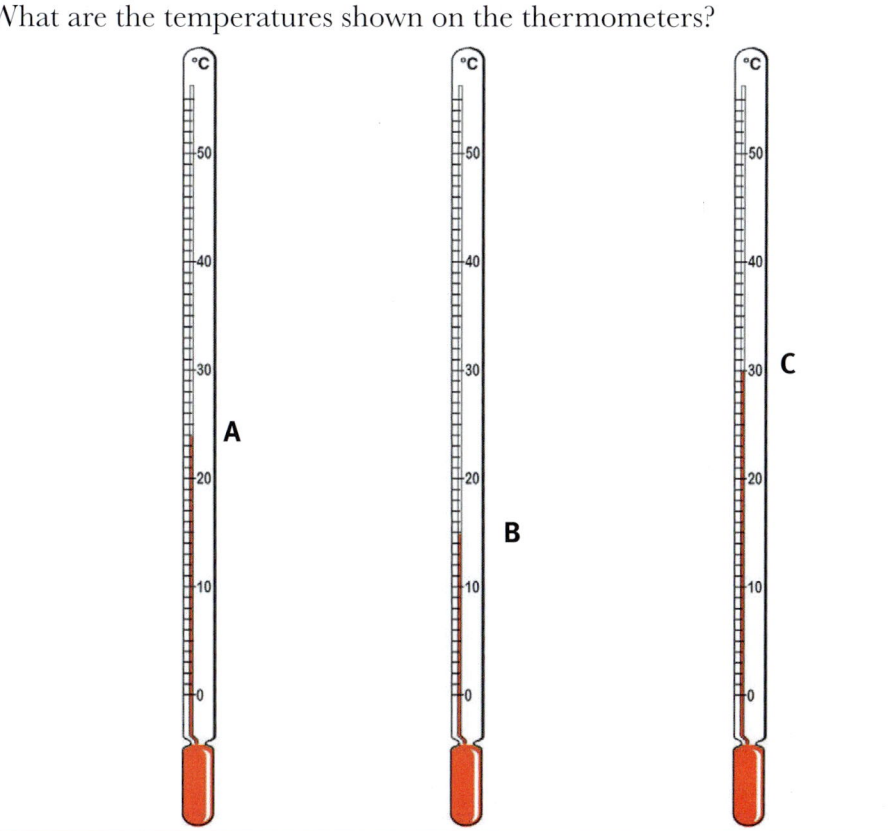

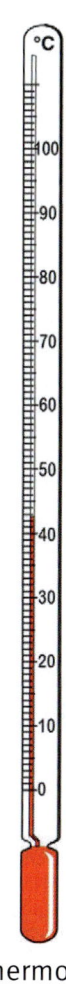

A thermometer.

5 States of matter

5.3 Changing state

Activity 5.3
Boiling water

Before you begin the activity, discuss in your group what safety measures you will take. Check these with your teacher.

1. Carefully measure 150 cm³ of water into a beaker.
2. Place a thermometer in the water.
3. Take the temperature.
4. Record this in a table. (Copy and extend the one below.)

Time / minutes	Temperature / °C
0	
1	
2	
3	
4	

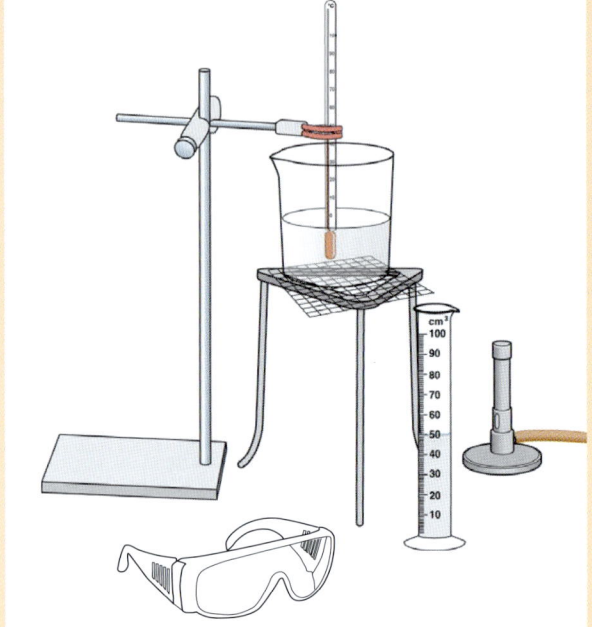

5. Heat the water.
6. Take the temperature every minute.
7. Repeat until the water is boiling strongly.

Questions

A1 Plot your temperature measurements on a graph.
A2 Describe your graph. (Mention how quickly the temperature rose and if the temperature rose by the same amount every minute.)
A3 What happened to the temperature of the water when it was boiling?

Summary
- Ice, water and water vapour are the three states of matter of water.
- Ice melts to form water.
- Water boils to form water vapour.
- Water vapour condenses to form water.
- Water freezes to form ice.

5.4 Explaining changes of state

Heating solids

When solids are heated they **expand**.

The particles in solids are arranged in a fixed pattern. The particles are held together strongly and are tightly packed.

The particles in the solid vibrate. The heat energy is **transferred** to the particles. The more energy the particles have, the more they vibrate. As the particles vibrate more, they take up more space. The particles are still held in position by the attractive forces between them.

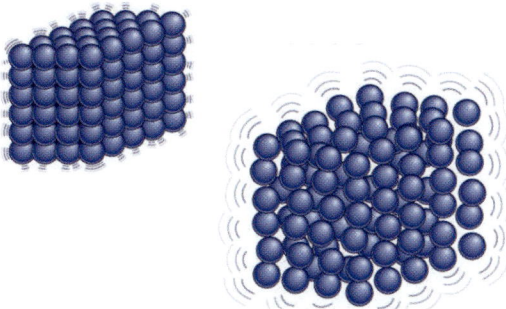

When a solid is heated the particles vibrate more and take up more space.

Melting solids

When solids are heated even more strongly they **melt.** They become liquid.

The particles in the solid vibrate more and more as heat energy is transferred to them. The particles vibrate so much that the attractive forces between them are no longer strong enough to hold them in a fixed pattern. They are able to slide past one another.

The forces are still strong enough for the particles to stay in touch with one another. The more the liquid is heated, the more energy is transferred to the particles and the more the particles move.

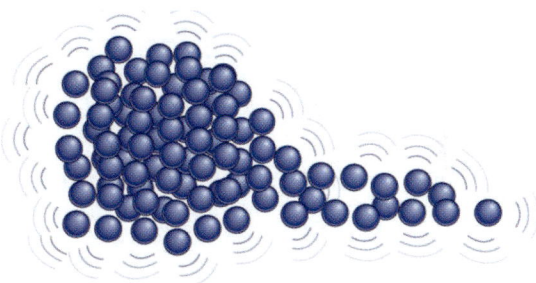

The particles vibrate so much that some escape the strong forces and can move around as a liquid.

Boiling liquids

When liquids are heated they **evaporate** and eventually **boil.**

In liquids the particles touch each other. The particles are held together weakly.

The particles move more as heat energy is transferred to them. Some particles have enough energy to break the weak attractive forces holding them together. These particles can escape into the air as gas particles.

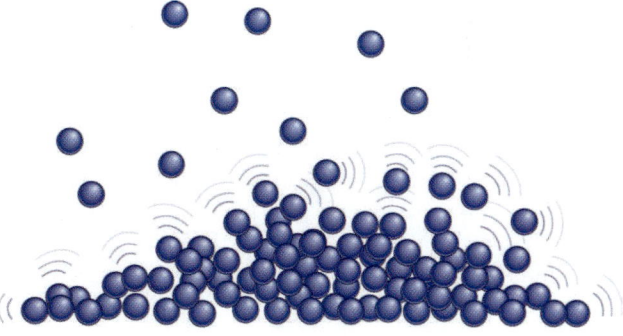

The particles move so quickly that some escape as a gas.

Questions

1. Describe the arrangement of particles in a solid.
2. What happens to the particles in a solid when they are heated?
3. How do the particles of a liquid behave when they are heated?
4. What happens to the particles when a liquid boils?

5.4 Explaining changes of state

Cooling gases

The particles in a gas are free to move anywhere and spread out. There are no forces holding them.

When a gas gets cooler it **condenses** to form a liquid.

When gas particles reach a cold surface, some of the heat energy transfers from the particles to the surface. The particles move less and get closer together. They form a liquid.

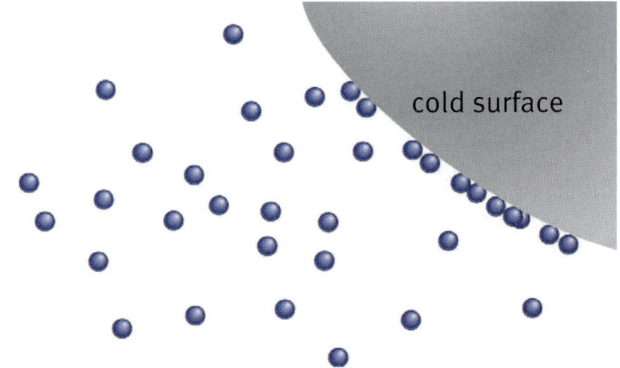

When the particles hit a cold surface their movement slows down.

Freezing liquids

When a liquid **freezes** it becomes a solid.

The particles in a liquid move and slide past each other. As heat energy is transferred from the particles to the environment, the particles move more slowly and the liquid gets cooler.

The cooler the liquid is, the less the particles are able to move or slide past each other. Eventually the particles have so little energy they can only vibrate. They become arranged in a fixed pattern to form a solid.

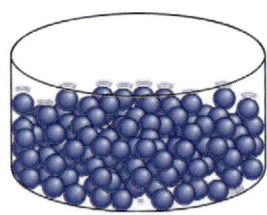 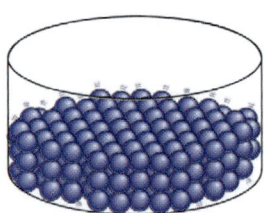

Particles in a liquid.   Particles in a solid.

Questions

5 What does 'condense' mean?
6 What happens to the particles in a gas when they touch a cold surface?

Activity 5.4
Modelling changes in state

Solid to liquid
1 As a group, arrange yourselves as if you are the particles in a solid.
2 Now imagine the particles are being heated. Move as if you are being heated gently. Move as the particle theory suggests.
3 Imagine the particles are now being heated strongly so that the solid melts and becomes a liquid. Remember to behave as the particle theory suggests.

Question

A1 Write down the way you had to behave to illustrate the behaviour of particles as a solid melts.

continued ...

5.4 Explaining changes of state

...Modelling changes in state

Liquid to gas
4 As a group arrange yourselves as if you are the particles in a liquid.
5 Imagine the particles are being heated. Move as if you are being heated gently.
6 Imagine the particles are now being heated strongly so that the liquid boils. Remember to behave as the particle theory suggests.

Question

A2 Write down the way you had to behave to illustrate the behaviour of particles as a liquid evaporates and then boils.

Gas to liquid
7 As a group arrange yourselves as if you are the particles in a gas.
8 Imagine a part of the room is a cold surface. As you move near to the surface you must behave as the particle theory suggests. You must start to condense to form a liquid.

Question

A3 Write down the way you had to behave to illustrate the behaviour of particles as a gas condenses to form a liquid.

Liquid to solid
9 Arrange yourselves as the particles in a liquid. Make sure you move as the particle theory suggests.
10 Now imagine the liquid has been placed in a freezer. Behave as the particle theory suggests as you become a solid.

Question

A4 Write down the way you had to behave to illustrate the behaviour of particles as a liquid freezes to form a solid.

Summary
- Particles vibrate or move depending on how much energy they have.
- Energy can be transferred to or from the particles.
- The energy of the particles can overcome the forces holding particles together.

Unit 5 End of unit questions

5.1 Copy and complete the following sentences.

    a A solid has a .... shape. A solid cannot be ....

        A liquid has a fixed .... and cannot be .... [4]

    b Which properties of a solid are shared with a liquid but **not** with a gas? [2]
    c Which property is shared by a gas and a liquid? [1]
    d Which property of a gas means it can be used in a car tyre? [1]
    e Which property of a liquid is used when petrol (gasoline) is pumped from the tank to the engine of a car? [1]

5.2 The diagrams below show the arrangement of the particles in a solid, a liquid or a gas.

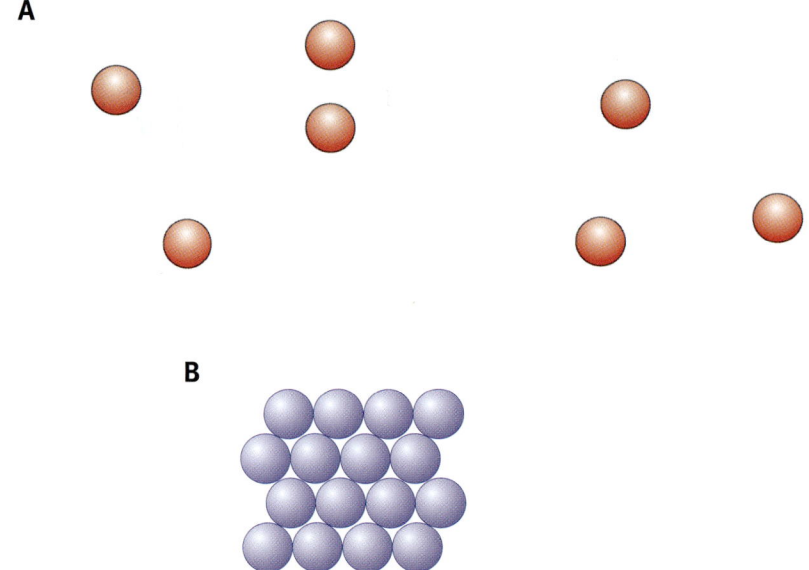

    a Is **A** a solid, a liquid or a gas? [1]
    b Is **B** a solid, a liquid or a gas? [1]
    c Explain, using the particle theory, what happens when a liquid is heated and then evaporates. [2]
    d Explain, using the particle theory, what happens when a liquid is frozen. [2]

5.3 For each of the following terms state which states of matter are involved. For example:

freezing – a liquid changing to a solid.

    a evaporation [1]
    b melting [1]
    c condensation [1]

5 End of unit questions

5.4 Mercedes heated a liquid and recorded the temperature every minute. Here are her results.

Time / minutes	Temperature / °C
0	20
1	25
2	19
3	39
4	47
5	56
6	58
7	59
8	58

a Copy the axes and labels below, on graph paper. Plot Mercedes's results on the grid. [4]
b Draw a line of best fit. [1]
c Which reading does not fit the pattern? [1]
d Suggest a reason for this. [1]
e What happens to the temperature between 5 and 8 minutes? [1]
f Explain why this happens. [1]

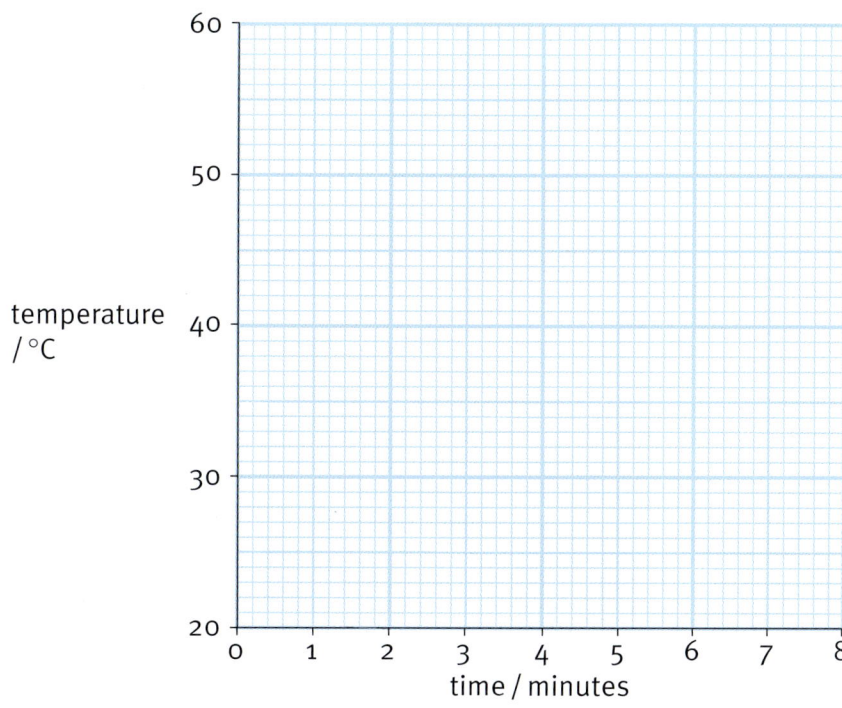

5 States of matter 79

6.1 Metals

Metals are very useful **materials**. Materials are the substances from which objects are made.

There are many different metals. Metals are used to do lots of different jobs.

Iron is used for bridges because it is strong.

Gold is used for jewellery because it is shiny.

Stainless steel does not rust and is strong so it can be used for cooking pans and bicycle frames. Stainless steel also conducts heat well, which is useful for pans.

Copper is used for electrical wiring because it conducts electricity well and it is flexible.

Properties of metals

All metals share some **properties.**

- Metals are usually **shiny** when polished or freshly cut.
- Metals ring like a bell when you hit them.
- Metals are strong and tough. They do not **shatter** when dropped and they do not crack easily. They can hold large weights without breaking.
- Metals can be shaped by bending them. They are **malleable**, which means that they can be hammered into shape. They are **ductile**, which means that they can be drawn out into wires.
- Metals don't melt easily. Mercury is the only metal that is a liquid at room temperature.

Iron is malleable.

A lot of heat is needed to melt metal.

6 Material properties

6.1 Metals

- Some metals are **magnetic.** Iron, steel, nickel and cobalt are magnetic.
- Metals are good **conductors** of heat. When you touch them they conduct heat energy away from the hand so they feel cold.

You can look for these properties when deciding if something is a metal or not.

You need to remember that:

- the surface of most metals will become dull after a while
- big lumps of metal are hard to test for bendiness
- bottles and cups ring when they are hit but they aren't made of metal.

Questions

1. List **ten** metals.
2. Why are gold and platinum used for jewellery?
3. Why is copper so useful?
4. What are Olympic medals made from?
5. What do 'malleable' and 'ductile' mean?

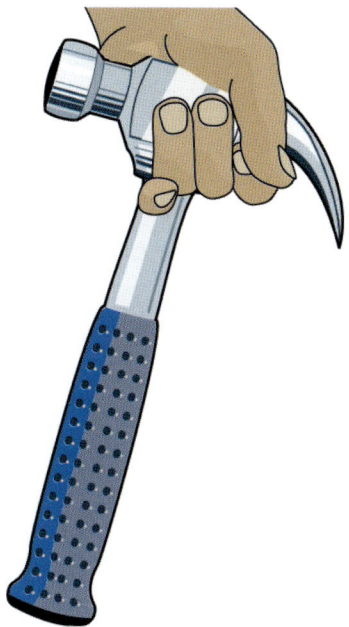

The metal of the hammer head feels colder than the rubber handle.

Activity 6.1
Properties of metals

Investigate the metal items you have been given.

- Describe each item.
- State which metal or metals it is made of.
- Suggest which property of the metal is important in the function of this item.

Make a table of your results like this.

Item	Metal	Useful property
electrical wire	copper	It conducts electricity. It is ductile.

Summary
- Metals are shiny and strong.
- Metals are malleable and ductile.
- Metals are good conductors of heat and electricity.

6 Material properties

6.2 Non-metals

Non-metals are useful, often because of their chemical reactions. There is a lot of variation between non-metals.

Properties shared by almost all non-metals
- Non-metals look dull. They do not reflect light very well and the surface is not as smooth as metals.
- Non-metals that are solids are **brittle**.
- Most non-metals do not **conduct** heat energy well. This is useful because some can be used to make handles for cooking pans, for example.
- Most non-metals do not **conduct** electricity. This is useful because some can be used to make coverings for electric cables and plugs, for example.

Properties shared by many non-metals
- Non-metals are not as strong or hardwearing as metals.
- Many non-metals are gases.
- The non-metals that are not gases have **low melting points** and **low boiling points.**

Sulfur is added to rubber to make it hard.

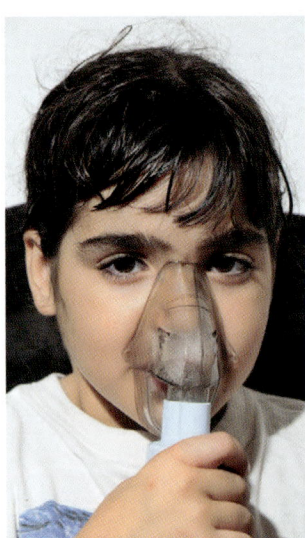

Pure oxygen is used in hospitals for people with breathing difficulties.

The balloons are filled with helium.

Chlorine is used to kill bacteria.

6 Material properties

6.2 Non-metals

Carbon is used to purify water.

Silicon is used to make computer chips.

Questions

1. Name **five** non-metals, other than sulfur and helium.
2. What is sulfur used for?
3. What property of the gas helium makes it useful in balloons?

Activity 6.2
Researching non-metals

Your teacher will give you a list of non-metals to choose from.

Choose **one** non-metal. Use reference books and the internet to find out about it.

Here are some questions you could research.

- What is it used for?
- What are its properties?
- Where is it found?
- Does the non-metal need to be processed before it can be used? If so, how is this done?
- Are there any interesting facts about it?

Present your research as a report or as a poster.

Summary
- **Non-metals have low melting points and are brittle.**
- **Many are gases.**
- **They do not conduct electricity or heat energy well.**

6 Material properties

6.3 Comparing metals and non-metals

Metals and non-metals have different properties.

Metals
- Most are solid at room temperature.
- They are shiny.
- They do not shatter.
- They conduct heat energy well.
- They conduct electricity.
- They are malleable.
- They are ductile.
- They make a ringing sound when hit.

Non-metals
- Many are gases at room temperature.
- They are dull.
- They are brittle.
- They do not conduct heat energy well.
- Most do not conduct electricity.

Where are metals and non-metals used here?

Questions
1 List **five** objects in the photograph that are made of metal and **five** that are made of a non-metal.
2 A material is dull, brittle and does not conduct electricity. Is it a metal or a non-metal?
3 Mercury is a metal. Why is it unusual?
4 Write down **two** things that a metal can do but a non-metal cannot.

6 Material properties

6.3 Comparing metals and non-metals

Activity 6.3
Investigating materials

Your teacher will give you several different materials.

Examine each material closely and test it to identify which are metals and which are non-metals.

You will need to ask a number of questions for each of the materials you investigate.

- What does the material look like? Is it shiny or dull?
- Does it make a ringing sound when you hit it?
- Is it brittle?
- Can you bend it?
- Does it feel hot or cold to the touch?
- Does it conduct electricity? To test this, set up a circuit as shown in the diagram. Before you start, check that the lamp is working by connecting the crocodile clips together with no test material. When you carry out a test, make sure you have good contact between the crocodile clips and your test material.

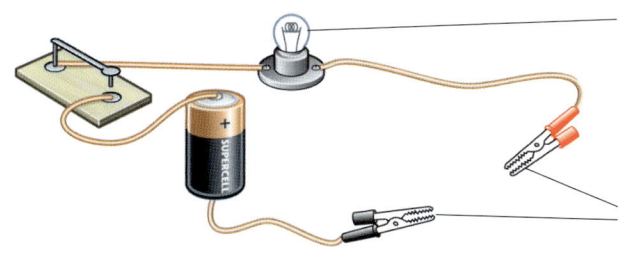

If the lamp goes on, the material conducts the electricity.

Connect the material you want to test here.

Testing a material to see if it conducts electricity.

Questions

A1 Construct a table for the collection of your results. Decide if each material is a metal or a non-metal.

A2 Were any of the materials hard to place in the metals or non-metals groups? Explain your answer.

A3 Which do you think was the best test to distinguish between metals and non-metals? Explain your answer.

Summary
- Metals and non-metals have different properties.
- When you investigate materials to see if they are metals or non-metals you need to look at more than one property.

6 Material properties

6.4 Everyday materials and their properties

Many different materials are used to make the clothes you wear, the buildings you live in and everything you use each day. We make things out of materials with the properties that we need for a particular purpose.

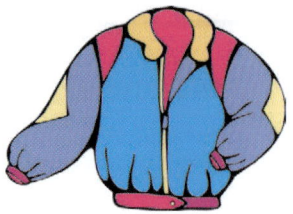

Plastics come in many different types, with different properties. Some plastics are **flexible**, lightweight and easily shaped.

Fibres can be natural (made from living materials, such as silk or cotton) or **synthetic** (made from other chemicals). Fibres are tiny threads so they can be strong and bendy.

Ceramics can withstand high temperatures. They are hard, brittle and very strong. Ceramics are used for floor tiles, sinks and the tiles on the outside of the space shuttle.

Glass is **transparent** or **translucent**. It is hard but very brittle. It can be coloured.

Let's think about two of these materials – glass and plastic. How do their properties help us to choose which one we should use to make an object?

Glass is used in windows, in bottles and jars for food and drink, glasses to drink from, beakers and other science equipment.

Plastics may be used for drinking cups, bowls for washing in, bottles and jars for food and for drink, hose pipes, window frames and many other uses.

Glass

Glass is usually **transparent**. This means you can see through it. This property is good for windows. It is also useful to see the contents of jars and bottles.

Glass is **waterproof**. It does not **react** with the food or drink inside the jar or bottle.

Glass is cheap to make and can be made in many shapes. It can be **recycled**.

But glass is heavy and can break easily. These properties may be a disadvantage for some uses. Some glass is treated so that it can be heated without breaking.

6.4 Everyday materials and their properties

Plastic

Plastic can be **transparent or opaque.** It can be moulded into many shapes.

Plastic can be used for containers for food and drink. It does not **react** with the food.

Plastic is light in weight, and can be coloured brightly. Some plastic can be recycled.

But plastic takes a very long time to break down and this causes problems with disposal and litter. Plastic may be affected by heat and may change shape.

Questions

1. **a** Give **two** properties that glass and plastic always share.
   b Give **two** properties that glass and plastic sometimes share.
2. What advantages do bottles made from plastic have?
3. What disadvantages are there when you use plastic bottles?
4. Why are plastic bowls not used for heating on a cooker?
5. Look at the photographs of the toys. Which type of material is most suitable for making a toy for a baby? Give reasons for your choice.
6. What are the disadvantages of using metal for a toy for a baby?
7. Why is plastic often used for children's toys?
8. What properties would you look for in materials to make a kite?

Toys made from different materials.

Activity 6.4
Materials and their properties

The properties of materials determine the use you can make of them.

For each of the materials you are given, list the properties and suggest a use for the material. Record your results in a table.

Summary
- There are many different materials.
- Different materials have different properties.
- The use you make of a material depends on its properties.

6 Material properties

Unit 6 End of unit questions

6.1 **a** Copy the paragraph and choose words from the list to complete it. Each word may be used once, more than once or not at all.

**brittle   conduct   cut   ductile
electricity   malleable   metal   ring**

Metals are shiny when freshly .... or polished. They are

strong and if you tap them they .... like a bell.

Metals .... heat energy and ....

Metals are .... , which means they can be beaten into shape.

They are .... , which means they can be drawn out into wires.   [6]

b State **three** differences between metals and non-metals.   [3]

6.2 The table gives information about the melting points and boiling points of some metals and non-metals.

Substance	Melting point / °C	Boiling point / °C
gold	1064	2850
lead	328	1750
copper	1082	2580
helium	−270	−269
oxygen	−219	−183
mercury	−39	357
aluminium	660	2400
nickel	1455	2150
sulfur	119	445
sodium	98	900

a Copy and complete the tally charts below.

up to 0	
0 to 499	
500 to 999	
1000 to 1499	

Boiling point / °C	Tally
up to 0	
0 to 999	
1000 to 1999	
2000 to 2999	

[2]

88 6 Material properties

6 End of unit questions

Use this grid to help you plan your own frequency diagrams.

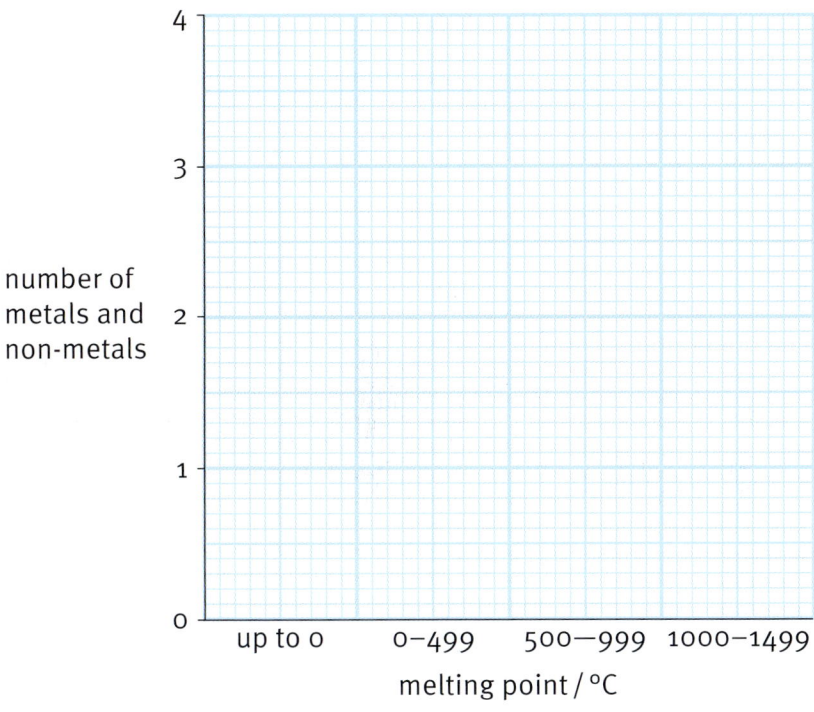

- **b** Plot the tallied figures on two separate frequency diagrams. [6]
- **c** Which metals and/or non-metals are gases at a room temperature of 25 °C? [1]
- **d** Which metals and/or non-metals are liquid at a room temperature of 25 °C? [1]
- **e** Which metals and/or non-metals are solid at a room temperature of 25 °C? [2]
- **f** Which metal or non-metal has the smallest difference between its melting point and its boiling point? [1]
- **g** Which metal or non-metal has the largest difference between its melting point and its boiling point? [1]

6.3 For each of the statements below choose **one** of the materials from the list. Each material may be used once, more than once or not at all.

**aluminium   glass   gold   helium   mercury
paper   plastic   steel   straw   wood**

- **a** This metal is very strong and is used to build bridges. [1]
- **b** This metal is used for jewellery because it stays shiny and can be made into many shapes. [1]
- **c** This is not a metal and is lightweight. It can be used for making bottles. [1]
- **d** This metal is very light and is used for building aircraft. [1]
- **e** This is not a metal and can be used for making the roofs of houses. [1]
- **f** This material is made from wood and can be made into thin sheets. You can write on it. [1]

6 Material properties

7.1 Acids and alkalis

Acids are everywhere

Many things contain **acid**. Some foods contain acid. They have a sour, sharp, tangy taste. Lemons and limes taste sour. They contain citric acid. This is a weak acid.

Common acids in the laboratory are hydrochloric acid, sulfuric acid and nitric acid.

Foods containing fruits often contain acids.

Questions
1. Name a food that contains an acid.
2. Describe the taste of lemons and limes.

Some acids are dangerous

Some acids are strong. They are **corrosive**. The bottles have a hazard warning label. If strong acid gets on your skin it will dissolve it. You will get a chemical burn. Always use eye protection when using acids.

Acids can be diluted with water. This makes them less dangerous.

Dilute acids are still **harmful** or **irritant**. The bottles have hazard warning labels.

If you spill acid, wash the area with lots of water. The water dilutes the acid.

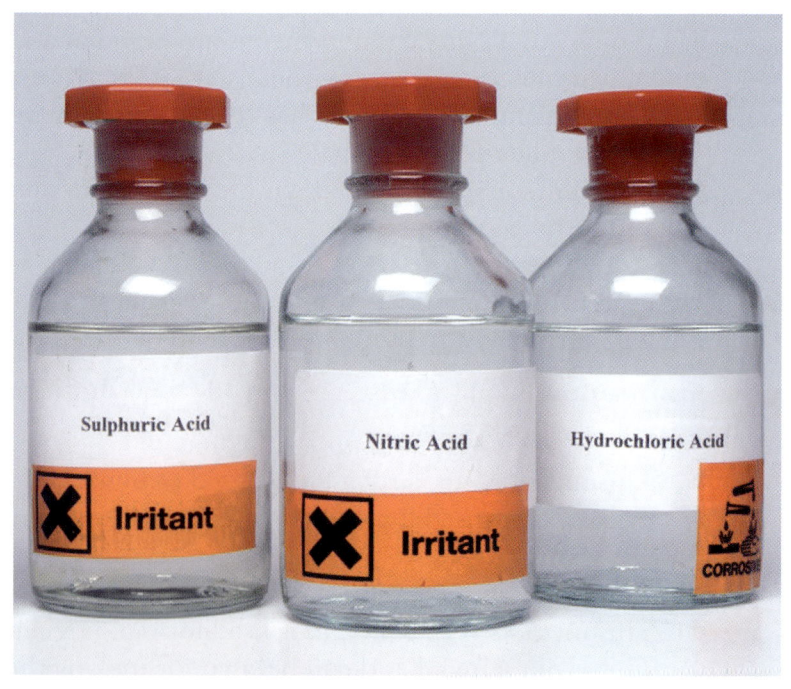

7 Material changes

7.1 Acids and alkalis

Alkalis are everywhere

Many cleaning products contain **alkali**. Sodium hydroxide is a strong alkali. Strong alkalis are dangerous. They are corrosive.

If strong alkali gets on your skin, it dissolves your skin. Your skin feels soapy. You get a chemical burn. Alkalis are harmful if you get them in your eyes. Always wear eye protection when using alkalis.

Alkalis can be diluted with water. This makes them less dangerous.

Common alkalis found in the laboratory are sodium hydroxide, potassium hydroxide and calcium hydroxide.

Acids and alkalis are chemical opposites. They can cancel each other out when they are mixed together.

> **Questions**
> 3 What does 'corrosive' mean?
> 4 What should you do if you spill acid?

All these products contain alkalis.

Working safely with acids and alkalis

When you handle chemicals you should:

- stand up to work, so that if you spill something it does not spill onto you
- wear safety glasses, so nothing gets into your eyes
- take the top off the bottle and place it upside down on the work surface, so that it does not get acid onto the surface or dirt into the acid
- replace the bottle top as soon as you finish using the bottle. This prevents spills and replacing the wrong top on the wrong bottle.

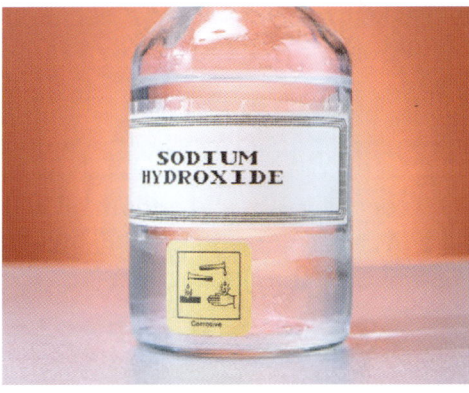

Strong sodium hydroxide is corrosive.

Activity 7.1
Produce a poster

Produce a poster about acids and alkalis. Make sure that your information is presented clearly and is accurate.

> **Summary**
> - Acids and alkalis are everywhere.
> - Some acids and alkalis are dangerous.
> - Dangerous chemicals have hazard warning labels.
> - Acids and alkalis are chemical opposites.

7.2 Is it an acid or an alkali?

These three containers all look the same. One contains water, one contains acid and one contains alkali.

Which is which?

You can tell them apart when you add a few drops of red cabbage juice.

Red cabbage juice can be used as an **indicator**. An indicator is one colour in an acid and a different colour in an alkali.

Indicators can be made from the brightly coloured berries, flowers and other parts of plants. These include:

- red cabbage
- blackcurrant
- beetroot.

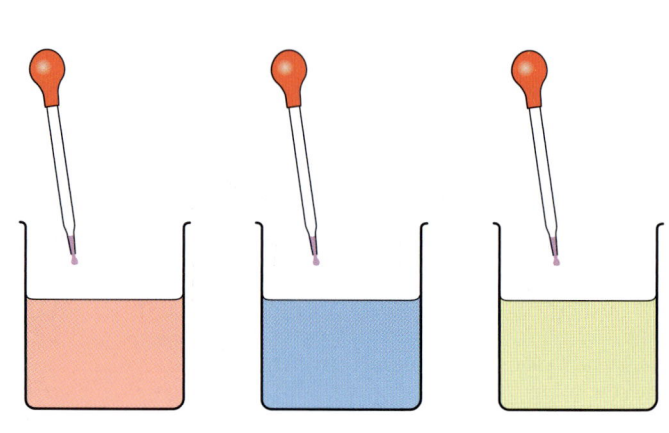

hydrochloric acid   water   sodium hydroxide

> **Questions**
>
> 1. How does an indicator show the difference between an acid and an alkali?
> 2. What colour does red cabbage juice go when it is added to lemon juice?

Litmus

Litmus is a very common indicator. It is a dye.

Litmus turns red in acids. Litmus turns blue in alkalis.

Litmus turns purple when it is in a **neutral** substance. This is a substance that is neither acid nor alkali.

Litmus turns purple in water. Water is neutral. This means water is neither an acid nor an alkali.

Substance	Litmus colour	Type of substance
hydrochloric acid	red	acid
sodium hydroxide	blue	alkali
water	purple	neutral
lemon juice	red	acid
calcium hydroxide	blue	alkali

7 Material changes

7.2 Is it an acid or an alkali?

Questions

3. What does litmus do when it is put into sodium hydroxide?
4. What colour does litmus change to in an acid?
5. Is water an acid, alkali or neutral? Give the reason for your answer.

Activity 7.2
Making your own indicator solution

1. Cut up the plant material you have been given.
2. Place some in a pestle and mortar and crush it.
3. Add a little methylated spirit. **Safety:** check with your teacher before you use this. It is flammable and dangerous if you breathe it in.
4. Crush the plant material again.
5. Use a pipette to transfer the liquid into a test tube.
6. Use the liquid you collect to test the substances you are given.
7. Make a table to record the chemicals you tested and the colours you see.

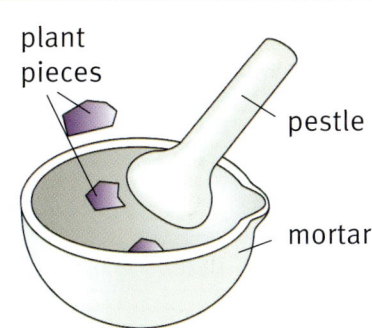

2. Crush the plant pieces.

3. Add a little methylated spirit.

4. Keep crushing until the colour comes out.

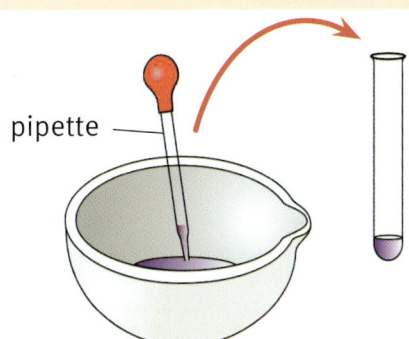

5. Use a pipette to put the liquid into a test tube.

Summary
- An indicator changes colour in an acid or alkali.
- Some plant materials make good indicators.
- Litmus is red in acids and blue in alkalis.
- Substances that are neither acid nor alkali are called neutral.

7 Material changes

7.3 The pH scale

Litmus shows if a substance is an acid or an alkali.

Universal Indicator shows how acidic or alkaline a substance is. This indicator can change to many different colours.

Type of substance	Colour of Universal Indicator
strongly acidic	red
weakly acidic	yellow
neutral	green
weakly alkaline	blue
strongly alkaline	purple

The strength of acids and alkalis is measured on the pH scale.

Universal Indicator changes colour and shows the pH of a substance.

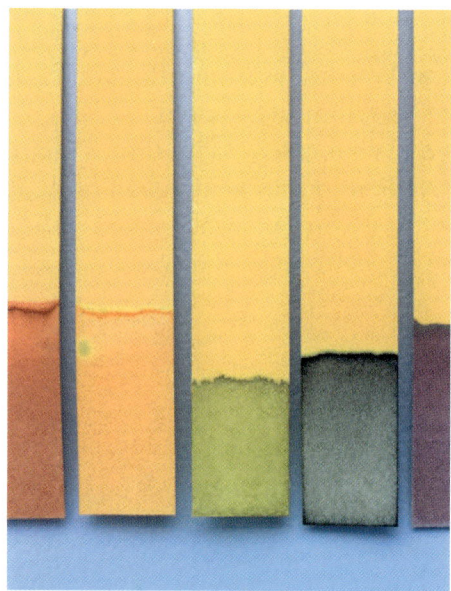

These are strips of paper soaked in Universal Indicator solution and then dried. The papers have then been dipped into different liquids.

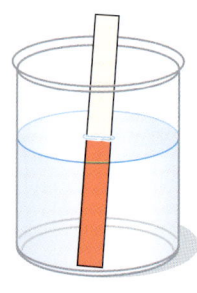
strongly acidic
pH = 1

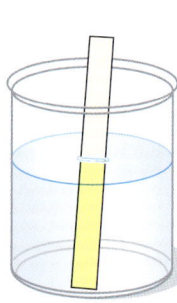
weakly acidic
pH = 4

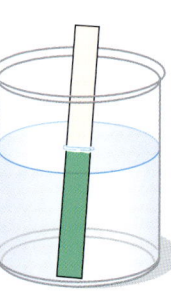
neutral
pH = 7

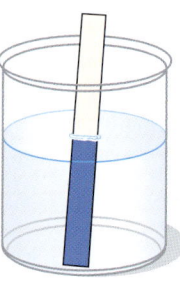
weakly alkaline
pH = 10

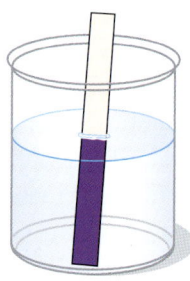
strongly alkaline
pH = 13

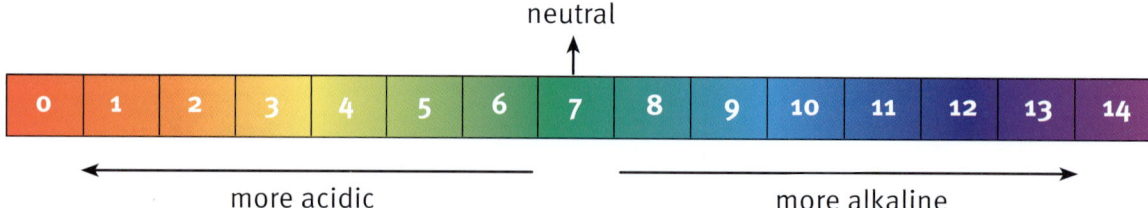

A colour chart for Universal Indicator showing the pH scale.

7.3 The pH scale

Questions
1. What does the pH scale measure?
2. What is the pH of a neutral solution?
3. A liquid has a pH of 1. What type of liquid is it?
4. What range of pH do strong alkalis have?
5. What colour does Universal Indicator go in a liquid with a pH of 9?
6. Which colours does Universal Indicator go in acids?

Activity 7.3
Investigating the pH of different substances

Your teacher will give you some different liquids. Use Universal Indicator to test the liquids.

Use a table like the one below to record the colour of the indicator and the pH.

Record the type of each liquid such as strongly or weakly acidic, neutral, strongly or weakly alkaline.

Liquid	Colour of Universal Indicator	pH	Type of liquid
lemon juice		4	weakly acidic
salt water	green		
soap solution		8	weakly alkaline
cola drink	yellow	4	

Summary
- The pH scale measures how acidic or alkaline a substance is.
- Universal Indicator changes to different colours in different pHs.
- A pH of below 7 is acidic.
- A pH of above 7 is alkaline.
- A pH of 7 is neutral.

7.4 Neutralisation

Acids and alkalis can cancel each other out. When you mix them together they make a neutral solution. This is called **neutralisation**.

If you add too much acid to an alkali, it makes an acidic liquid. If you add too little acid to an alkali, it stays an alkaline liquid.

You can add the acid very slowly and a few drops at a time. This makes it easier to judge exactly when it becomes neutral.

> **Questions**
> 1. What colour is Universal Indicator when the solution is neutral?
> 2. What sort of reaction happens when an acid and an alkali are mixed?

Making a neutral solution

You can use a special piece of science equipment called a **burette** to neutralise an alkali very accurately. You add Universal Indicator to the alkali in the flask.

In the first diagram the pH in the flask is about 13. As the acid is added, the pH becomes lower. The acid is added slowly. The flask is shaken slightly each time some acid is added.

In the second diagram 25 cm³ of acid has been added to the flask. The pH in the flask is now 7. The liquid is now neutral.

The acid has **reacted** with the alkali and **neutralised** it. The acid and alkali have cancelled each other out.

In the third diagram a little more acid has been added to the flask. The pH in the flask is now about 6. The liquid is weakly acidic.

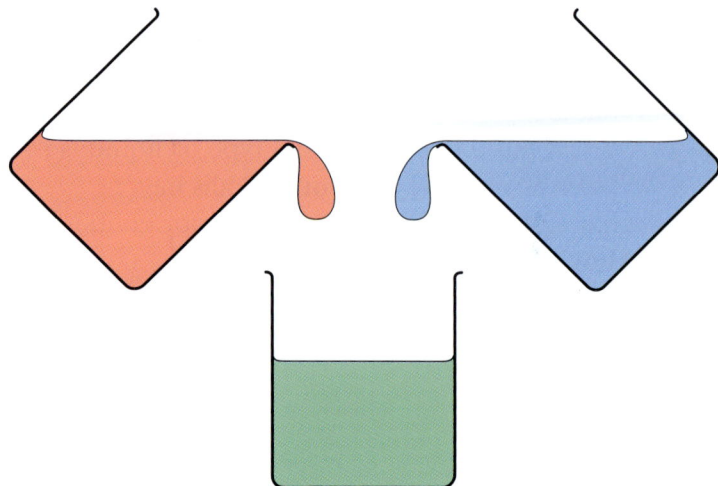

Mixing acid and alkali to make a neutral solution.

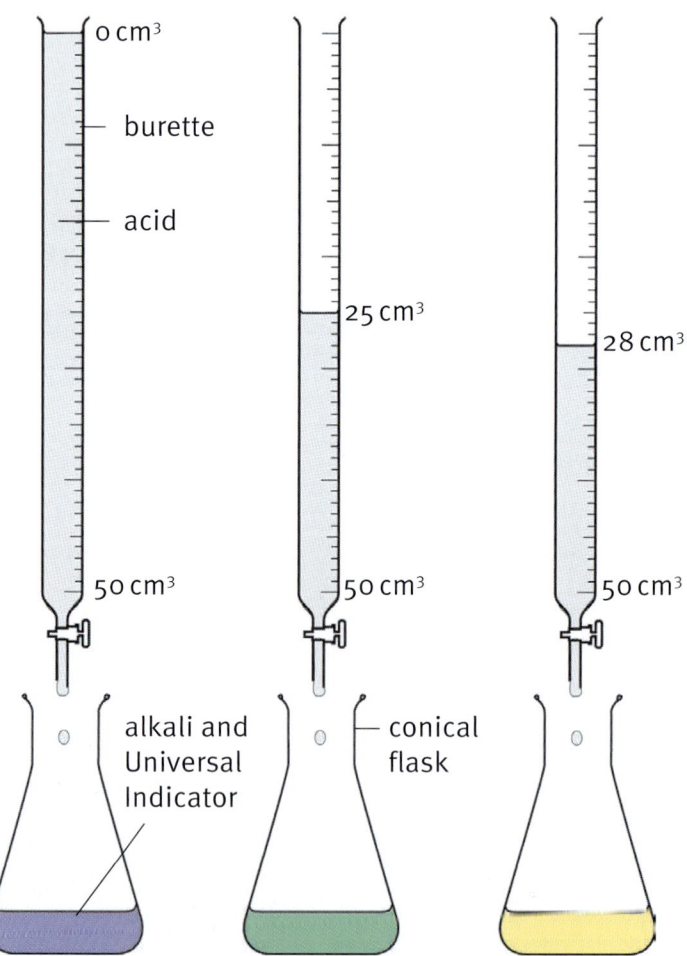

Using a burette to add acid to a flask of alkali.

7.4 Neutralisation

Activity 7.4
Rainbow neutralisation

1. Place a crystal of washing soda in the bottom of a test tube.
2. Carefully add some water until the tube is about two-thirds full.
3. Put in a few drops of Universal Indicator.
4. Carefully pour some acid on the top.
5. Do not shake the tube.
6. Leave the tube to stand for a few days.

How does the rainbow happen in the test tube?

At the bottom of the tube
The washing soda has dissolved in the water around it. The Universal Indicator is purple or dark blue around the washing soda. The washing soda solution is a strong alkali. The particles of washing soda gradually move up the test tube. They mix with more water and the Universal Indicator turns a lighter blue. This shows it is more weakly alkaline.

At the top of the tube
The acid has turned the Universal Indicator red at the top of the tube. This shows it is strongly acidic. The acid particles gradually move down the tube. They mix with more water and the Universal Indicator turns yellow. This is more weakly acidic.

In the middle of the tube
The acid and the washing soda solution mix. The Universal Indicator is green. The washing soda solution and acid have neutralised each other.

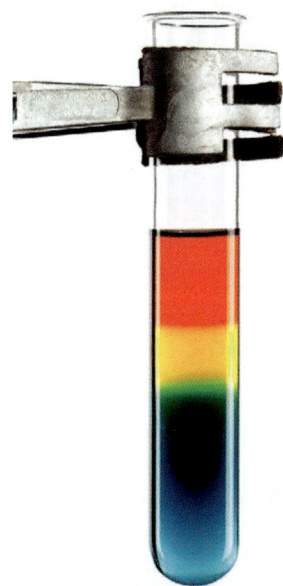

The experiment in Activity **7.4** after a few days.

Questions
3. What is the pH of the top part of the test tube?
4. What is the pH of the bottom of the test tube?
5. Which is the most alkaline part of the tube?

Summary
- Acid and alkali can cancel each other out.
- When they react together, they neutralise each other.
- To neutralise an alkali you must use exactly the right amount of acid.

7 Material changes

7.5 Neutralisation in action

Indigestion
Your stomach produces hydrochloric acid. This acid gives the stomach the right conditions to **digest** your food. When your stomach produces too much acid you have **indigestion**. It can be very uncomfortable. There are many medicines that can help. They are all alkalis and they neutralise the acid. Sometimes these medicines are called antacids.

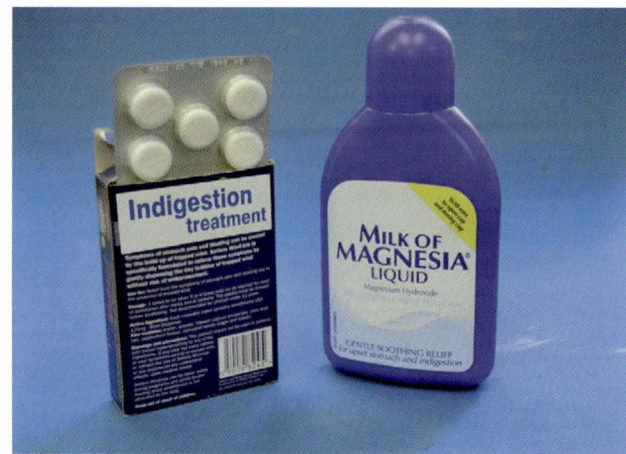

Some medicines for indigestion.

Toothpaste
There are millions of **bacteria** in your mouth. These bacteria feed on the food pieces left on your teeth. The bacteria produce acid when they feed. This acid damages your teeth and makes them **decay**. Toothpaste contains alkali and this helps to neutralise the acid.

> **Questions**
> 1. Why is toothpaste alkaline?
> 2. Where does the acid in your mouth come from?

Toothpaste helps to neutralise the acid in your mouth.

Neutralising lakes
In some parts of the world there are harmful chemicals in the air that make the rain acidic. This acid rain damages trees and changes the pH of the lakes, rivers and ponds. The plants and animals that live in the lakes cannot live in acid conditions. Some countries drop alkalis into the lakes to neutralise the acid.

Growing crops
In some areas the soil is very acidic and plants do not grow well. Farmers spread lime on the soil to neutralise the acid so that plants can grow better.

> **Questions**
> 3. Why is an alkaline substance dropped into lakes in some countries?
> 4. What do farmers spread onto acidic soil? Explain why they do this.

Lime is added to acidic soils, to neutralise the acid.

7.5 Neutralisation in action

Activity 7.5
Testing the pH of soil

1. Take a sample of soil in a test tube and add some water.
2. Shake the tube.
3. Filter the mixture in the tube.
4. Add a few drops of Universal Indicator to the **filtrate**. (The filtrate is the liquid that comes through the filter paper.)
5. Record your results.

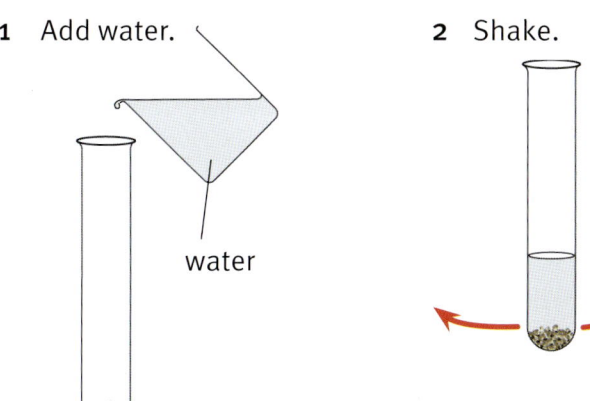

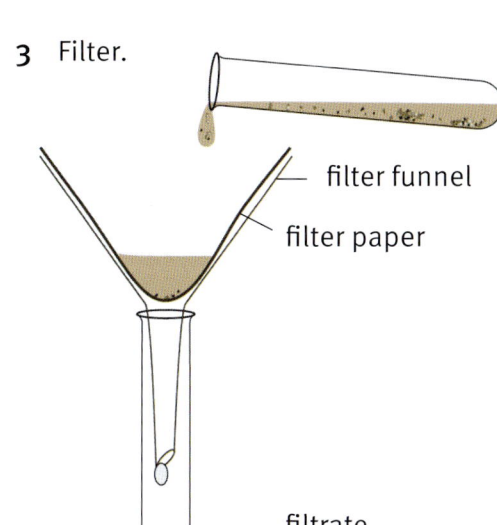

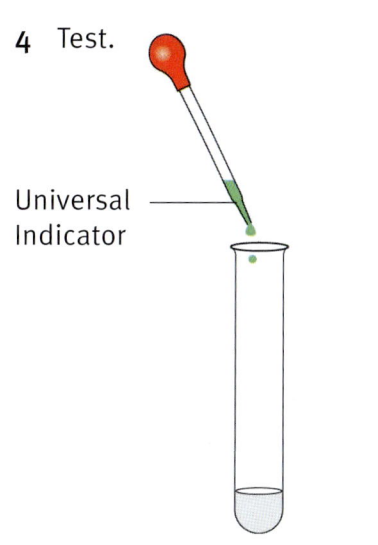

Question
A1 Use books or the internet to find out what sort of plants will grow well in this type of soil.

Summary
- Antacids are used to neutralise acid in the stomach.
- Toothpaste is alkaline and helps to neutralise acid in the mouth.
- A neutralisation reaction can be used to change the pH of lakes and soils.

7 Material changes

7.6 Investigating acids and alkalis

Asking questions

Scientists ask questions. These are some questions scientists might try to answer:

- How much lime should be added to an acid lake to neutralise it?
- Which is the best indigestion remedy?
- How much toothpaste is needed to neutralise the acid in your mouth?

Which is the best indigestion remedy? This is not a very precise question. Does it mean the most pleasant tasting, the cheapest, the most effective or the most cost effective?

Scientists need to put their questions in a way that they can test. For example:

- 'Which indigestion powder neutralises the acid using the least powder?'

Activity 7.6A
Asking questions

In a small group, discuss and write down **four** questions about acids and alkalis that you could investigate. Discuss your ideas with the rest of the class.

Could each of your questions be investigated?

Planning an investigation

When you plan to do an investigation you have to design an experiment. If you are investigating the effect of indigestion powders on stomach acid you must use a **model** because you cannot use your stomach acid. You will have to use a beaker of acid instead.

There is a lot to think about.

- How will you make your test fair?
- What will you change in your investigation?
- What will you keep the same?

The things that can change are called **variables**.

- How will you know when the powder has neutralised the acid?
- What will you see happen?
- How will you carry out the investigation?
- How will you record your results?

Activity 7.6B
Planning

Choose one of the questions from Activity **7.6A** and plan how you could carry out the investigation.

7 Material changes

7.6 Investigating acids and alkalis

Which powder is best at neutralising acid?

Two students put 20 cm³ of hydrochloric acid into each of three beakers. The acid has a pH of 1. This is like the strong acid in your stomach. They also put a few drops of Universal Indicator in each beaker.

They add the indigestion powder spatula by spatula until the acid is neutralised and the Universal Indicator is green. They do this with each of the three powders A, B and C. They record the number of spatulas used.

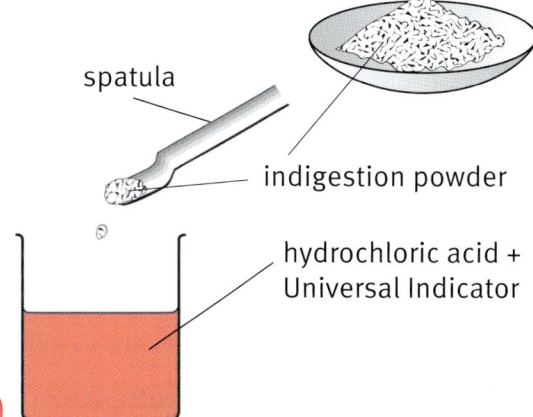

Questions

1. a What is being kept the same in this investigation?
   b What is being changed?
   c What is being measured?
2. a Which is the most effective powder? Which is the least effective powder?
   b Do you think there is enough evidence to be certain of your answers to part **a**?

Powder	Number of spatulas used to neutralise the acid
A	10
B	6
C	24

The students repeat their investigation two more times. The table shows all of their results.

Powder	Number of spatulas used to neutralise the acid			
	1st try	2nd try	3rd try	Mean
A	10	9	11	10
B	6	17	16	13
C	24	23	25	24

Questions

3. Now which powder do you think is the most effective?
4. Which result looks 'wrong'?
5. Suggest why the students might have got this 'wrong' result.

Summary

- Scientists put a question for investigation in a way that can be tested.
- An investigation must be planned to make it a fair test.
- Results can be recorded in a table.
- Results are used to provide evidence to answer the question being investigated.

7 Material changes

Unit 7 End of unit questions

7.1 Litmus is a dye made from a living organism.
It is red in an acid.
It is blue in an alkali.
It is purple in a neutral solution.
    a What is the correct scientific term for a substance that changes colour in this way? [1]
    b What colour is litmus in a solution of pH 4? [1]
    c What colour is litmus in pure water? [1]

7.2 Each of these words or phrases is associated with acids or with alkalis.

makes Universal Indicator turn blue
makes Universal Indicator turn red
pH 2   pH 9   toothpaste
soapy   sour   lemon juice

Copy the table. Then write each word or phrase in the correct column.

Words associated with acids	Words associated with alkalis

[4]

7.3 This truck is unloading acid at a factory.

    a The driver has placed a warning notice nearby.
Explain why this is important. [1]
    b Suggest what could be done if there is an accident and some acid is spilt onto the ground. Explain your answer. [2]

7 Material changes

7 End of unit questions

7.4 Aron and Ben put 50 cm³ of alkali into a conical flask.
They added Universal Indicator solution to the alkali.
They used a burette to add acid to the alkali.
The acid was added 10 cm³ at a time. The students stirred the contents of the conical flask each time they added some acid.
Aron and Ben recorded the pH after each addition of acid.
The table shows their results.

Volume of acid added / cm³	0	10	20	30	40	50
pH of solution	12	11	10	9	8	7

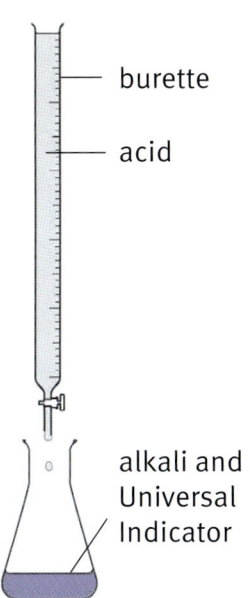

- burette
- acid
- alkali and Universal Indicator

a What colour was the solution at the start? [1]
b What was the colour of the solution at the end? [1]
c Which **one** of these statements is correct?
  - The acid was stronger than the alkali.
  - The alkali was stronger than the acid.
  - The acid and alkali were equal in strength.
  Explain your answer. [2]
d Draw a line graph of the students' results on graph paper.
  Place the pH on the vertical axis. [5]

7 Material changes

8.1 Rocks, minerals and soils

The surface of the Earth is covered by a layer of rock. This layer is called the Earth's **crust**.

Scientists who study rocks are called **geologists**.

Rocks

Geologists study a number of different materials that they call 'rocks'.

The photographs show some different kinds of rocks.

Minerals

Rocks are made up of grains of different materials. These different materials are called **minerals**. When you look closely at some rocks you can see the different minerals.

Each mineral is made of one chemical substance. In some rocks the minerals form small **crystals**. In other rocks the crystals are much larger.

Granite is a rock made from quite large crystals of three different minerals. Granite is sometimes polished and used as flooring or work surfaces because it looks attractive.

The three minerals in granite are called quartz, feldspar and mica.

This is granite. The glassy crystals are quartz. The large pink and white crystals are feldspar. The small black crystals are mica.

Questions

1. What is a geologist?
2. How can you tell the difference between a rock and a mineral?
3. Name **three** different minerals and describe where you can see them.

8.1 Rocks, minerals and soils

Soil

Soil is made up of small particles of rock and minerals. Soil also contains the remains of plants, animals and waste products such as dung. All the material that comes from living things is called **humus**. Many bacteria, fungi and small animals live in the soil. The bacteria and fungi break down the dead plant and animal materials. The particles in soil may be different sizes. **Sand** particles are large. **Clay** particles are small. Soils also contain different amounts of humus.

These differences give soils different **properties**. These properties are important for growing crops.

Soil is made from tiny rock particles and humus.

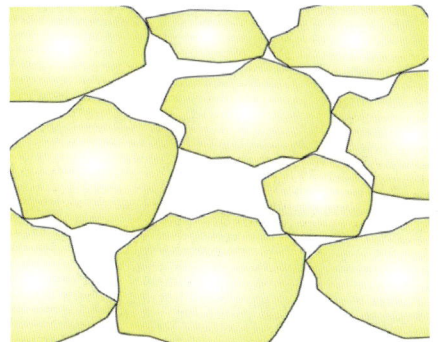

Sandy soils contain a lot of large sand particles. There are big air spaces between the particles.

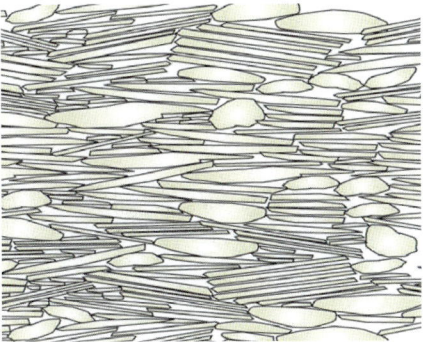

Clay soils contain a lot of tiny clay particles. There are only tiny air spaces between the particles.

Activity 8.1
Looking at rocks and minerals

1. Look at the rocks and minerals you have. A hand lens helps you look closely.
2. Describe each rock and mineral carefully.
3. Use reference books and the internet to help you identify the rocks and minerals.

Question

4. Why do you think the properties of different soils are important for growing crops?

Summary
- The surface of the Earth is covered with rocks, minerals and soil.
- Rocks are made of grains of minerals.
- Soil is made from rocks, minerals and humus.

8 The Earth

8.2 Soil

What is soil?

Soil is made up of pieces of rock and minerals, humus, bacteria, fungi and small animals. **Humus** is the remains of dead plants and animals. This is sometimes called **organic matter**.

Activity 8.2A
Looking at different soils

Spread each soil on a dish or on some white paper. Look carefully at it using a hand lens.

Describe what you can see. You could draw a labelled diagram and write a description of each soil.

Activity 8.2B
Looking at the composition of soils

1. Place some soil from one sample in a glass jar with a lid.
2. Add some water so that the jar is about two-thirds full. Put the lid on firmly. Shake the jar.
3. Leave the jar and its contents to settle. This may take a day. The particles in the soil settle with the heaviest particles at the bottom. The lighter particles may still hang in the water. The humus is the lightest part. It floats on the top.
4. Repeat the investigation with the other soil sample.

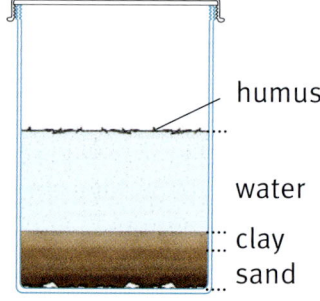

Questions

A1 When you repeat this investigation with the second sample, what must you do to make sure the investigation is a fair test?
A2 Where are the heaviest particles?
A3 Which part of the soil is floating on the top of the water?
A4 Compare the two soils.

Soils and water

Some soils allow water to pass through them very quickly. These soils drain quickly. Other soils may hold water for a long time.

This property depends on the composition of the soil. Sandy soils drain very quickly but soils containing lots of clay particles hold water for a long time.

Sandy soils have good drainage.

8.2 Soil

Drainage of water is important for the survival of crops. Farmers sometimes treat the soil to improve the drainage. This helps them grow the crops.

Clay soils have poor drainage.

Activity 8.2C
Investigating soil drainage

1. Place a measured volume of soil in a filter paper in a filter funnel.
2. Pour a measured volume of water onto the soil.
3. Collect the liquid that comes through in a measured amount of time.
4. Repeat for different soils.

Questions
- **A5** What are you trying to find out?
- **A6** Which variables did you keep the same?
- **A7** Which variable did you measure?
- **A8** How did you know which soil has better drainage?
- **A9** Compare the soils.

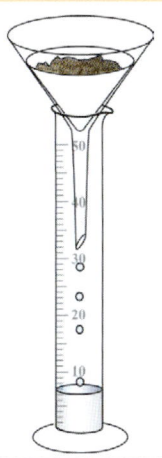

Explaining drainage

Soils that have poor drainage have particles of sticky clay which are very small and pack closely together. These particles hold the water and it cannot move.

Soils that drain quickly have bigger spaces between the particles so water drains freely.

A farmer could mix more sandy particles into a sticky soil so that the water drains more easily.

Humus helps to hold water. A farmer could add more organic matter to a soil that drains very quickly to stop it drying out too quickly.

Summary
- Soil contains pieces of rock and minerals, dead and decaying organic matter and living things.
- The proportion of clay and sand particles in a soil affects its properties.

8.3 Igneous rocks

Rocks are classified by the way they are formed. Here, we will look at rocks that are made from melted material deep inside the Earth.

Magma

The crust of the Earth is made of solid rock. But deep inside the Earth it is very hot. When rock is very hot it melts to form liquid. Beneath the crust the rock is **molten** (hot and liquid). The molten rock is called **magma.**

Igneous rocks

When magma cools, it solidifies and forms rocks. Rocks that have been made in this way are called **igneous rocks**.

Magma is a mixture of different minerals. Different samples of magma may contain different minerals in different quantities. This means that magma can form different kinds of rocks when it cools and becomes solid.

The way that the magma cools also affects the kind of rock that is formed.

When magma cools deep underground, it cools very slowly. This is because the magma is surrounded by hot rock. The slow cooling gives plenty of time for large **crystals** to grow.

When magma forces its way nearer to the surface through cracks in rocks, it cools more quickly. There is only enough time for small crystals to form.

Granite forms when magma cools deep underground.

Basalt forms when magma cools near the surface.

8.3 Igneous rocks

When the magma comes out of a hole in the Earth's surface as a liquid, it cools very quickly. There may not be enough time for any crystals to form at all.

Volcanoes

When magma reaches the surface of the Earth it is called **lava**. The lava **erupts** from volcanoes.

Obsidian forms when magma cools very quickly.

A volcano in Hawaii with lava flows.

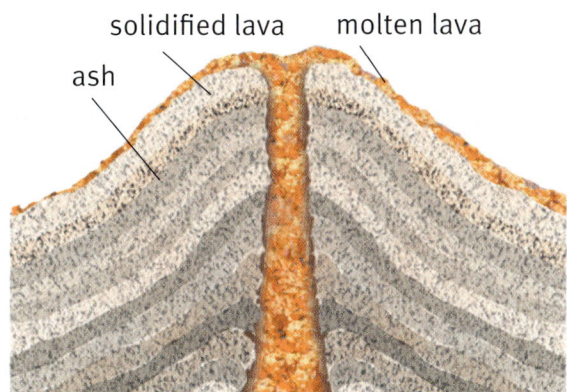
Some volcanic cones are formed from ash and lava.

Questions

1. Which of the rocks in the photographs cooled most slowly when it was formed? How can you tell from looking carefully at the rock?
2. Obsidian and pumice are igneous rocks that contain no crystals. What does that tell you about how they were formed?
3. How does magma get onto the surface of the Earth?

Summary

- Igneous rocks are formed from magma.
- When the magma cools slowly, rocks containing large crystals are formed.
- When the magma cools quickly, rocks with small crystals or no crystals are formed.

8 The Earth

8.4 Sedimentary rocks

Sediment

Rivers often carry lots of **sediment**. Sediment is made up of little fragments of rocks. Eventually, the sediment settles out of the water, perhaps when the river reaches the sea.

Sedimentary rocks

Layers of fragments of rocks or mud collect on the sea bed. As more layers build up on top of them, the weight of the new layers presses the particles in the deeper layers together. Solid rock is formed. It is called a **sedimentary rock**.

Sometimes, the remains of dead plants and animals fall into the sediment. They become part of the rock. They may form fossils.

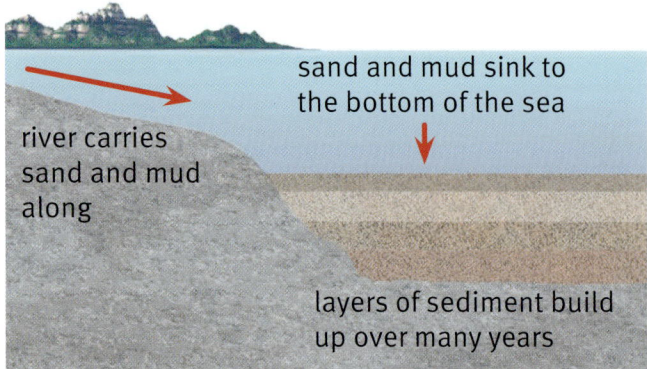

Layers of sediment form on the sea bed.

The weight of new sediments presses down on older sediments. The pressure presses water out. Chemical changes form solid rock.

How can you tell that a rock has been formed like this? There are three important clues.

- Sedimentary rock has layers.
- Sometimes, these layers contain **fossils.**
- Sedimentary rock is made of **grains** or particles that are stuck together. There are often tiny gaps in between the grains, so the rock is **porous**. Water can soak into the rock, into the little gaps between the grains.

Sandstone is a sedimentary rock formed when grains of sand were pressed together.

These sandstone rocks are made of orange sand particles compressed together.

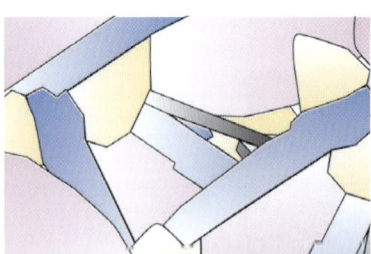

Crystals in an igneous rock have no gaps between them.

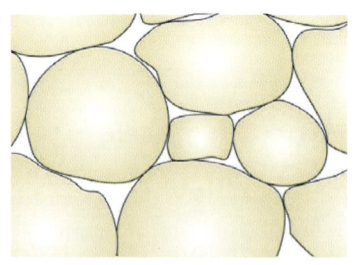

Grains in a sedimentary rock have tiny gaps between them.

8.4 Sedimentary rocks

Limestone is a sedimentary rock formed from little fragments of shells from animals, such as corals. The grains are made of calcium carbonate.

Limestone is often almost white, because it is made of calcium carbonate.

This limestone is full of fossils of animals.

Activity 8.4
Porous rocks

Your teacher will give you two samples of rocks. Find out which one is more porous.

1. Weigh each rock. Record its mass in a results table.
2. Soak each rock in a container of water for five minutes. The rock must be completely covered.
3. Blot off any excess water quickly and reweigh each rock. Record the new mass in the table.
4. Calculate how much water has been taken up by each rock.

Questions
- **A1** How can you tell which rock is more porous?
- **A2** Which variables should you keep the same to have a fair test?
- **A3** Which variables are difficult to keep the same?

Questions
1. What clues would you look for to show a rock is sedimentary?
2. Explain why sedimentary rocks are porous.
3. Explain why fossils are never found in igneous rocks.
4. Pumice is an example of an igneous rock that is porous. How do you think pumice became porous?

Summary
- Sedimentary rocks are made from little grains of sediment that are stuck together.
- Sedimentary rocks are made up of layers.
- Sedimentary rocks sometimes contain fossils.
- Sedimentary rocks are porous.

8 The Earth

8.5 Metamorphic rocks

Rocks look so hard and strong that it is difficult to believe they could be squashed.

But rocks sometimes get buried very deep under the ground. Here, it is very hot and the pressures are very high.

The high temperatures and pressures change the rocks. They often squash the grains closer together. They make the rock harder. The rock has no gaps so it is no longer porous.

Rocks that have been changed like this are called **metamorphic rocks**.

As you go deeper into the Earth the temperature and the pressure increase. In this gold mine, the miners can only work for a few hours at a time.

You can see grains that do not fit perfectly together in this limestone.

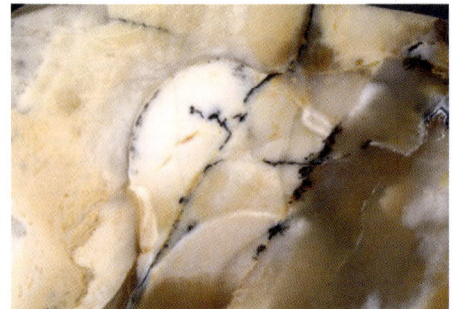

Marble is a metamorphic rock formed from limestone. It is hard with no pores.

Sandstone is made of sand grains with tiny gaps between them.

Quartzite is a metamorphic rock formed from sandstone.

Questions

1. Marble and limestone are both made of calcium carbonate, but they have different properties. Why is this?
2. How is quartzite formed?
3. Do you think that a metamorphic rock could contain fossils? Explain your answer.

8.5 Metamorphic rocks

Metamorphic rocks don't only form deep underground. They can also form when hot lava flows close to rocks near the surface of the Earth. The heat from the lava affects the rock and makes it change.

Rocks can also be changed when the Earth's surface moves. For example, in an earthquake, rocks may get pushed against each other. If this keeps on happening, they may get squashed and folded. The grains in the rocks may get crushed and forced very close together.

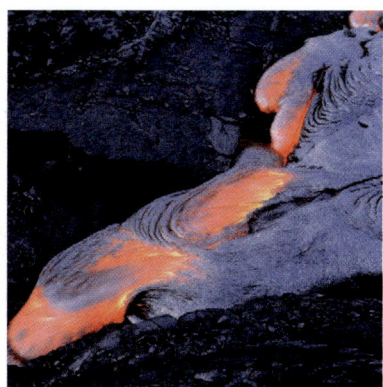

The rocks next to the hot lava will be changed to metamorphic rocks.

Movements of the Earth's crust cause heating and squashing of rocks.

Activity 8.5
Properties of rocks

Your teacher will give you some samples of different kinds of rocks. They may be igneous, sedimentary or metamorphic rocks.

You are going to look carefully at each rock sample and record some of their **properties**.

1. Look at the samples of rock you have.
2. Make a list of the questions you will ask about the samples. Think about properties such as:
   - how smooth or rough it is
   - the colour
   - what the rock is made of (Can you see crystals or grains? How big are they? Are they all the same, or are there different sorts?)
   - how porous it is
   - how hard or soft the rock is. Test the hardness by scratching the rock with a metal nail.
3. Make a table to record the information.
4. Now look carefully at the samples of rocks. You could use a hand lens to help you. Record the properties that each rock has.

Summary
- Metamorphic rocks are formed when heat and pressure change other rocks.
- Metamorphic rocks are usually harder than the rocks from which they were formed.

8.6 Weathering

Rocks do not stay the same forever. They get worn away slowly. Rain, wind, frost and temperature changes can all wear away rocks. When rocks are worn away by these things we call it **weathering**.

Chemical weathering

Rainwater is slightly acidic. When rainwater attacks limestone a chemical reaction takes place. This is an example of **chemical weathering**.

Limestone is made of calcium carbonate. When acid reacts with it, carbon dioxide gas, water and a salt are produced. The carbon dioxide gas goes into the air and the other products are washed away by the rain. Rain is a very weak acid so the reaction is only very slight. It takes many years to notice the differences caused to the limestone.

This carved stone face is 500 years old.

Activity 8.6
Acid and rocks

You will be given several different kinds of rocks. Place a piece of each kind on a dish. Place a few drops of acid on the rock. Record what happens in a table. Note any changes in the appearance of the rock.

Questions

A1 Which rocks did the acid react with?
A2 Which rocks were not affected by the acid?

Questions

1. What is weathering?
2. What is chemical weathering?
3. Give an example of how chemical weathering is caused.

Physical weathering

Water gets into the spaces and cracks in rocks. When this water freezes, it expands. This makes the cracks larger. When the water melts the larger cracks are left. When this happens many times the rocks are broken up. This is an example of **physical weathering**.

The water inside the crack freezes and expands. When the temperature rises the ice melts and bits of rock fall off.

8.6 Weathering

The heat of the Sun can make rocks expand. At night the temperature falls and the rock contracts. When this happens over and over again the rocks can crack.

Wind and running water can wear away rocks. Rocks are made smooth by water running over them.

Biotic weathering

Living organisms can cause rocks to break apart. This is called **biotic weathering**.

Plants can grow in the cracks in rocks. The growth of the plant's roots causes cracks and damage to the rocks.

The details of the carving on the Sphinx have been worn away.

The river has worn away the rock.

A tree growing and splitting limestone rock.

Questions

4 Describe the process of physical weathering caused by rainwater freezing in cracks.
5 Describe how and why the statue of the Sphinx has changed since it was made.
6 Describe **one** example of biotic weathering.

Summary
- **Rocks are worn away by weathering.**
- **Weathering can be chemical, physical or biotic.**
- **Weathering is caused by rainwater, changes in temperature, rivers, wind and plants.**

8 The Earth

8.7 Moving rocks

Moving pieces of rock

Rocks can be broken up into pieces by weathering. These pieces of rock are called **rock fragments**.

These fragments are often moved away from where they were produced. They can be moved by gravity, water and wind. This movement of rock fragments is called **erosion**.

Gravity makes the fragments fall down slopes.

Wind blows tiny rock fragments about.

Rainwater washes rock fragments down slopes. Once rock fragments get into a stream or river they can be carried away. The smaller rock fragments are carried a long way. The larger ones are left behind.

> **Questions**
> 1 How are rock fragments formed?
> 2 How are rock fragments moved?

Forming sediment

The speed of a river or stream depends on how steep the slope is and how much water is in the river. A fast-flowing river can carry large rocks. A slow-flowing river can only carry small rock fragments.

When the slope of the land gets less steep, the river flows more slowly. Some rocks then settle on the bed of the river because they are too heavy to be carried. This is called **deposition**. The deposits build up and form **sediments.**

> **Questions**
> 3 What does 'deposition' mean?
> 4 Explain why some rock fragments are carried further than others.

The photographs show deposition at the different stages of a river's journey.

In the hills, streams flow quickly. Streams carry smaller rock fragments away and leave the large fragments behind.

Further downstream, we see beaches made of pebbles.

On flatter land, the river flows more slowly so it deposits sand.

The river deposits fine sand and mud as it gets nearer to the sea.

8.7 Moving rocks

Layer upon layer

When you stir up a mixture of different sized rock fragments and water, the fragments spread out into the water. When you stop stirring, the fragments settle with the heaviest fragments at the bottom and the lightest at the top.

Different layers are formed.

The same thing happens with the rock fragments deposited by rivers. The sediment is deposited on the bed of the river, or on the sea bed.

Over millions of years there are changes in what is carried and deposited by the rivers. The sediments at the bottom were deposited before the ones on top. In the diagram on the right you can see the different layers of sediment that have formed the different sedimentary rocks.

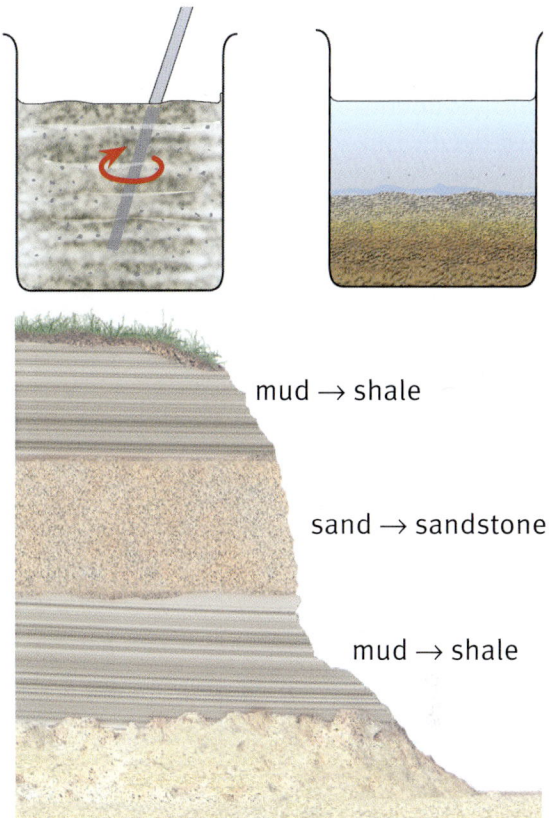

Rivers sometimes carry sand and sometimes mud to the sea.

Smoothing fragments

When the rock fragments are first formed, they have sharp edges. When the fragments rub against each other the edges become smoother. This is called **abrasion**.

When there is a sand storm the particles of sand are moved by the wind at high speed. When they hit anything in the way they damage it.

Sometimes sand is mixed with air and is blown at buildings and pavements to clean them. This is called sand blasting.

These pebbles have been worn smooth by rubbing against one another.

Questions

5 Where there are layers of sediment laid down over many years, which layer is the oldest? Give a reason for your answer.
6 What is meant by 'abrasion'?

Summary
- Rock fragments are moved by gravity, water and wind.
- Rivers carry fragments to the sea.
- Smaller fragments are carried further than large ones.
- Layers of mud and sand build up at the bottom of the sea and form sedimentary rocks.

8.8 Fossils

When animals and plants die, their bodies may fall into sediments. Usually, they just decay. But sometimes they can become part of sedimentary rocks.

As the rock layers build up, the rock becomes solid. The minerals in the rock may replace the minerals in parts of the dead bodies. This takes place over millions of years.

These remains of living organisms that have changed to rock are called **fossils**.

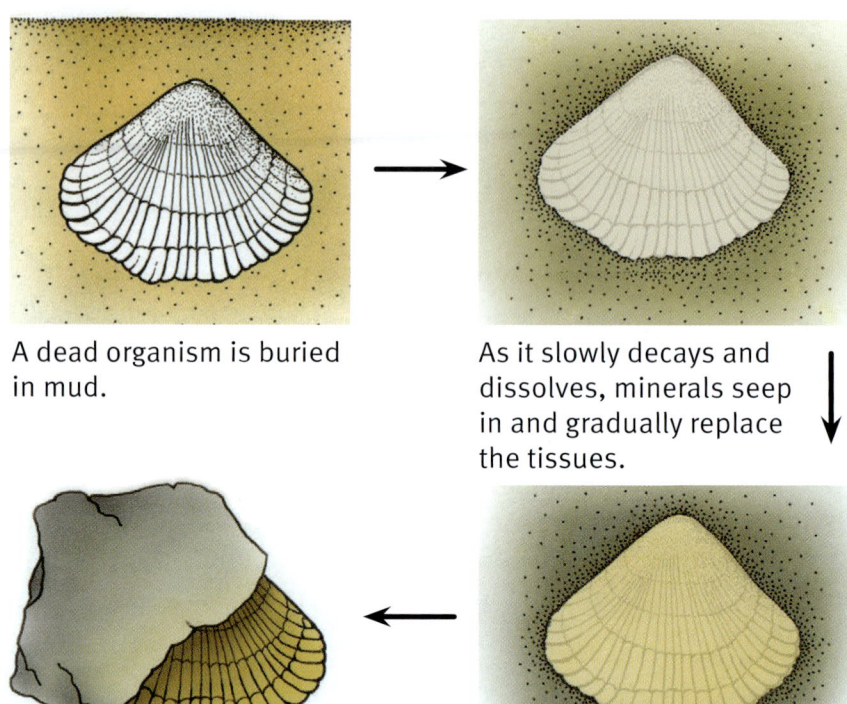

A dead organism is buried in mud.

As it slowly decays and dissolves, minerals seep in and gradually replace the tissues.

The mud around the shape also turns into rock. A fossil has been formed.

The minerals become rock in the shape of the organism.

Fossils can also be made when an animal leaves an imprint of its footprint or burrow in wet sand or mud. When more sediment is deposited on top of the imprint and the rock hardens, there may be a mark in the rock.

Clues from fossils

Fossils can help us to work out how a rock formed.

Limestone contains fossils from sea animals and plants. So we know limestone was formed under the sea.

A dinosaur footprint from Arizona USA.

This limestone contains fossils of delicate sea animals called crinoids.

8 The Earth

8.8 Fossils

Coal sometimes contains fossils of plants that look like ferns. So we know that coal was not formed under the sea. Coal was formed when trees and other plants fell into swamps millions of years ago.

Fossils tell us about the plants and animals that lived millions of years ago. Some of them were very similar to those found today. This tells us that those types of plants and animals have been on Earth for millions of years. But other fossils show us strange organisms that do not live on Earth today.

Fossil fern in coal.   Modern fern.

Lepidodendron (scale tree) fossil in coal.

Questions

1. What is a fossil?
2. Which type of rock are fossils found in?
3. Describe how fossils are made.
4. How do we know that coal was not formed in seas?
5. What do fossils tell us?

Activity 8.8
Looking at fossils

Look at the fossils (or photographs) provided. For each example:

- describe the type of rock it is in
- state what type of organism it is the remains of
- name any organisms alive today that are similar to the fossil.

You may need to use reference books or the internet to help you.

Summary
- Fossils are formed from dead organisms that become part of a rock.
- Fossils tell us how some rocks were formed.
- Fossils tell us about life on Earth millions of years ago.

8.9 The fossil record

Fossils have been found all over the world. There are many different types of animal and plant fossils. They were formed at different times over many millions of years.

All the fossils in the different rocks make up the **fossil record**. We can learn a lot about organisms that lived on Earth long ago by looking at the fossil record. We can see when species first appeared, when species disappeared, and how species changed over time.

The oldest fossils that have been found so far are of simple bacteria. They lived about 3.5 billion years ago.

Fossils form in sedimentary rock. New sedimentary rocks form on top of old rocks. So usually the deeper a rock is, the older it is. The deeper the rock in which a fossil is found, the older the fossil.

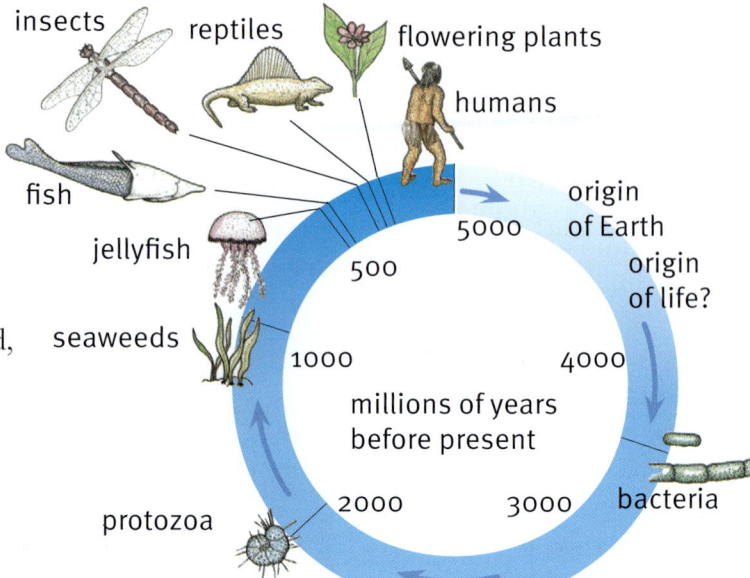

This diagram shows time from 5000 million years ago. The label lines indicate when different kinds of organisms appeared on the Earth.

Questions

1. What is the Latin name of the oldest species of horse in the fossil record?
2. Which species of horse is older – *Pliohippus* or *Mesohippus*?
3. How long ago did *Equus*, the modern horse, appear on the Earth?

This diagram shows the fossils of horses that have been found at different levels in rocks. The deeper the rock, the older it is. The fossils show that horses have changed over millions of years.

8.9 The fossil record

Sometimes fossils that are found in older rocks are not found in younger rocks. This tells us that this type of organism has died out.

For example, flying reptiles called pterosaurs lived between 220 and 65 million years ago. Fossils show that there were many different kinds of pterosaurs. Some of them had wing spans of 10 meters.

A fossil of a pterosaur.

Questions

4. Are there any animals alive today that are like the pterosaurs?
5. When did fish first appear on the Earth?
6. Which came first – the insects or the flowering plants?
7. When did the first seaweeds appear on Earth?

Activity 8.9
Researching the fossil record

Choose a group of organisms.

Use reference books and the internet to find out about this group from the fossil record.

Here are some questions you could research:

- When did this group first appear?
- What were the conditions like on the Earth at this time?
- How do you know this?
- Are organisms from this group still alive today?
- Was there ever a time when this group was the dominant group of organisms on the Earth? If so, when was it?
- How has this group of organisms changed over millions of years?

You can present your findings as a report, a poster, or a talk.

Summary
- The fossil record tells us when different species of animals and plants first appeared on the Earth.
- The fossil record tells us how species of animals and plants have changed over millions of years.
- The fossil record tells us when species disappeared from the Earth.

8.10 The structure and age of the Earth

What do we know about the Earth?

Geologists have worked out that the Earth is about 4500 million years old. They have also worked out what the Earth is like inside.

The Earth has a **crust** of solid rock. Beneath the crust is the **mantle**, which is molten. In the centre of the Earth is the **core**. It is made of the metals nickel and iron. The outer part of the core is molten. The inner part of the core is solid.

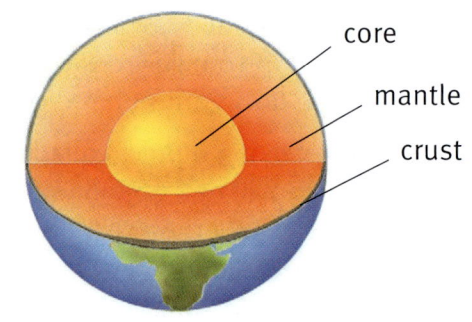

> ### Questions
> 1. What is the scientific name for the area at the centre of the Earth?
> 2. Which metals are found in this area?

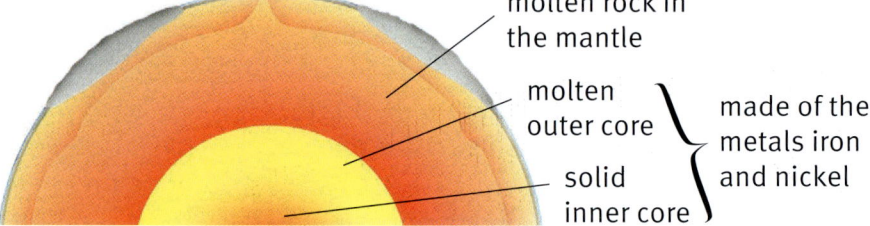

Changing ideas

People used to think that the Earth was only a few thousand years old. They thought that the Earth never changed.

In 1912 a German scientist called Alfred Wegner suggested that millions of years ago all the land was one large continent. Over millions of years the land broke up and drifted apart. This idea is called **continental drift**.

His evidence for this idea was that:
- the shapes of the continents fit together
- the types of rocks on the different continents match up where they fit together
- the fossils on the different continents match up where they fit together.

Wegner could not explain how continental drift happened so not everyone believed his ideas.

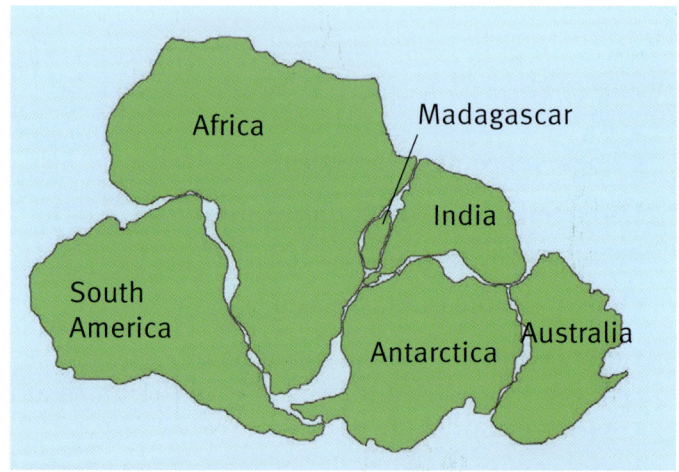

How the continents were joined a long time ago.

Tectonic plate ideas

In the 1960s, a new theory of **tectonic plates** was developed. The theory is that the Earth's surface is made up of large plates. These plates move slowly on the molten magma underneath them. The plates move only a few centimetres each year.

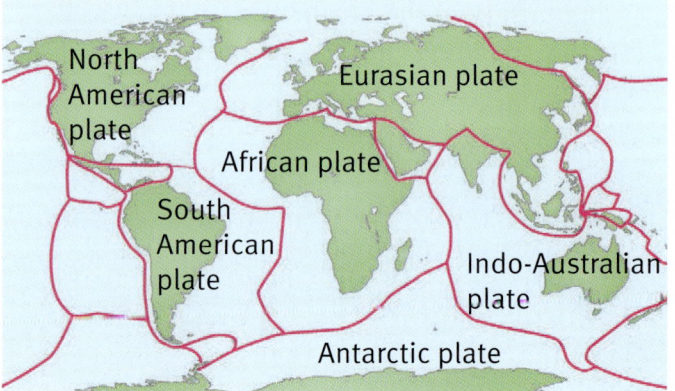

The red lines show the edges of the tectonic plates.

8.10 The structure and age of the Earth

> **Questions**
> 3 What evidence did Wegner have for his idea of continental drift?
> 4 Why did some people reject his idea?
> 5 Which plate do you live on?
> 6 What is the connection between the plate boundaries and where earthquakes and volcanoes occur?

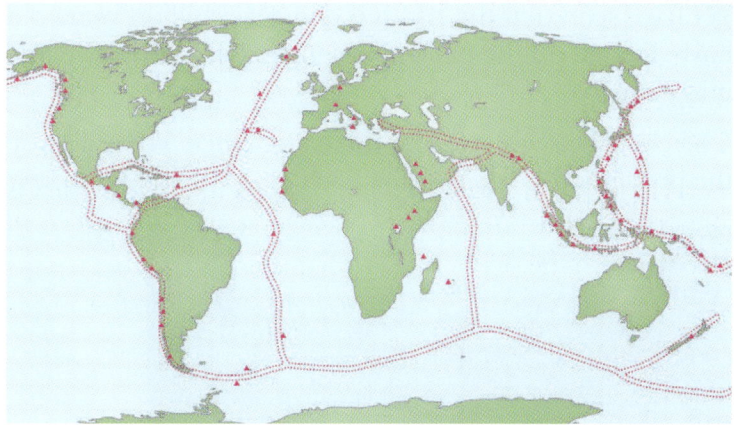

some of the World's volcanoes
main earthquake zones

The age of the Earth

Scientists can use the proportions of different substances in rocks to work out how long ago the rocks were formed. The oldest rocks that have been discovered are 4.28 billion years old. They are in Canada.

It is difficult to find rocks that are the same age as the Earth because rocks are recycled and changed over and over again

Scientists believe that the Earth was formed at the same time as the rest of the solar system. To help them discover the age of the Earth, they have also studied rocks from the Moon and from **meteorites**. A meteorite is a fragment of rock from space that falls to Earth.

Scientists have found meteorites that are 4.5 billion years old. They think the Earth is the same age as these meteorites.

A fragment of the Canyon Diablo meteorite which fell in Arizona, USA.

Activity 8.10
Research on the origin of the Earth

Use reference books and the internet to find out how scientists believe the Earth was formed. Remember to include some of the evidence for their ideas. Present your findings as a report, a poster or a talk.

> **Summary**
> - The Earth is made up of the core, the mantle and the crust.
> - The Earth is more than 4.28 billion years old.
> - The surface of the Earth is made up of tectonic plates, which move slowly.
> - Scientists have studied rocks and meteorites to work out the age of the Earth.

8 The Earth

8.11 The geological timescale

We have seen that the Earth is about 4.5 billion years old. Geologists have divided up the enormous lengths of time between then and now into **eras**.

The chart below shows the three eras since 542 million years ago, up to the present. You can see that each era is divided into several **periods**.

This is what we think the Earth looked like in the Carboniferous period.

era	period	millions of years ago
Paleozoic	Cambrian	488–542
Paleozoic	Ordovician	444–488
Paleozoic	Silurian	416–444
Paleozoic	Devonian	359–416
Paleozoic	Carboniferous	299–359
Paleozoic	Permian	251–299
Mesozoic	Triassic	200–251
Mesozoic	Jurassic	146–200
Mesozoic	Cretaceous	65–146
Cenozoic	Paleogene	23–65
Cenozoic	Neogene	1.8–23
Cenozoic	Quaternary	0–1.8

Geological timescale.

Questions

1. What era are we living in today?
2. How long ago did the Mesozoic era begin?
3. In which era did the Devonian period occur?
4. Suggest why it is helpful to divide the Earth's history into eras and periods.

8.11 The geological timescale

Rocks from different eras

We have seen that younger rocks are usually formed on top of older rocks. But, as the tectonic plates move and bump into one another, old rocks can be brought to the surface. Erosion can also wear away rocks, exposing older ones underneath them.

This means that we can sometimes find very old rocks at the surface.

The diagram shows a simplified map of the rocks that are found at the surface in different parts of North America.

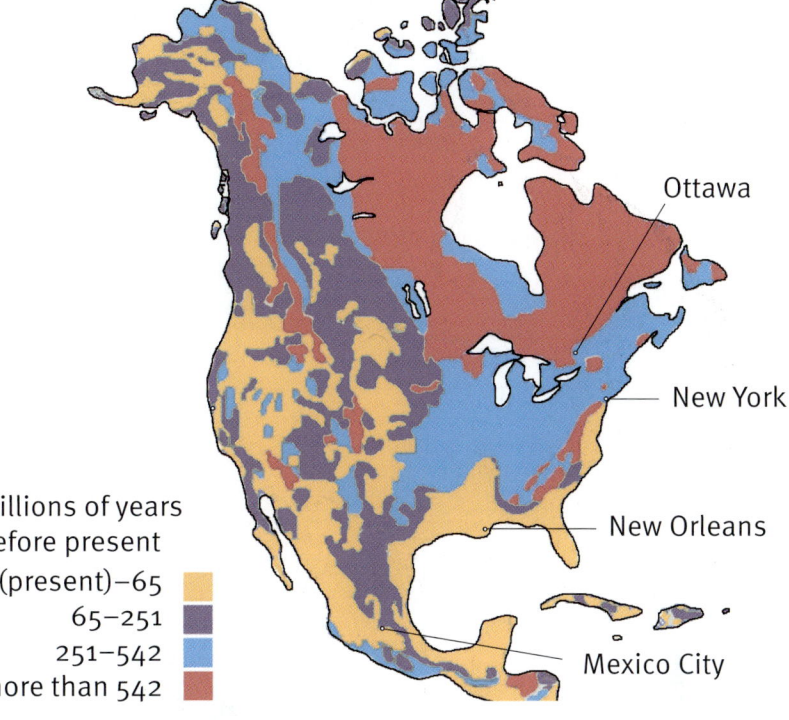

millions of years before present
- 0 (present)–65
- 65–251
- 251–542
- more than 542

Simplified geological map of North America.

Questions

5 **a** How old are the oldest rocks in North America?
 b In which part of North America are the oldest rocks found?
6 What is the age of the rocks that are found at the surface close to New Orleans?

Activity 8.11
Investigating local rocks

Find out what kind of rocks are closest to the surface near where you live. You may be able to go out and collect samples of the rocks.

Use books and the internet to find out:
- how long ago the rocks were formed
- what kind of rocks they are (igneous, sedimentary or metamorphic)
- how the rocks were formed.

Summary
- The huge lengths of time in the history of the Earth are divided into eras and periods.
- The rocks closest to the surface in different parts of the world were formed at different times.

8 The Earth

Unit 8 End of unit questions

8.1 The diagram below shows a vertical section through an area of land.

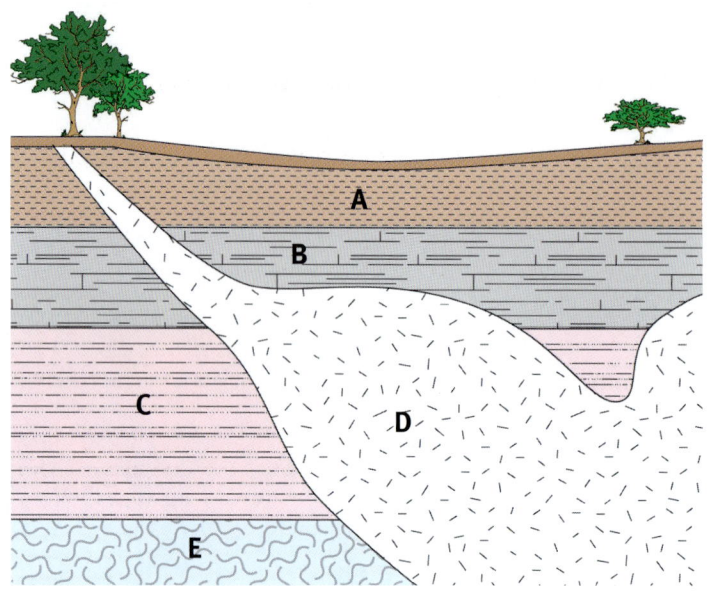

Rocks **A**, **B** and **C** are sedimentary rocks. Rock **D** was formed from hot lava that cooled. Rock **E** was changed by the heat from the lava.

- **a** What type of rock is rock **D**? [1]
- **b** What type of rock is rock **E**? [1]
- **c** Rock **A** contains fossils.
  - **i** What is a fossil? [2]
  - **ii** Which other **two** rocks could contain fossils? [1]
- **d** Explain how the sedimentary rocks were formed. [4]
- **e** Give **two** ways in which the properties of rocks of the same type as rock **D** differ from the properties of sedimentary rocks. [2]

8.2 Two geologists investigated the transport of rock fragments by moving water. They set up 50 m of tubing cut in half. They arranged the tubing so that the slope got gradually less steep. The diagram below shows how they did this.

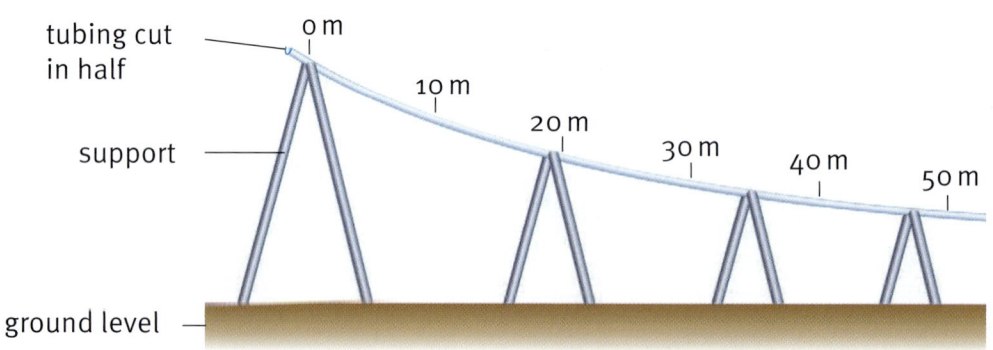

8 The Earth

8 End of unit questions

The geologists then mixed rock fragments of different sizes into the water. They poured the mixture of water and rock fragments into the top of the tubing, at point 0 m.

As the mixture flowed down the tubing, the rock fragments gradually dropped out of the water.

The geologists recorded the mass and diameter of the rock fragments deposited at different distances from the starting point. At each of these distances they examined the individual fragments and worked out the mean mass and mean diameter for fragments found at each distance.

Distance from starting point / m	Mean mass of rock fragments / g	Mean diameter of rock fragments / mm
5	0	no fragments deposited
10	0	no fragments deposited
15	16	4.0
20	23	3.5
25	27	3.0
30	31	2.5
35	36	2.5
40	39	2.0
45	45	1.5
50	48	0.5

a On graph paper, draw line graphs to show these results.
- Put 'Distance from starting point' on the horizontal axis.
- Put 'Mean mass of rock fragments' on the left-hand vertical axis.
- Put 'Mean diameter of rock fragments' on the right-hand vertical axis.
- Choose suitable scales for each of the axes. Label them fully, including the correct units.
- Use a neat cross, ✗, to plot the points for 'Mean mass of rock fragments'.
- Use a dot with a circle around it, ⊙, to plot the points for 'Mean diameter of rock fragments'.
- Join each set of points with a carefully drawn line. [6]

b Describe how the mean mass of the rock fragments at each distance varies with the distance from the start of the tubing. [2]

c Describe how the mean diameter of the rock fragments varies with the distance from the start of the tubing. [2]

9.1 Seeing forces

The photograph shows a logging truck in New Zealand. The truck's engine must pull with a big force to make its heavy load of logs move along the road.

Pushing and pulling, stretching and turning – these are some of the things a **force** can do.

- You use a force to **push** a broken-down car.
- You use a force to **pull** a drawer open.
- You use a force to **stretch** a rubber band.
- You use a force to **turn** a door handle.

Push, pull, stretch and turn – these are some of the ways in which a force can act. (We say that a force 'acts' on an object.)

> **Questions**
>
> 1 The sentences above give examples of how forces are used. Think up some examples of your own. Write four more sentences, one for each of the words 'push', 'pull', 'stretch' and 'turn'.
> 2 Look at the pictures. They show some people making use of forces. Write short sentences to describe what each force is being used for.

We use forces in many everyday activities.

128 **9** Forces and motion

9.1 Seeing forces

Forces cannot be seen

Our bodies allow us to feel forces. There are nerve endings in our skin which can detect pressure.

Press gently with your finger on the tip of your nose. You will feel the force of your finger pushing on your nose.

Sit on a chair. You can feel the upward push of the chair.

Put your hand on the chair and sit on it. Your hand is squashed by two forces: the force of your body pushing downwards and the force of the chair pushing upwards.

We can't see these forces but we can feel their effects. In the drawings, the forces are represented by arrows.

A **force arrow** is a good way to represent a force because it shows the direction in which the force is acting.

We use a force arrow to show the direction of a force.

Labelling force arrows

A force arrow shows us the direction of a force. We label the arrow to show two things: the object that the force is acting on and the object that is producing the force.

The picture shows an example. The woman is pushing the shopping trolley. The force arrow is labelled to show which object is doing the pushing, and which object is being pushed.

This helps us to understand where forces come from. Forces appear when two objects **interact** with each other.

A magnet can attract an iron nail. The magnet and the nail interact. The magnet is pulling. The nail is being pulled.

The picture shows the force of the magnet on the nail.

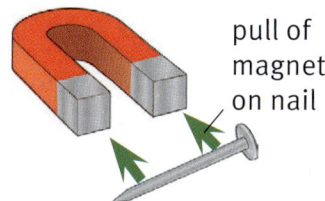

The label on a force arrow shows how the two objects are interacting.

> **Question**
>
> **3** Draw a simple picture of your foot kicking a ball. Add a force arrow to show the push of your foot on the ball. Label the arrow correctly.

9.1 Seeing forces

Activity 9.1
Labelling forces

Find some forces and label them with force arrows.

1. Make three force arrows out of card or paper. They should be about 20 cm long.
2. Find somewhere where a force is acting. Decide which direction the force is acting in.
3. Write a label for the force on one of your arrows.
4. Stick the label in place so that it is pointing in the direction of the force.
5. Repeat with your other arrows.

Questions

A1 Invite another student to look at one of your arrows. Do they agree with the direction of your arrow? Do they think you have labelled it correctly?

A2 Now look at one of their arrows and discuss it.

Questions

4. While they are playing together, Sam picks up his little brother Joe. Think about the force that acts on Joe.
   a. In which direction does this force act?
   b. What are the two objects that are interacting?
   c. Draw a diagram to show the force that acts on Joe. Take care to label the force arrow correctly.

Summary
- Forces act on objects to push, pull, stretch and turn.
- Forces happen when two objects interact with each other.
- A force arrow shows the direction of a force.

Sam is lifting Joe.

9 Forces and motion

9.2 Forces big and small

Forces can make things move. You have to push a shopping trolley to start it moving around the shop. You have to pull on a handle to open a drawer.

The pictures show some forces making things move. Which of these things needs the biggest force?

> **Question**
>
> 1 Look at the pictures. Put the forces in order, from smallest to biggest.

Measuring forces

In science, if we want to know if one force is bigger than another, we don't simply guess. We make measurements. How can we measure forces?

We use an instrument called a **forcemeter** to measure a force. (Another name for this is a **newtonmeter**.) The picture shows one type of forcemeter.

This is how you use it to measure the force needed to pull a block of wood along the bench.

- Check that the forcemeter reads zero before you start.
- Attach the hook of the forcemeter to the block.
- Hold the ring at the other end of the forcemeter and pull the block.
- Read the value of the force from the scale.

How a forcemeter works

There is a spring inside a forcemeter. The pulling force stretches the spring and this moves the indicator along the scale. The bigger the force, the further the indicator moves.

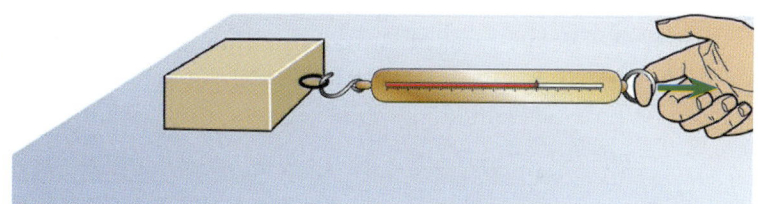

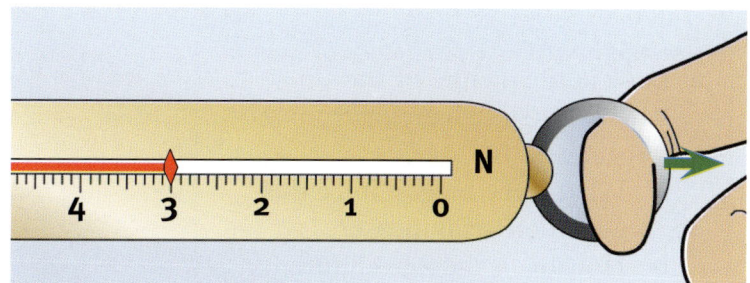

A forcemeter is used to measure forces, such as the force needed to pull a block.

9 Forces and motion

9.2 Forces big and small

The unit of force

We measure forces in **newtons**. This unit is named after Isaac Newton, an English scientist who explained how forces affect the way things move. To make it easy, we can write N instead of 'newton'.

How much is a newton? If you hold an apple on the palm of your hand, it presses down with a force of about 1 N. If you hold 5 apples, that's about 5 N.

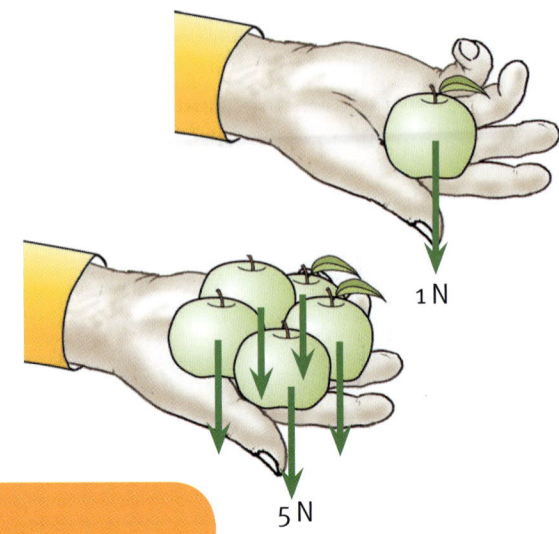

Activity 9.2A
Measuring forces with forcemeters

1 Measure some pulling forces using forcemeters.
 - Find the force needed to pull open a drawer or a door.
 - Find the force needed to lift a heavy stool.
 - Find the force needed to pull a block along the bench and then up a slope.

 Record your measurements in a table.

2 Lift a heavy book. Estimate the force in newtons needed to lift the book. Ask your partners to do the same.
 When everyone has made a guess, measure the force. Who got nearest to the correct answer?

Question

2 Look at the picture of the laboratory stool hanging from the forcemeter.
 a What is the biggest force this forcemeter can measure?
 b How big is the force lifting the stool?

Finding the force needed to lift a laboratory stool.

9.2 Forces big and small

Measuring pushing forces

If you stand on weighing scales, you press down on the scales and the reading on the dial increases. You can use scales like this to measure pushing forces.

You need a set of scales which measures in newtons. If it gives readings in kilograms, you need to know that 1 kg means 10 N, 2 kg means 20 N, and so on. (There is more about this on pages **134–135**.)

The pictures show three ways of using weighing scales to measure forces.

- You can stand on the scales to measure the downward force of your weight.
- You can use your hands to press the scales against the wall. This measures the pushing force of your arms.
- You can use your feet instead. This measures the pushing force of your legs.

Weighing scales can be used to measure a pushing force.

Activity 9.2B
The biggest push

How hard can you push?
Use weighing scales to answer this question.
Compare your answer with the rest of the class.

Question

3 The reading on a set of weighing scales is 5 kg. What force is pressing on the scales?

Summary
- Forces are measured in newtons (N).
- Forces are measured using forcemeters.

9 Forces and motion

9.3 Weight – the pull of gravity

We live on the Earth. It is difficult to get away from the Earth. If you jump upwards, you fall back down again. The Earth's **gravity** pulls you downwards.

The Earth's gravity causes a force that pulls any object downwards. This force is called **weight**. Like any other force, weight is measured in newtons (N).

Gravity always pulls you towards the centre of the Earth. It doesn't matter where you are on the surface of the Earth.

When we draw a force arrow to represent an object's weight, the arrow points towards the centre of the Earth.

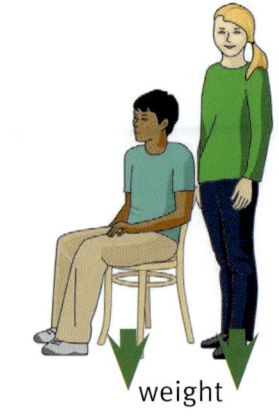

Our weight is caused by the pull of the Earth's gravity.

> **Questions**
> 1. Draw a diagram to show yourself, standing on the ground. Add a force arrow to show your weight.
> 2. Draw a diagram to show the Earth. Mark the centre of the Earth. Show yourself, standing on the Earth. Add a force arrow to show your weight.

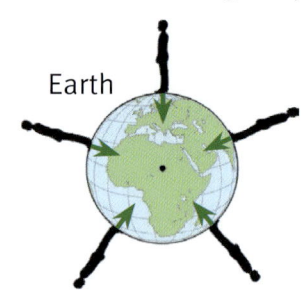

An object's weight is a force acting towards the centre of the Earth.

Falling through the floor

The Earth's gravity is pulling on us all the time. It pulls us downwards, but we don't fall through the floor. Why not?

The floor pushes upwards on us with a force. This force is called the **contact force**.

Any object that you push on pushes back with a contact force. Usually the force is big enough to balance the pull of gravity. But if you stand on something that isn't very strong, its upward push may not be enough to support you.

> **Question**
> 3. Go back to the diagram you drew for Question 1. Add a contact force arrow, to show the force of the ground acting on you.

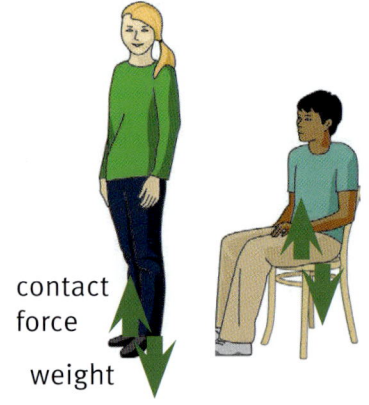

The floor pushes up on you with a contact force. So does a chair.

Mass and weight

When you weigh yourself at home, the scales show the value in kg. You might say, 'I weigh 50 kg.' However, in science, we would say that your **mass** is 50 kg.

The mass of an object is measured in kilograms (kg). It tells you the amount of matter the object is made of.

The Earth's gravity pulls on each kg with a force of about 10 N. So, if your mass is 50 kg, your weight on Earth is about 500 N.

9 Forces and motion

9.3 Weight – the pull of gravity

Imagine going to the Moon. The Moon's gravity is weaker than the Earth's. You weigh a lot less up there. You can jump much higher on the Moon – but you still fall back downwards.

If you go far out into space, far from the Earth, Moon or any other object, your weight is zero. Your mass stays the same, however – you are still made of 50 kg of matter.

Astronauts on the Moon experience much lower gravity than on Earth.

Questions

4 Copy the table.

Quantity	Description	Units
	a force caused by gravity	
	an amount of matter	

In the first column, write the words 'mass' and 'weight' in the correct spaces. Add the correct units in the last column.

5 A set of weighing scales gives values in kilograms. Are the scales measuring mass or weight?

6 When astronauts went to the Moon, they found it much easier to lift heavy objects than on Earth. Explain why.

Activity 9.3
Determining mass and weight

Use balances and forcemeters to find the mass and weight of a variety of objects.

Object	Mass /	Weight/

Record your answers in a table like the one shown here. Write the units in the headings of the columns.

Remember: weight (N) = mass (kg) × 10

$$\text{mass (kg)} = \frac{\text{weight (N)}}{10}$$

Summary
- Mass is the amount of matter in an object, measured in kg.
- Weight is the force of gravity on an object, measured in N.

9.4 Friction – an important force

Press your hands together. Rub them together. You should be able to feel the force of **friction** that each hand exerts on the other.

Rub your hands together hard and they will start to get warm. You have observed the heating effect of friction. That's useful on a cold day.

Rubbing your hands together – the force of friction causes them to warm up.

Friction is a force than can appear when two objects are in contact with each other. ('In contact' means 'touching'.)

The picture shows a heavy box lying on the floor. Imagine that you try to push it. If you try to push it to the right, the force of friction pushes back in the opposite direction – to the left.

Eventually, if you push hard enough, the box will move. Your pushing force is greater than the force of friction.

The force of friction makes it difficult to move a heavy object.

> **Question**
> 1 If you try to push the box to the left, in which direction will friction act? Draw a diagram to show the two forces.

The direction of friction

We say that friction acts to oppose motion. To draw a force arrow to represent friction, you must ask yourself: Which way is an object moving or trying to move?

For example, the heavy weight in the picture is trying to slide down the slope. This tells us that friction acts up the slope.

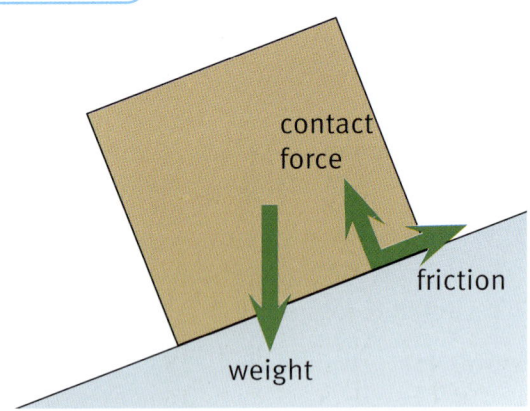
Without friction, the box would slide down the slope.

> **Question**
> 2 Omar is sliding along the school corridor. Draw a picture of Omar sliding along the floor. Add a force arrow to show the force of friction acting on Omar.

9 Forces and motion

9.4 Friction – an important force

Investigating friction

You can use a forcemeter to measure the force of friction. The diagram shows how. Place a wooden block on the bench and pull it with a forcemeter. When the block just starts to move, the forcemeter will show you the value of the force.

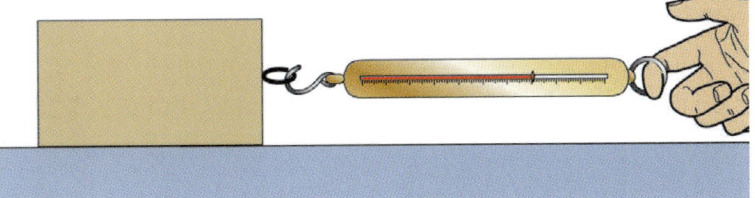

Measuring friction.

You can investigate the different **factors** that affect the size of the force of friction. Here's how.

- Add weights on top of the block to make it heavier.
- Turn the block so that a different face is in contact with the bench. This changes the area of contact.
- Use a material such as paper or cling film to cover the surface, making it rougher or smoother.

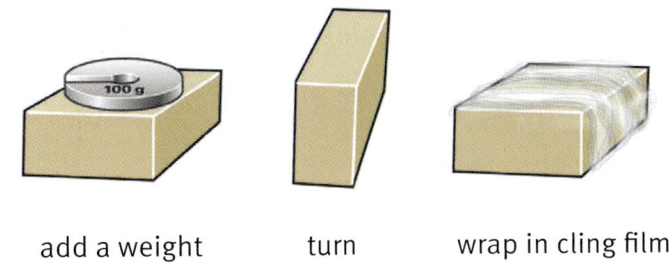

add a weight   turn   wrap in cling film

Investigating the factors which affect friction.

Activity 9.4
Factors affecting friction

1. You are going to investigate how friction depends on two of the factors mentioned above. Start by changing the weight of the block.
2. First, make a prediction. If you increase the weight of the block, will friction increase, decrease or stay the same? Give a reason for your prediction.
3. Carry out an experiment to test your prediction.
4. Now investigate how friction depends on the area of contact between the block and the bench.

Question

3. Press your hands very gently together and rub them. Now press much harder and rub again. Describe what you observe. What does this tell you about the force of friction?

Summary
- Friction is a force that acts when two surfaces are in contact with each other.
- Friction acts to oppose motion.

9 Forces and motion

9.5 Air resistance

If you drop something, it falls to the ground. Its weight – the pull of the Earth's gravity – makes it fall.

The photograph shows some parachutists falling. Eventually, they will reach the Earth's surface.

The parachutists will not be travelling very fast when they hit the ground. This is because they are falling through the air. This means that there is another force acting on them.

This extra force is the force of **air resistance**. This slows them down to a safe speed.

A parachute helps a parachutist to fall safely from a great height.

Balanced forces

As the parachutist falls, air pushes upwards on the inside of the parachute. We can represent this force using a force arrow, pointing upwards.

There are two forces acting on the parachutist. They are equal in size but point in opposite directions, so they cancel each other out. The parachutist falls at a safe speed.

When forces cancel each other out like this, we say that the forces are **balanced**.

Two forces act on the parachutist. Their effects cancel each other.

> **Question**
> 1 Name the two forces that act on a parachutist who is falling towards the ground. Give the direction of each force.

Moving through air

It is easy to wave your hand through the air. Air is a very 'thin' substance, so we can move easily through it. That's why a parachute must have such a big area – a small parachute would be useless.

> **Question**
> 2 Explain why a parachute would be useless if you went to the Moon.

The flying squirrel uses air resistance to help it glide through the air.

9 Forces and motion

9.5 Air resistance

Air resistance and friction

Air resistance is like friction. It tends to slow down anything that is moving.

A large area gives a lot of air resistance. A thistle seed will float slowly downwards. The wind will carry it far from the parent plant.

The aircraft in the photograph is designed to move easily through the air. A shape like this is described as **streamlined**.

There is a lot of air resistance when thistledown falls through the air.

A streamlined aircraft.

> **Question**
>
> **A+I**
>
> 3 Draw the outlines of two cars, one with a streamlined shape to reduce air resistance, and one whose shape is not streamlined. Explain why one may be able to go faster than the other.

Activity 9.5
Falling through air

SE

In this activity, you will try to make an object fall as slowly as possible.

1 Take a sheet of A4 paper and cut it into four equal rectangles.
2 Take one rectangle and fold it as shown, to make a 'seed'. (Some trees have seeds which are shaped like this so that they spin slowly downwards.)
3 Use a stopwatch to time your 'seed' as it falls. Change the design to make it fall more slowly – for example, give the 'wings' a twist. You will need to drop the 'seed' from the same height each time.
4 For each design, measure the time of fall 3 times and find the mean (average). To do this, add the 3 times together and divide by 3.
5 Compare your best design with others in the class. What makes a 'seed' fall slowly?

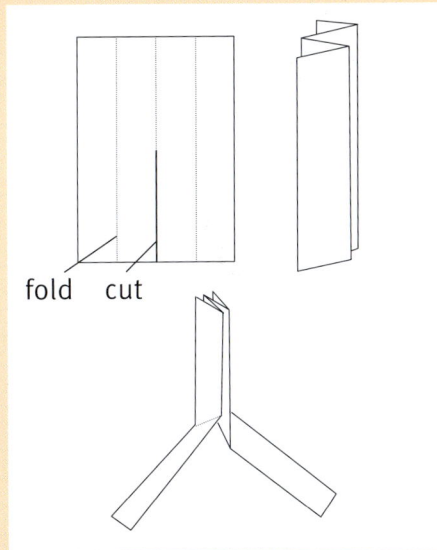

A 'seed' like this can be designed to fall slowly through the air.

Summary
- Air resistance is a force that acts on objects moving through air.
- A streamlined shape reduces air resistance.

9.6 Patterns of falling

When you drop a ball, it is difficult to see exactly what is going on. It leaves your hand and, almost immediately, it hits the ground.

One way to see the pattern of a falling object is to film it and then slow it down so that you can see it in slow motion. The picture shows the pattern.

The picture show the positions of a ball as it falls. Seven photographs of the falling ball were taken at equal intervals of time. As the ball falls, the photographs get farther apart. This shows that the ball is speeding up.

The ball speeds up because the the force of its weight pulls it downwards. (Air resistance on the ball is very small.)

These photographs show a falling ball.

Galileo and the Leaning Tower

Galileo was one of the first true scientists. He lived in Italy, 400 years ago. He investigated how things fall.

Galileo performed a famous experiment. He climbed to the top of the Leaning Tower of Pisa. From there, he dropped two iron balls, one much bigger than the other.

Most people expected the bigger ball to land first, but they were wrong. As Galileo predicted, they landed at the same time.

Why did people have the wrong idea? They were used to seeing lightweight objects falling slowly. Air resistance slows them down. But very little air resistance acts on an iron ball, so balls of different sizes fall at the same rate.

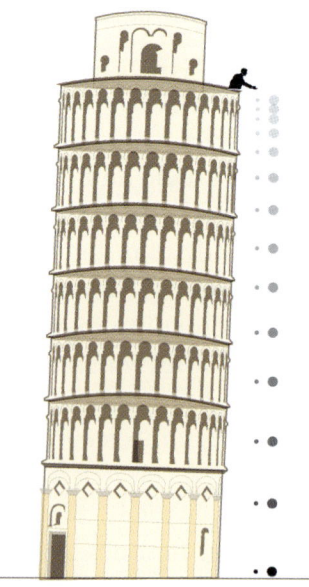

A small metal ball falls at the same rate as a big one

9.6 Patterns of falling

Activity 9.6
Investigating falling

In this activity, you will measure the time it takes for different objects to fall to the floor.

1. Find a selection of objects which you can safely drop, for example, a marble, a shuttlecock, a rubber ball, a pebble, a crumpled sheet of paper, a table tennis ball.
2. Use a stopwatch to time each falling object. You must start timing when the object is released and stop when it reaches the floor. Try this out and find the best way to do it.
3. Before you start your investigation, think about these things.
   - All the objects should fall from the same height. Why?
   - The greater the height, the better. Why?
   - Put your objects in order, starting with the one you think will fall in the shortest time. Discuss your ideas with your partners.
4. Draw up a table to show your results: for each object, record the distance it has fallen and the time taken. To be more sure of your answers, time each fall three times and find the mean. (This means that your table will need six columns.)
5. Now make your measurements.
6. Study your completed table of results. Do some objects fall more slowly than others? Do they show the pattern you predicted?
7. Try to explain your findings using ideas about forces (weight and air resistance). It will also help if you think about the result of Galileo's experiments.

Measuring the time taken for an object to fall.

Question

1. Explain why a feather falls at the same rate as a hammer on the Moon.

Summary
- A falling object speeds up as it falls, provided there is no air resistance to balance its weight.

9 Forces and motion

Unit 9 End of unit questions

9.1 The table below includes descriptions of four kinds of forces.

Name of force	Description of force
	the push of one object on another when they are touching
	the force produced when one surface slides over another
	the force on an object when it moves through the air
	the pull of Earth's gravity on an object

Copy the table. Use words from the list to fill the spaces in the first column.

friction   **weight**   **contact force**   **air resistance** [4]

9.2 a The diagram shows a stone falling through the air.

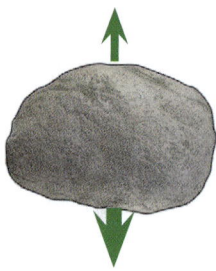

Copy the diagram. Label each force arrow with the name of the force it represents. [2]

b The diagram shows a boy pushing a box along the ground.
Copy the diagram. Add a labelled force arrow to represent each of the following forces:
- the push of the boy (label **P**)
- the weight of the box (label **W**)
- the contact force of the ground on the box (label **C**)
- the friction of the ground on the box (label **F**).

[4]

c The drawing shows a book hanging from a forcemeter.

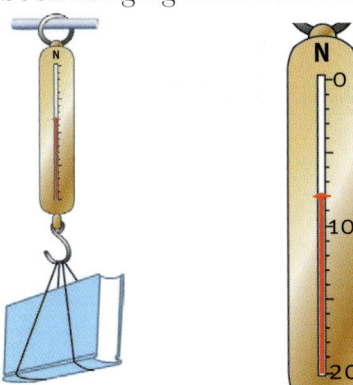

What is the weight of the book? Give the value and the unit. [2]

d The Earth's gravity pulls with a force of 10 N on each kilogram of an object's mass.
Calculate the weight of a 15 kg sack of potatoes. [2]

9.3 Jon is investigating the force of friction acting on a metal block as it slides on a wooden board.

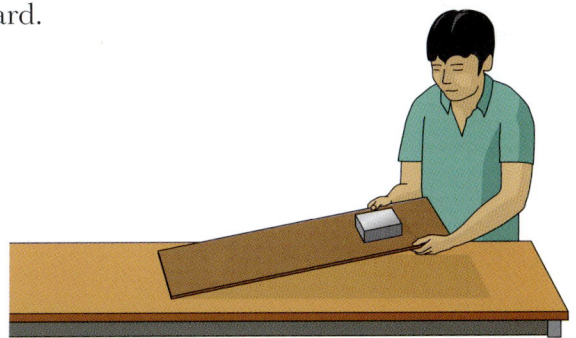

a Here are steps **1** to **4** in his method. They are in the wrong order.

He stops lifting the board when the block starts to slip.
He places the block on the board.
He measures the angle of the board.
He carefully lifts the end of the board upwards.

Write the steps in the correct order, numbering them from **1** to **4**. [4]

b Jon wants to know how the force of friction will change when he changes the surface of the board.
He spreads a thin layer of cooking oil over the board. Then he repeats the experiment.
What will happen to the angle at which the block slips? Choose one answer.
- The angle will stay the same.
- The angle will decrease.
- The angle will increase. [1]

Explain your answer. [1]

10.1 Using energy

Every day, from the time you get up to the time you go to bed, you are doing things. Lifting things, pushing things, climbing the stairs, walking around – all these activities require **energy**.

To lead an active life, you must have energy stored in your body. If you have studied Topic 3.2, you will already know that we get our energy from the food we eat.

> **Question**
> 1 Think of two more activities which require energy, to add to the examples above.

You need energy to pull a sledge uphill.

Activity 10.1A
Activities requiring energy

Try out some activities that require energy.

- Use a pulley to raise a heavy load.
- Squash or stretch a spring.
- Blow up a balloon.

As you carry out these activities, think about how you are using the energy stored in your body.

Energy supplies

There are many things we can only do with the help of machines. For example, we can fly through the sky in an aeroplane. We can travel fast along the road in a car or a bus.

Aeroplanes, cars and buses need an energy supply. They get their energy from the **fuel** in their tanks.

A car being refuelled at a petrol station in India.

10.1 Using energy

Electricity brings energy

Electricity is a good way of moving energy from place to place. Electricity is usually produced in large power station.

The power station may be far from the people who use the electricity it produces. The electricity is carried to the users along metal cables (wires).

The electricity produced by this power station is carried away in cables hanging from the tall pylons.

Activity 10.1B
Energy world

As countries become more developed, people use more and more energy.

In this activity, your task is to think about the energy supplies in the world around you. In a group, discuss the following questions and list your ideas. Be prepared to share them with the rest of the class.

- Where are there petrol (gasoline) stations in your neighbourhood? How does the petrol get to the petrol station?
- Do you use any fuels in your home – for example, gas or paraffin? How do these get to your home?
- Do you know where there is a power station that generates electricity? Have you seen electricity cables bringing electricity to your neighbourhood?
- Have you seen any oil wells or coal mines?

Defining energy

Thinking about the energy supplies we use helps us to understand what we mean by 'energy'. You need an energy supply to make something happen.

In the rest of this unit, we will look more closely at how energy is needed to make things happen.

> **Summary**
> - Energy is required to make something happen.
> - We make use of many different energy supplies.

10 Energy

10.2 Chemical stores of energy

To lead an active life, you need the energy that is supplied by your food.

We use other energy supplies, for example, when we cook, or heat our homes, or travel by car or bus. The aircraft in the picture is being supplied with fuel.

Fuels have to be burnt to release their store of energy.

An aircraft needs an energy supply. It uses kerosene fuel.

> **Question**
> 1. We often burn fuels for cooking. Name some different fuels used for cooking.

Activity 10.2
Energy from fuels

To get the energy from a fuel, it must be burnt. You can use the energy from burning fuel to heat some water.

1. Put a beaker of cold water on a tripod. Put a thermometer in the water. Note the temperature reading.
2. Put a candle below the beaker.
3. Light the candle and start a stopwatch.
4. Record the temperature of the water every minute. Put your results in a table.
5. Display your results in a graph.
6. Use your results to help you decide: Did the candle supply energy to the water at a steady rate? Explain your ideas.

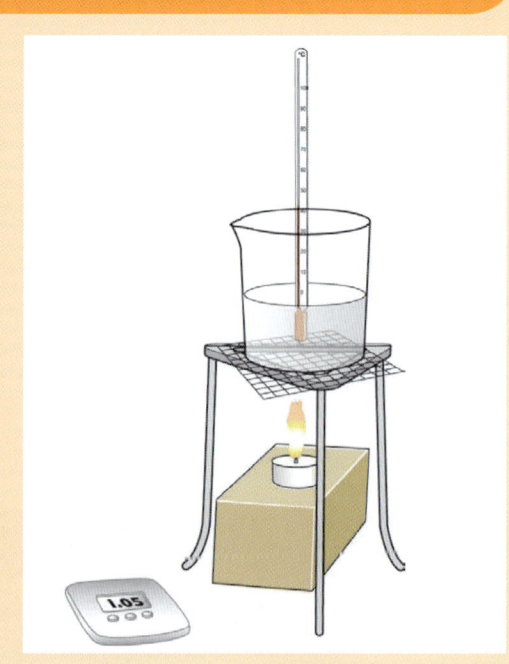

10 Energy

10.2 Chemical stores of energy

Batteries store energy

A torch (flashlight) is something else that needs an energy supply. It uses batteries to supply the energy needed to make it light up.

When all the energy stored in the batteries is used up, we say that the batteries are 'flat' or 'dead'.

Some batteries are rechargeable. This means that, when they have run down, they can be recharged so that they can supply energy again.

Batteries are a convenient energy supply.

> **Question**
> 2 Name **three** devices, other than a torch, that use batteries as their energy supply.

Energy stored in chemicals

Foods, fuels and batteries are all stores of energy. They have something else in common. They are all made up of chemical substances. We say they are **chemical stores of energy**.

To get the energy out of a fuel such as petrol or gas, it must be burnt. Burning is a chemical reaction.

To get the energy out of your food, there must be a chemical reaction inside you.

Inside a battery, there are chemical substances. They react together to produce electricity.

(The chemicals inside a battery can be hazardous, so it is not safe to open one. Your teacher may show you the chemicals inside a battery in a safe way.)

A battery contains chemical substances.

> **Question**
> 3 When you throw away a used battery, the chemicals in it may escape and harm the environment. Explain why using rechargeable batteries is less harmful to the environment.

Summary
- Foods, fuels and batteries store energy.
- They are all chemical stores of energy.

It's a good idea to put used batteries in a recycling bin if possible.

10 Energy

10.3 More energy stores

A clock needs a store of energy to keep it working. Many clocks use batteries to supply the energy they need.

The pictures show two other types of clocks.

- One uses a wound-up spring to store energy. The spring slowly unwinds to make the clock work.
- One uses a heavy weight which has to be pulled upwards. The weight slowly drops to make the clock work.

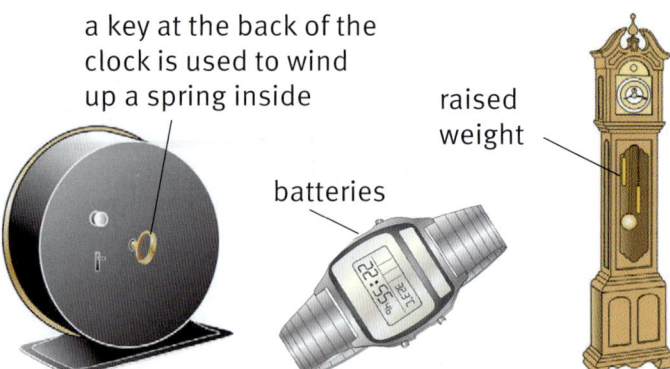

Different clocks use different energy supplies.

Activity 10.3A
Energy toys

Each toy needs an energy store to make it work.

Examine some different toys. Make sure you know how each one works.

Can you find the energy store used by each toy?

- Which toys use batteries?
- Which toys use squashed or stretched springs?
- Which toys use something which has been lifted upwards?

Storing energy in a spring

You may have to work hard to squash or stretch a spring, so that it stores energy. When you let go, the spring returns to its original length. That releases its energy.

We say that a stretched spring is a store of **elastic energy**.

Stretching a chest expander is hard work and strengthens your muscles.

Questions

1. An elastic band can store energy.
   a. Explain how the elastic band can be made to store energy.
   b. How can its energy be released?
2. Describe a toy that uses an elastic band as its energy store.

10.3 More energy stores

Storing energy in a raised object

A hammer is a heavy object. To hammer in a nail, you lift the hammer up so that it stores energy. Then, when you let the hammer fall, its energy can be used to bang in a nail.

To lift a hammer, you have to overcome the force of gravity pulling it downwards. So we say that a raised object is a store of **gravitational potential energy**.

Water stored behind a dam is a store of gravitational potential energy. As the water flows downwards, its energy can be used to turn a millwheel or to generate electricity.

Hitting a nail with a hammer.

Questions

A+I 3 A toy car needs a source of energy to move. How could you give gravitational potential energy to a toy car so that it will move when you let it go?

A+I 4 Imagine that you are jumping up and down on a trampoline.
   a Name the store of energy when you are pressing downwards on the stretchy skin of the trampoline.
   b Name the store of energy when you are high up in the air.

Activity 10.3B
Toy designer

Draw designs for two toys which would be suitable for a young child.

- One toy must use a store of elastic energy.
- The other must use a store of gravitational potential energy.

Add notes to your drawings to show how each toy works and how energy is stored.

Summary
- An object which is stretched or squashed is a store of elastic energy.
- An object which has been lifted upwards is a store of gravitational potential energy.

10.4 Thermal energy

If you heat something up, it gets hot. We say that it is a **thermal energy** store.

The hotter it is, the more energy it is storing.

Here is a way people used to heat water to cook their food.

- They put large stones in a fire.
- The stones became very hot. They stored a lot of thermal energy.
- Then they put the hot stones into water. The water became hot. The thermal energy of the stones spread out into the water.

A thermal imaging camera can show up which things are storing a lot of thermal energy.

Question

1. If you heated a big stone and a small stone in a fire, which would store more energy? Explain your answer.

Activity 10.4A
Sharing thermal energy

In this activity, you will investigate what happens when you mix two thermal energy stores.

1. Pour 100 cm³ of cold water into a large beaker. Mark the level on the outside. Add another 100 cm³ of cold water and mark the level again. Empty the beaker.
2. You have a jug of hot water and another jug of cold water. Measure the temperature of the hot water and of the cold water. Record your answers.
3. Now mix equal volumes of hot and cold water, as follows. Pour cold water into the beaker, up to the first mark. Then pour in hot water up to the second mark. Make a prediction: what will the temperature of the mixture be?
4. Stir and measure the temperature of the mixture. Was your prediction correct?
5. Can you predict the final temperature if you mix 50 cm³ of cold water with 100 cm³ of hot water?

second mark (200 cm³)

first mark (100 cm³)

10.4 Thermal energy

Thermal energy escaping

A good energy store is one which stores its energy for a long time, until it is needed.

A battery can store its energy for years after it has been made.

The energy in petrol or gas has been stored for millions of years.

Thermal energy stores are not like that. Their energy spreads out into the surroundings, so that a hot object cools down. If you hold your hands close to a hot object, you will feel the energy spreading out from it.

If your food is too hot to eat, just wait – its energy will soon spread out into the surroundings.

> **Questions**
> 2 What happens to the temperature of a hot object as energy spreads out from it?
> 3 Energy spreading out from a hot object, far away, keeps the Earth warm. Which object is that?

Activity 10.4B
Water cooling

In this activity, you will find out how the temperature of hot water changes as its store of energy spreads out.

Discuss with your teacher how you will carry out the experiment.

Record your results and display them in a suitable way.

Try to explain the pattern of your results.

Summary
- A hot object is a thermal energy store.
- Energy spreads out from a hot object to its surroundings.

10 Energy

10.5 Kinetic energy

If you ride a bicycle, you have to push on the pedals to make it move. Push some more and you will go faster.

Cycling can be hard work. It uses up your energy.

Your energy is transferred to the bike. When it is moving, we say that it has **kinetic energy**. The person riding the bike also has kinetic energy, because they are moving. Any moving object has kinetic energy.

When an object stops moving, it no longer has kinetic energy.

A moving cyclist has kinetic energy.

> **Question**
> 1 a In the picture of the cyclists, which student has kinetic energy?
>   b How could you give yourself kinetic energy without using a bicycle? Suggest **two** different ways.

Kinetic energy, more or less

If an object is moving faster, it has more kinetic energy.

If two objects are moving at the same speed, the one with more mass has more kinetic energy. (Remember: mass is measured in grams or kilograms.)

It takes a lot of energy to get an elephant moving quickly.

Activity 10.5A
Kinetic energy comparisons

SE

The picture shows one way to investigate kinetic energy.

A glass marble is dropped on to a tray of damp sand. The marble makes a mark in the sand. The more kinetic energy the object has, the bigger the mark it makes.

You have two tasks.

1 Show that an object has more kinetic energy if it is moving faster.
2 Show that an object with a large mass has more kinetic energy than an object with a smaller mass moving at the same speed.

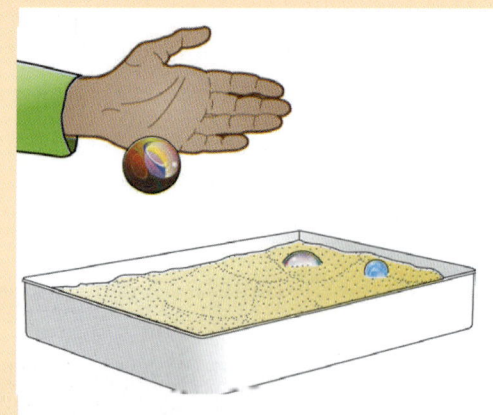

10 Energy

10.5 Kinetic energy

> **Question**
>
> 2 A car and a heavy truck are moving along a main road, side-by-side. Which has more kinetic energy? Explain your answer.

Slowing down

When a cyclist slows down, they have less kinetic energy. What happens to the kinetic energy?

To stop a bicycle, the cyclist presses on the brakes. The brake blocks press on the wheels. The force of friction slows the bike until it stops. The brake blocks get hot. That is where the kinetic energy goes.

> **Activity 10.5B**
> **Friction causing heating**
>
> Try these two short activities to find out how the force of friction slows things down and heats things up.
>
> 1 Rub your hands together. You will feel them getting hotter. How can you get them really hot?
> 2 Outside the classroom, a member of the class rides their bicycle and brakes to a halt. Touch the brake block and the wheel rim. Do they feel warm?

Friction resisting movement

You should remember from Unit **9** that the force of friction tends to slow things down.

Friction reduces a moving object's kinetic energy. Friction makes things hot.

For example, when a car travels along the road, there is friction between the air and the car. This makes the air hotter and stops the car from going faster and faster.

> **Question**
>
> 3 a When a car slows down, the brakes get hot. Use energy ideas to explain why.
>   b Explain why the brakes of a car get much hotter than the brakes of a bicycle.

> **Summary**
> - A moving object has kinetic energy.
> - The greater the mass and the greater the speed, the more kinetic energy an object has.
> - Friction reduces kinetic energy and makes things hotter.

10.6 Energy on the move

So far, you have studied various ways of storing energy. Now we will look at how we can **transfer** energy from one place to another.

Electricity transfers energy

Batteries are useful because they are stores of chemical energy. Connect a battery in a circuit. Then the electricity in the wires can make a lamp light up or a motor spin round.

Most homes have a supply of mains electricity. This can supply energy to operate lights, heaters, washing machines, televisions and many other appliances. Mains electricity can supply energy much more quickly than a battery can.

We say that the electricity in the wires carries **electrical energy** to where it is needed.

The fans this man sells use energy from electricity.

> **Question**
>
> 1. The list shows some useful things you might find in an office:
>
>   **desk lamp**   **telephone**   **scissors**
>   **computer**   **stapler**
>
>   Which are supplied with electrical energy to make them work?

Energy spreading out

When an object is hot, we say that it is a thermal energy store. If it is hotter than its surroundings, its energy gradually spreads out.

Energy spreading out from a hot object is called **heat energy**. It spreads out from a hot object.

If an object is very hot, it may start to glow. It gives out **light energy**.

A light bulb is a good example. Inside a bulb there is a hot wire or a hot gas. Light from the bulb spreads out in all directions.

Light energy spreads out in all directions from these colourful lights.

10 Energy

10.6 Energy on the move

> **Question**
>
> **2 a** What type of energy must be supplied to a light bulb to make it work?
> **b** What **two** types of energy spread out from the bulb when it is switched on?

Sound spreading out

If you bang a drum, it vibrates. We hear the bang of the drum.

Vibrations carry the sound of the drum through the air to our ears.

The drum soon stops vibrating. Its energy has been transferred through the air as **sound**.

Electricity, heat energy, light energy and sound energy are examples of energy carriers. They are carried in different ways.

A drummer drumming.

Activity 10.6
Energy transfers

Try out some short experiments that show different ways in which energy can be transferred. For each, decide which type of transfer it is:

- transfer by electricity
- transfer by radiation
- transfer by sound.

For each type of transfer, think up another example.

Summary
- **Energy can be transferred from one object to another.**
- **There are different ways in which energy can be transferred:**
  by electricity
  by heat
  by light.

10.7 Energy changing form

Here is what you have learnt so far about energy.

- We need a supply of energy to make things happen.
- Energy can be stored in different ways.
- Energy can be transferred in different ways.

We can think of energy coming in different forms, some for storing and some for transferring. The table shows these different forms.

Form of energy	Description
chemical energy	energy of a chemical substance
elastic energy	energy of a stretched or squashed object
electrical energy	energy carried by electricity
gravitational potential energy	energy of an object that has been lifted
heat energy	energy spreading out from a hot object
kinetic energy	energy of a moving object
light energy	energy spreading out from a bright object
thermal energy	energy of a hot object
sound energy	energy coming from a vibrating source

Question

1. Which forms of energy are stores and which are transfers? Make two lists.

Activity 10.7A
Energy changes in a rollercoaster ride

A rollercoaster ride can be exciting. The car starts high up. Then it runs downhill, moving faster and faster. At the end, the brakes come on and it slows to a halt.

The energy of the car keeps changing as it goes up and down.

With a partner, discuss how the car's energy changes.

- What form of energy does it have when it is high up?
- What form of energy does it have when it is moving quickly?
- The brakes become hot as the car slows down. What energy change is happening?

10.7 Energy changing form

Keeping track of energy

When energy is being transferred, it can change from one form to another. For example, if you listen to music on the radio, we can say that:

- electrical energy is transferred to the radio
- sound energy comes out of the radio.

Electrical energy has been transformed into sound energy. We can show this change in a diagram like the one on the right.

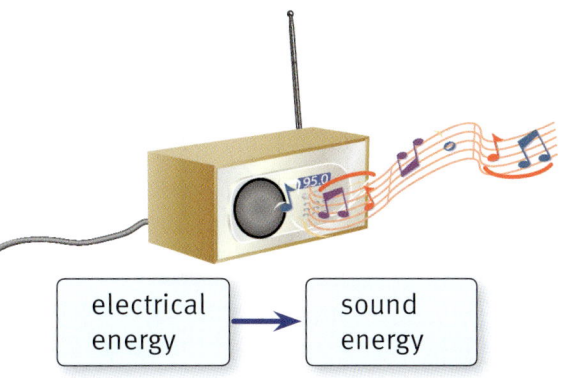

A television set transforms electrical energy to sound and light energy.

Questions

2 When a car starts, it uses its fuel (a chemical store of energy) to make it move (kinetic energy). Copy and complete the diagram to show the energy change that happens when a car starts.

3 What energy change happens in a light bulb? Draw a diagram to show this.

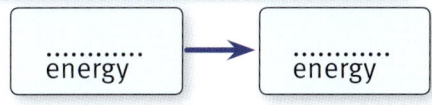

Activity 10.7B
Energy changes

Your teacher will show you some examples of energy changes. For each one:

- name the forms of energy before and after the change
- draw a diagram to represent the energy change.

Summary
- Energy can be stored and transferred.
- Energy can change form as it is transferred.

10 Energy

10.8 Energy is conserved

We measure energy in units called **joules**. The shorthand for joules is **J**.

Where does energy go?

The digger in the photograph is used on a building site. It digs and pushes soil. It lifts bricks.

The digger needs a supply of energy to do these things. It gets its energy from the diesel fuel in its tank.

> **Question**
>
> 1 Diesel is an energy store. What form of energy is stored by diesel?

When the digger lifts things, pushes things or pulls things, it is doing work. For example, when it lifts some bricks, it is increasing their gravitational potential energy.

The digger's engine gets hot, and this requires energy. Because the digger is warmer than its surroundings, heat energy spreads out from it into the surroundings.

If the digger's fuel supplies it with 10 million joules of energy, those 10 million joules will be transferred as work and heat.

> **Question**
>
> 2 In the picture, how can you tell that the digger is doing work?

10 million joules (from fuel) → 5 million joules transferred as work

10 million joules (from fuel) → 5 million joules transferred as heat

Conservation of energy

A torch uses a battery as its energy supply. If you use the torch, the battery will eventually run out.

The chemical energy stored in the battery is first transformed into electrical energy (there is electricity in the wires of the torch). Then the electrical energy is transformed into two other forms of energy:

- light energy (light shines from the bulb)
- heat energy (the bulb also gets hot).

10 Energy

10.8 Energy is conserved

If we could work out how much energy the battery stored and how much light and heat energy come from the bulb, we would find that the totals were the same. All of the chemical energy stored in the battery becomes heat and light energy.

Energy never disappears. It just gets changed from one form to another. This is a very important idea in science.

We call it the **Principle of Conservation of Energy**.

Here are two ways of stating this idea.

- Energy cannot be created or destroyed. It can only be changed from one form to another.
- In any change, there is the same amount of energy after the change as there was before the change.

Energy never disappears

If you do a lot of hard work, you use up some of the energy stored in your body. If you leave a torch on for a long time, you use up the energy stored in the battery.

However, this doesn't mean that the energy has disappeared. It has gone from the store, but it has been changed into other forms.

The unit in which we measure energy is named after James Joule, who made important discoveries about energy in the nineteenth century.

Question

3. A battery supplies 100 J of energy to make a torch work. If the torch produces 10 J of light energy, how much heat energy will it produce?

Activity 10.8
Energy poster

The Principle of Conservation of Energy is one of the most important ideas in science.

Make a poster to help you to remember this important principle.

Your poster might show energy changing from one form to another but never being used up.

Summary
- Energy is conserved.
- Energy cannot be created or destroyed. It can only be changed from one form to another. This is the Principle of Conservation of Energy.

Unit 10 End of unit questions

10.1 Our bodies need a supply of energy to be active.
  a How do we get our supply of energy? Choose from:
  - from our food
  - by drinking water
  - by wearing warm clothes
  - directly from sunlight. [1]

  b Fuels are useful stores of energy. How do we get the energy from a fuel? Choose from:
  - by moving it
  - by storing it
  - by burning it
  - by eating it. [1]

  c What type of energy store is a fuel? Choose from:
  - thermal
  - chemical
  - gravitational
  - elastic. [1]

10.2 A battery can be used in an electrical device such as a torch.

  a What type of energy store is a battery? [1]
  b When the torch is switched on, energy is transferred from the battery to the bulb. What type of energy is transferred to the bulb? [1]
  c Which **two** types of energy are transferred from the bulb when the torch is switched on? [2]

10.3 Jamil works in a circus. He runs along the ground, jumps onto a trampoline and goes high up into the air.

  a Name the type of energy Jamil has when he is running. [1]
  b Name the type of energy stored by the trampoline when it is stretched downwards. [1]
  c Name the type of energy Jamil has when he is high up in the air. [1]

10.4 Energy can be transferred in different ways. Copy the table and use words from the list to complete the first column.

heat   sound   electricity

Energy transfer	Description
	A battery is used to make a motor spin round.
	A gas burner is used to boil water in a pot.
	A musician blows a trumpet.

[3]

10.5 Ella had a beaker of warm water. Its temperature was 70 °C. She poured in some cold water and stirred the mixture. When she measured the temperature of the water, it had fallen to 40 °C.
  a Ella said, 'A lot of the energy in the hot water has disappeared.' Explain why Ella's statement is wrong. [2]
  b Explain why the temperature of the water decreased when the cold water was added to the hot water. [2]

10.6 Energy spreads out from a hot object. In an experiment, some hot water was poured into a metal container. Its temperature was recorded every minute and a graph was drawn to show the results.

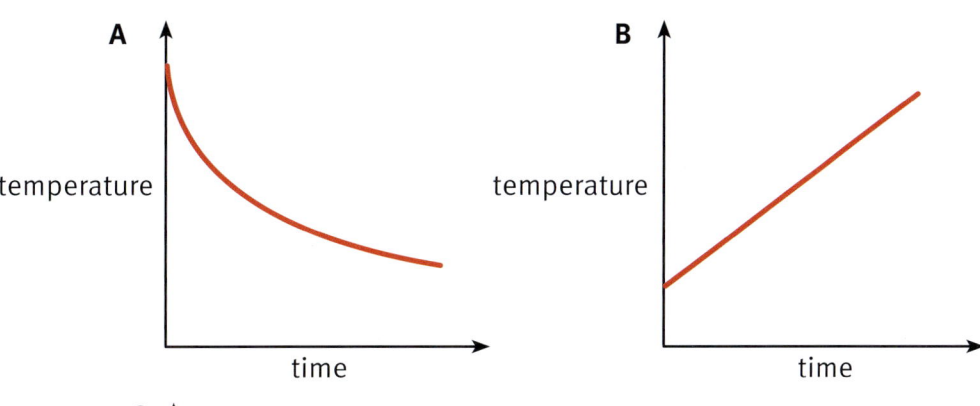

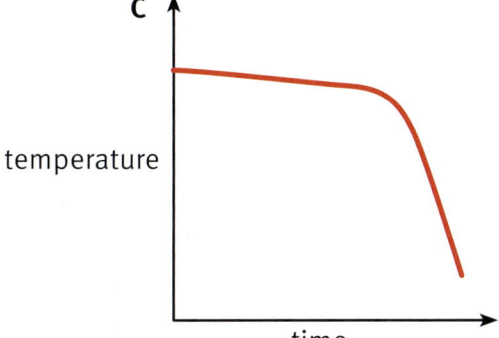

Which graph shows the pattern of the results? Explain your choice. [3]

11.1 Day and night

We live on the Earth. During the day, we can see the Sun in the sky. Sometimes we can also see the Moon.

At night, the sky is dark. We can see stars. Sometimes we can also see the Moon.

The Sun, Moon and stars are all objects in space, far from the Earth. By observing these objects, **astronomers** have been able to discover a lot about space.

An astronomer at work, studying objects in space through a telescope.

> **Questions**
> 1 Which word means 'scientists who study space'?
> 2 Nadia says, 'We see the Sun during the day and the Moon at night.' Is she correct? Explain your answer.

The pattern of a day

Every day, the Sun rises in the east. It travels across the sky and sets in the west. It is highest in the sky at midday.

How can we explain this pattern?

There are two ways to explain the pattern. One is correct, the other is wrong.

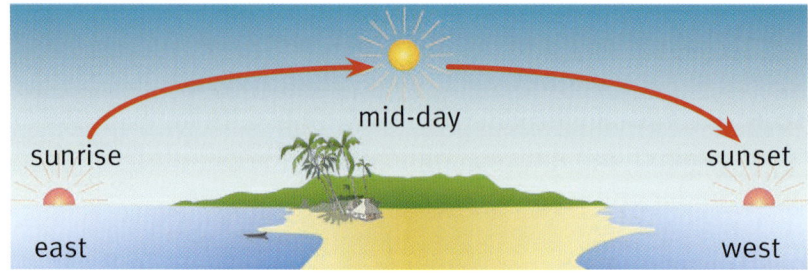

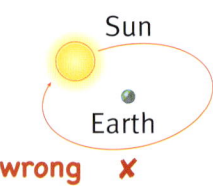

wrong ✗

right ✓

Here is the wrong explanation. The Earth sits still in space. The Sun travels around the Earth once every day.

Here is the correct explanation. The Earth is not still. It spins around on its axis, once every day. This makes the Sun **appear** to travel around the Earth.

The Earth's **axis** is the line joining the North Pole to the South Pole. It is as if there was a long stick passing through the Earth from top to bottom.

The Sun appears to travel from east to west. This tells us that the Earth must be turning the other way, from west to east.

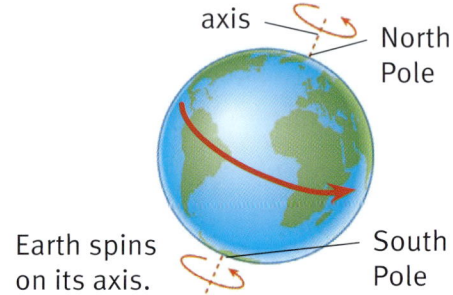

Earth spins on its axis.

162 11 The Earth and beyond

11.1 Day and night

Activity 11.1
The turning Earth

If you watch the stars in the night sky, you will see that they also move across the sky, from east to west. Here is a way to model this.

One student sits on a revolving office chair. They represent the Earth. They must keep looking straight ahead.

The rest of the students stand at different positions around the chair. One represents the Sun. The others represent the stars.

The teacher turns the chair towards the right. The 'Earth' student describes what they see.

Predict what they will see if the chair is turned to the left.

Around the world

At any moment, only the half of the Earth that faces the Sun is in daylight. As the Earth turns, this part moves into darkness. This is night-time.

In the picture, it is day-time in Africa and Europe. India is just moving into darkness. It is the middle of the night in Australia.

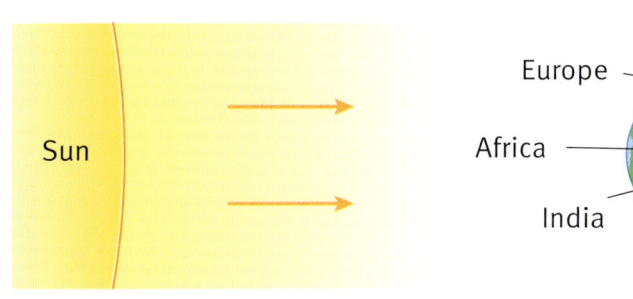

Questions

3 If your part of the Earth is turned away from the Sun, is it day or night?
4 Look at the picture of the Earth turning. Who will see the Sun rise first, someone in India or someone in Australia?

Summary
- The Sun appears to move across the sky during the day, from east to west.
- This happens because the Earth is turning, from west to east.

11 The Earth and beyond

11.2 The starry skies

At night, if there are no clouds, you can see the stars. They appear as bright spots of light in the night sky.

We cannot see the stars during the day. This is because light from the Sun makes the sky too bright.

Moving stars

If you sit and watch the stars, you will see that they seem to move across the sky. The photograph on the right shows how the stars appear to move.

This photograph was made using a camera which recorded the tracks of the stars for two hours.

> **Questions**
>
> **A+I** 1 Each star follows a path across the sky from east to west, just like the Sun. Suggest an explanation for this.
>
> **A+I** 2 Look at the photograph of the star tracks. How can you tell that some stars are brighter than others?

Star patterns

The brightest stars in the night sky seem to form patterns. These patterns are called **constellations**.

Although the stars of a constellation look close together in the sky, they may be very far apart in space.

The pictures on the right show two constellations with shapes that are easy to remember. Many constellations were given their names by the ancient Greeks, over 2000 years ago.

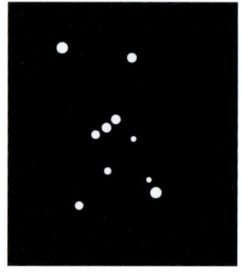

The stars of the Orion constellation.

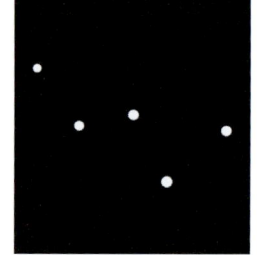

The stars of the Cassiopeia constellation.

Activity 11.2A
Constellations

It is useful to be able to recognise the patterns of some constellations. Then you will be able to see how the night sky changes during the year.

1 Use a reference book to find pictures of the constellations. Using black paper and aluminium foil, make a chart of your chosen constellation.
2 Share your chart with others in the class. How many constellations can you learn in 10 minutes?
3 A constellation may look different depending on where you view it from on the Earth's surface. Try to explain why this is.

11.2 The starry skies

Through the year

We see different constellations at different times of the year. For example, Orion is easy to see from November to February but it cannot be seen from May to July.

This happens because of the movement of the Earth. The Earth is in orbit around the Sun. It follows a path through space. This path is called its **orbit**.

It takes one year for the Earth to travel all the way round its orbit. The diagram shows the position of the Earth in January and in July.

To see the stars, you need to be on the dark side of the Earth. The diagram shows why you will see different stars in January and July.

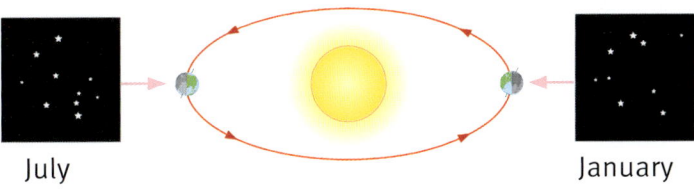

July   January

Question

3 Orion cannot be seen in July. Make a simple copy of the diagram and mark where you think Orion is in July.

Activity 11.2B
The Earth in its orbit

Your class is going to make a model of the Earth in its orbit around the Sun. You can use the diagram above to guide you.

1 Put a large ball or a lamp in the centre of the room to represent the Sun.
2 Use a smaller ball to represent the Earth. Use chalk, or perhaps string, to mark a circle on the floor about two metres across, with the 'Sun' at the centre This represents the Earth's orbit around the Sun. Mark the Earth's positions in January and July.
3 Stick your constellation diagrams from Activity **11.2A** around the walls of your classroom. Find out how to put them in the correct order.
4 Take it in turns to carry the 'Earth' around its orbit. As you do so, keep your back to the 'Sun'. (In this way, you will be on the night-time side of the Earth.) Note the stars that you can see at different times of the year.

Summary
- The stars appear to move across the sky during the night, from east to west. This happens because the Earth is turning, from west to east.
- We see different constellations of stars at different times of the year. This is because the Earth travels along its orbit round the Sun once each year.

11 The Earth and beyond

11.3 The moving planets

For thousands of years, people have watched the stars in the night sky. They tried to make sense of the patterns of the constellations.

They noticed that the patterns of stars stayed the same from one year to the next. But they also noticed something surprising. Five of the stars gradually changed their positions.

They called these the 'wandering stars' or 'planets'. Now we know that the **planets** are not stars at all.

Through the telescope

The stars look like tiny points of light in the night sky. If you look at a star through a telescope, it still looks tiny.

If you look at the planets through a telescope, you can see that each planet looks different. Some are small, some are large. Some have rings.

Today, we have photographs of all the planets. These were taken using cameras on board spacecraft which flew through space to take a closer look.

Mercury

Venus

Earth

Mars

Jupiter

Saturn

Uranus

Neptune

> **Questions**
> 1 Which planet do we live on?
> 2 Which planet has rings?

What is a planet?

The Earth is one of eight planets in our solar system. A planet is a large object that orbits a star. All of the planets orbit the Sun. Each planet has its own orbit.

The planets do not drift off into space. They are held in their orbits by the pulling force of the Sun's gravity.

The solar system

The Sun and all the orbiting planets and their moons make up the **solar system**.

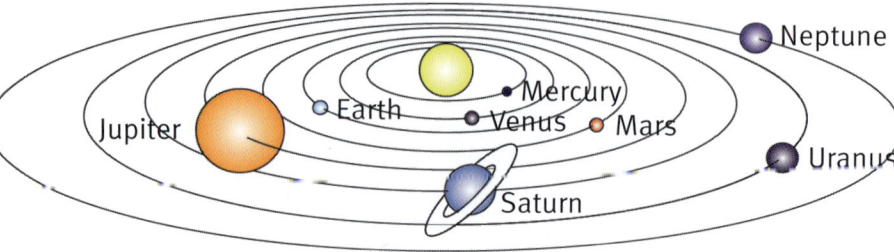
The solar system.

11 The Earth and beyond

11.3 The moving planets

> **Question**
> 3 Read the strange sentence below. How could it help you to remember the order of the planets?
> **M**y **V**ery **E**ducated **M**other **J**ust **S**howed **U**s **N**ature

Two types of planets

The four planets closest to the Sun (Mercury, Venus, Earth and Mars) are the warmest. They are called the **rocky planets** because their surfaces are made of rock.

The four planets further from the Sun (Jupiter, Saturn, Uranus and Neptune) are big, cold planets. They are called the **gas giants** because they are made of frozen carbon dioxide and other substances which are normally gases on Earth.

> **Question**
> **A+I**
> 4 Uranus and Neptune were not discovered until after the telescope was invented. Suggest a reason for this.

Activity 11.3
The orbits of the planets

The planets orbit the Sun. Their orbits are not quite circular. They have a shape called an ellipse.

Here is how to draw circles and ellipses.

1 Place a large piece of paper on a board. Push a nail through the paper into the board. This represents the Sun.
2 Join the ends of a piece of string or ribbon to make a loop. Place one end around the nail.
3 Use your pencil to stretch the loop out. Move the pencil round, keeping the string stretched. This will draw a circular orbit around the Sun.
4 To draw an ellipse, push a second nail through the paper into the board, a few centimetres from the first. Now draw an orbit as before, with the string looped around both nails.
5 Look at your ellipse.
   • Mark the point where the planet is closest to the Sun.
   • Mark the point where the planet is furthest from the Sun.

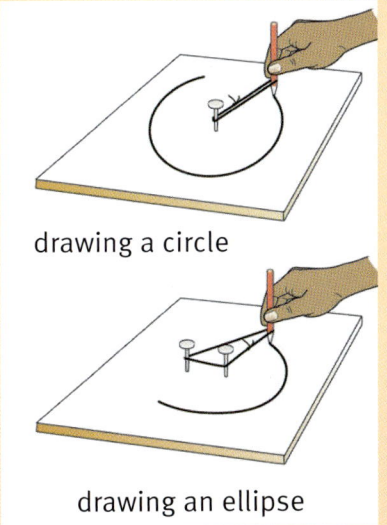

drawing a circle

drawing an ellipse

Summary
• The planets orbit the Sun.
• The Sun and the planets together make up the solar system.

11 The Earth and beyond

11.4 Seeing stars and planets

What is a star?

A star is a giant ball of hot, glowing gas.

- The surface of a star may be as hot as 10 000 °C.
- Inside, its temperature may be over 10 million °C.

The Sun is a star

The Sun is our local star. It is much closer to us than the other stars. This means that it looks much bigger and brighter than them.

It is dangerous to look directly at the Sun. Its light could blind you. Astronomers never look directly at the Sun.

Astronomers have used specially adapted telescopes to photograph the surface of the Sun. Sometimes you can see giant flares of hot gas, leaping up into space.

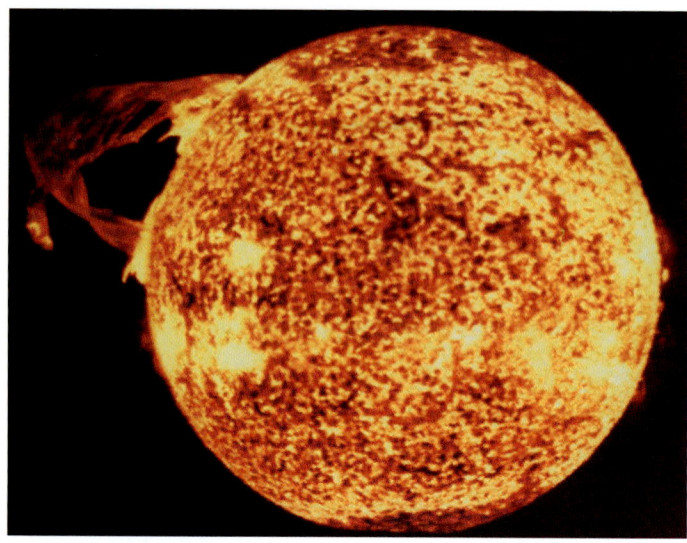

The Sun, photographed by a spacecraft showing a huge solar flare.

Questions

1. Why do we describe the Sun as 'our local star'?
2. Neptune is the furthest planet from the Sun. If you lived on Neptune, would the Sun look bigger or smaller than when we see it from Earth?

Activity 11.4A
An image of the Sun

It is dangerous to look at the Sun with the naked eye, or using binoculars or a telescope. Here is a safe way to make an image of the Sun.

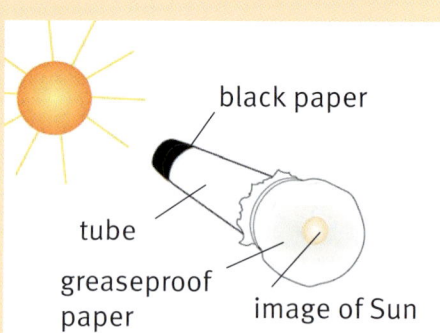

1. Stick a piece of black paper over one end of a long cardboard tube.
2. Stick a piece of greaseproof paper over the other end of the tube, to make a screen.
3. Using a pin, make a hole in the centre of the black paper.
4. Point the pinhole towards the Sun and look at the screen. Move the tube around a little until you see a bright circle on the screen. This is an image of the Sun. Light from the Sun is passing through the pinhole and making the image on the screen. You could investigate: Which gives a bigger image, a short tube or a long tube? A wide tube or a narrow tube?

11 The Earth and beyond

11.4 Seeing stars and planets

How we see stars and planets

The stars are hot. They glow with light. We say that the stars are **sources** of light.

We see the stars because their light travels through space and enters our eyes.

Planets are much colder than stars. They do not glow.

So how do we see the planets? Light from the Sun spreads out into space. When sunlight reaches a planet, it **reflects** off the planet. Some of the reflected light reaches our eyes.

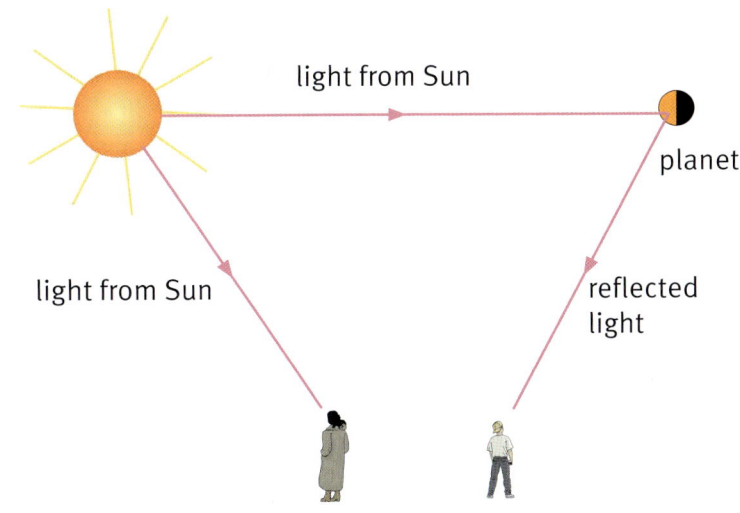

Activity 11.4B
Planet in a box

You are going to look into a cardboard box through a small slit. There are two things inside the box:

- a ball, to represent a planet
- a lamp, to represent the Sun.

1. Look into the box through the slit, with the lamp switched off. Can you see the planet?
2. Switch on the lamp. Can you see the planet? Is the whole of the planet lit up?
   Describe and explain what you see. Include a diagram.

Question

3. Damisi says, 'We see planets because sunlight bounces off them.' Give the scientific word she should use instead of 'bounces'.

Summary
- The Sun and the other stars are sources of light.
- Planets are not sources of light. We see the planets because they reflect sunlight to our eyes.

11 The Earth and beyond

11.5 The Moon and its phases

What is the Moon?

The Moon is a ball of rock which we can see in the sky. Sometimes we see it shining brightly in the night sky. Sometimes it appears in the sky during the daytime.

People have different ways of describing the Moon. Some people think that the full Moon looks like a person's face. In other parts of the world, people say they can see a rabbit, a moose or a dragon.

The Moon's changing face

The shape of the Moon seems to change as the days pass. We say that the Moon shows different **phases**. There is a pattern in these changes.

The **full Moon** is when the Moon's face is a complete circle.

The **new Moon** is when the Moon's face is completely dark.

It takes about two weeks for the Moon to change from new Moon to full Moon. After another two weeks, it returns to being a new Moon.

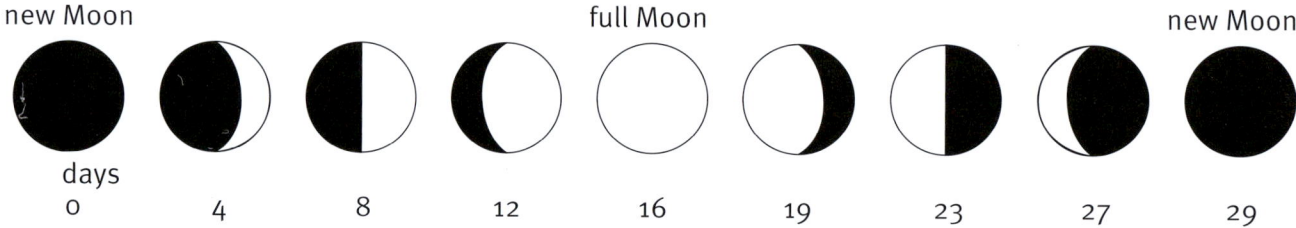

It takes about a month for the Moon to show all its phases.

> **Question**
> 1 How many weeks are there between one full Moon and the next?

Reflecting sunlight

The Moon is a cold object. It does not give out its own light. We see the Moon because it reflects sunlight.

The Moon is shaped like a sphere. Only half of the Moon is lit up by sunlight. The other half is in darkness, so we cannot see it.

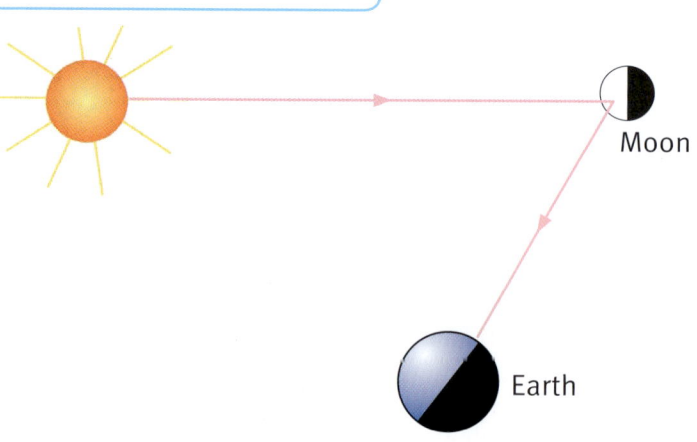

The Moon reflects light from the Sun to our eyes.

11.5 The Moon and its phases

Activity 11.5
A model of the Moon

You can use a model to show why the Moon has phases.

1. You need a cardboard box with a ball hanging inside, to represent the Moon. Cut one hole in the cardboard box to shine a torch (flashlight) through. The torch represents the Sun.
2. Cut four other holes for looking through, as shown.
3. Shine the light of the torch so that it lights up one side of the ball. Look through the first viewing hole. Describe what you see.
4. Draw a diagram of the box, viewed from above. Show the torch and its light, reflecting off the ball. Include a drawing to show how the ball looks from the viewing hole.
5. Look through each of the other viewing holes in turn and record your observations.

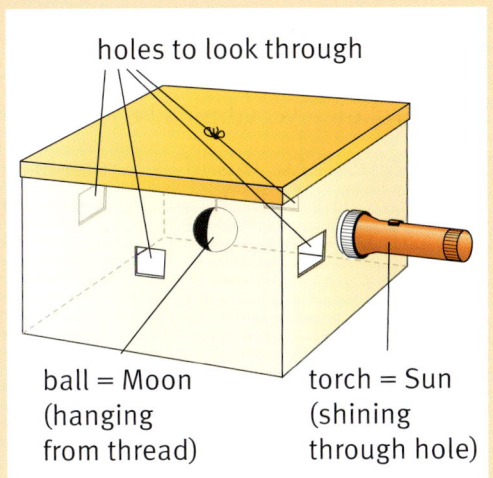

Explaining the Moon's phases

The Moon is in orbit around the Earth. It takes about one month to complete an orbit.

The diagram shows the Moon at different points in its orbit. The side of the Moon facing the Sun is always bright. The phase of the Moon changes because we see it from different angles.

- When the Moon is in the same direction as the Sun, its dark side faces Earth. This is when we see a new Moon.
- When the Moon is in the opposite direction to the Sun, its sunlit side faces Earth. We see a full Moon.

Question

2. Draw a diagram to show the positions of the Sun, Moon and Earth when we see a half Moon.

Summary
- The Moon is a rocky object in orbit around the Earth.
- The side of the Moon facing the Sun is lit up. We see the Moon because it reflects sunlight.
- The phase of the Moon changes as it travels around its orbit, because we see it from different angles.

11.6 A revolution in astronomy

Today, all scientists agree that the Earth and planets move around the Sun. But it took many centuries to convince everyone of this.

We are used to seeing the Sun, Moon and stars moving across the sky. The Earth doesn't feel as if it is spinning. So it was natural for people to think that the Earth was stationary and everything else orbited the Earth.

The picture shows this idea, which lasted for over 1500 years. It is called a **geocentric model** because the Earth is at the centre. (The Earth is called *geos* in Greek.)

> **Question**
> 1 List some other words that start with geo- and give their meanings. Are they all connected with the Earth?

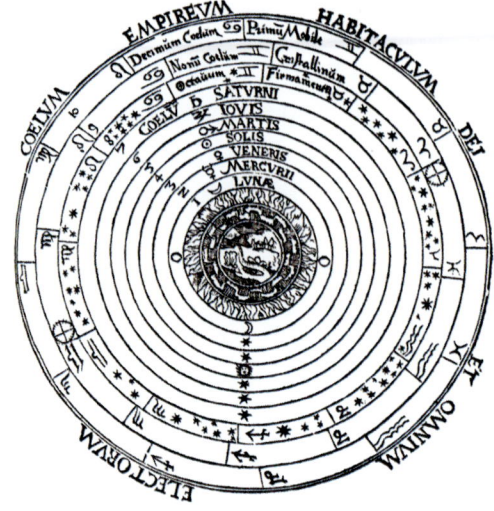

A diagram of the solar system, published in 1524. The Earth is at the centre with the Moon, planets and Sun orbiting it.

The problem of the planets

People have made careful observations of the planets and stars for thousands of years. There was a problem with the geocentric model of the solar system. It could not explain the unusual motion of the planets.

As we saw in on pages **166**–**167**, the planets change their positions in the sky. For example, sometimes we see Mercury and Venus at dawn, before the Sun rises. Sometimes we see them at sunset. This shows that they do not move at a steady speed around the Earth.

Astronomers made up complicated ways to explain this. But in about 1510 a Polish astronomer called Copernicus came up with a simpler answer. He suggested that the Earth and planets all travel round the Sun. He also suggested that the other stars were very, very far away.

This is called a **heliocentric model** because the Sun is at the centre. (The Sun is called *helios* in Greek.) There is a picture of the heliocentric model on page **166**.

Nicolaus Copernicus.

> **Questions**
> 2 Copernicus only knew of six planets, the ones closest to the Sun. Name them.
> 3 In the heliocentric model, only one object orbits the Earth. What is it?

11 The Earth and beyond

11.6 A revolution in astronomy

It's the Earth that moves

Copernicus realised that, as the Earth travels around the Sun, we get a different view of the planets and stars. That's why we see different stars at different times of year.

Copernicus's idea is a simple way of explaining complicated observations. Scientists usually prefer a simple explanation if it will explain all the available information.

> **Activity 11.6**
> How the planets move
>
> You need to go outside to do this activity. Work in a group of five students. One represents the Sun, the others represent the first four planets.
>
> The planets move around the Sun, each in its own orbit. The person who represents the Earth needs a notebook to record observations.
>
> Find out how Mercury, Venus and Mars seem to change their positions as seen from Earth.

Galileo and the telescope

Galileo was an Italian astronomer who lived 100 years after Copernicus. He was lucky. The telescope had just been invented and, in 1609, he became the first person to use a telescope to look at the Moon and stars.

Galileo discovered that Jupiter had four moons orbiting it. This showed that not everything orbits the Earth.

Many people were unhappy with the ideas of Copernicus and Galileo. They wanted to believe that the Earth was at the centre of the Universe.

Galileo didn't really have enough evidence to prove his ideas, but today we know that much of what he believed is correct.

Galileo demonstrating his telescope in Venice.

> **Summary**
> - In the geocentric model, the Sun, Moon and planets orbit the Earth.
> - In the heliocentric model, the eight planets, including the Earth, orbit the Sun.

11.7 400 years of astronomy

Four centuries have passed since Galileo first looked at the sky through his telescope.

In that time, astronomers have made many interesting discoveries about the **Universe**. The Universe is made up of all the matter and energy that exist. It is everything that we can see or ever hope to see in space.

- They discovered two more planets, Uranus and Neptune.
- They discovered the asteroid belt between Mars and Jupiter. An **asteroid** is a small lump of rock in orbit around the Sun.
- They discovered that the Sun is just one of the stars which make up a **galaxy** called the Milky Way. A galaxy is made up of many billions of stars, clustered close together in space.
- They discovered that there are many billions of galaxies in space. That means that there is an enormous number of stars in the Universe.

> **Question**
>
> 1. Put these items in order, from smallest to biggest:
>
>   **a star   a planet   an asteroid
>   the Universe   a galaxy
>   the solar system**

Galaxies come in different shapes and sizes.

Our galaxy, the Milky Way, is shaped like this one, with spiral arms.

The expanding Universe

You need a powerful telescope to see the distant galaxies. A hundred years ago, two American astronomers made an amazing discovery when they looked at galaxies through a big telescope.

- Henrietta Leavitt measured how far away the galaxies were.
- Edwin Hubble measured how fast the galaxies were moving.

Their results showed that all of the galaxies are spreading out in space. The Universe is getting bigger and bigger – it is expanding!

Henrietta Leavitt.

11.7 400 years of astronomy

This means that, a long time ago, the Universe was much smaller than it is today.

Now we know that the Universe started about 13.7 billion years ago. The start is called the Big Bang. The Universe started to expand from a tiny point in space.

The Universe is still expanding. It may go on expanding for ever. Nobody knows.

Edwin Hubble.

Activity 11.7
Galaxies spreading apart

This activity will help you to imagine how the galaxies which make up the Universe are spreading apart.

1. Draw six galaxies on paper, making each about 2 cm across.
2. Cut them out.
3. Use sticky tape to stick them to a toy balloon.
4. Carefully blow up the balloon. As it expands, what happens to the galaxies?

Can you think of another way to represent the expanding Universe, using a long, wide elastic band?

Some galaxy shapes you could copy.

Questions
2. What name is given to the time when the Universe started?
3. How old do scientists believe the Universe is?

Summary
- The Universe consists of all the matter and energy that exist. It is expanding.
- The Universe is made up of billions of galaxies. Each galaxy is made up of billions of stars.

11 The Earth and beyond

11.8 Journey into space

The first person to go into space was a Russian called Yuri Gagarin, in 1961. Since then, hundreds of people have been into space.

To get into space, you have to travel above the Earth's **atmosphere**. This is the thin layer of air around the Earth.

If you go more than 10 km above the Earth's surface, the air is too thin to breathe. There is no air in space.

A spacecraft must be equipped with supplies of oxygen so that the astronauts on board can breathe.

Yuri Gagarin in his spacecraft.

Question

1. Suggest some other things that will be needed if people are to spend several days in a spacecraft.

We have lift-off

If you throw a ball upwards, it falls down again. The harder you throw the ball, the higher it goes. But it will never go into space.

It takes a big force to push a spacecraft into space. This is because a spacecraft is heavy – it weighs several tonnes.

Giant rockets are needed to push the spacecraft upwards. Each rocket can push with a force of thousands of newtons.

The rockets contain chemicals which burn. They supply the energy needed to lift the spacecraft into space.

Questions

2. What type of energy store does a rocket have?
3. The rockets push the spacecraft upwards. The spacecraft's energy increases. What type of energy does it gain?

A rocket takes off, carrying a spacecraft into space.

11 The Earth and beyond

11.8 Journey into space

On the Moon

In 1969, the Apollo 11 spacecraft took the first people to the Moon. They explored part of its surface. It was a dangerous journey but they returned safely.

The Moon has no atmosphere. An astronaut showed that a feather fell at the same speed as a hammer. There was no air resistance to make the feather fall more slowly. The Moon's gravity is much weaker than the Earth's. This made it much easier for the astronauts to move around, even though they were wearing spacesuits.

Astronaut on the surface of the Moon.

> **Question**
>
> 4 Astronauts on the Moon must carry a supply of oxygen. Explain why.

Activity 11.8
Journey to Mars

One day, astronauts may travel to the planet Mars. This will be a difficult and dangerous journey. It will take several months to get there. Plan the trip to Mars. Think about these questions.

- What will the astronauts need during the journey?
- What will they do when they land on Mars?
- How will they communicate with Earth?
- How will they get back to Earth?

The information in the table may help you.

Present your ideas to the rest of the class.

This rover explored the surface of Mars in 2006.

On Mars ....
There is no atmosphere to breathe.
There are no rivers, lakes or seas.
Gravity is less than half as strong as on Earth.

Summary
- Rockets provide the force needed to lift a spacecraft into space.
- Despite the difficulties and dangers of space travel, astronauts have visited the Moon.

Unit 11 End of unit questions

11.1 **a** In which direction is the Sun when it rises? [1]
    b During the day, we see the Sun appear to move across the sky.
        Choose the correct explanation from the list below.
- The Sun orbits the Earth once every day.
- The Earth orbits the Sun once every day.
- The Earth turns around once every day.
- The Sun turns around once every day. [1]

    c Describe how the stars move in the sky at night. [2]

11.2 Choose words from the list to answer the questions below.

Moon   Jupiter   Milky Way   Earth   Sun

    a What is the Moon in orbit around? [1]
    b What is the name of our galaxy? [1]
    c Which object in the list is a star? [1]
    d Which **two** objects in the list are planets? [2]
    e Which **two** objects in the list are sources of light? [2]
    f Which objects in the list are parts of the solar system? [2]

11.3 The diagram shows the Sun, Earth and Mars. We see Mars because it reflects light from the Sun.
Copy the diagram. Complete it to show the path of sunlight which allows us to see Mars.

Sun

Mars

Earth

[2]

Unit 11 End of unit questions

11.4 The drawing shows the Earth and the Sun. It shows the Earth's position in January.

Make a copy of the diagram and answer the following questions.

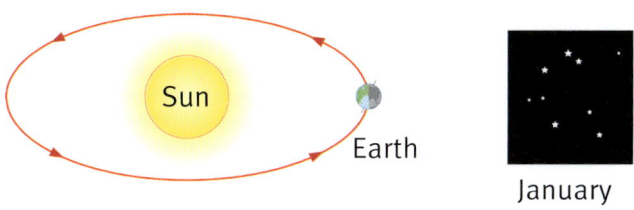

- **a** Mark a point on the Earth where it is night-time. Label this 'night'. [1]
- **b** A person on the Earth looks at the stars in the night sky. Add an arrow to the diagram to show the direction in which they will see stars. [1]
- **c** Draw the position of the Earth six months later, in July. Label this 'July'. [1]
- **d** Use the diagram to explain why the stars we see in July are different from the stars we see in January. [2]

Reference

Laboratory apparatus

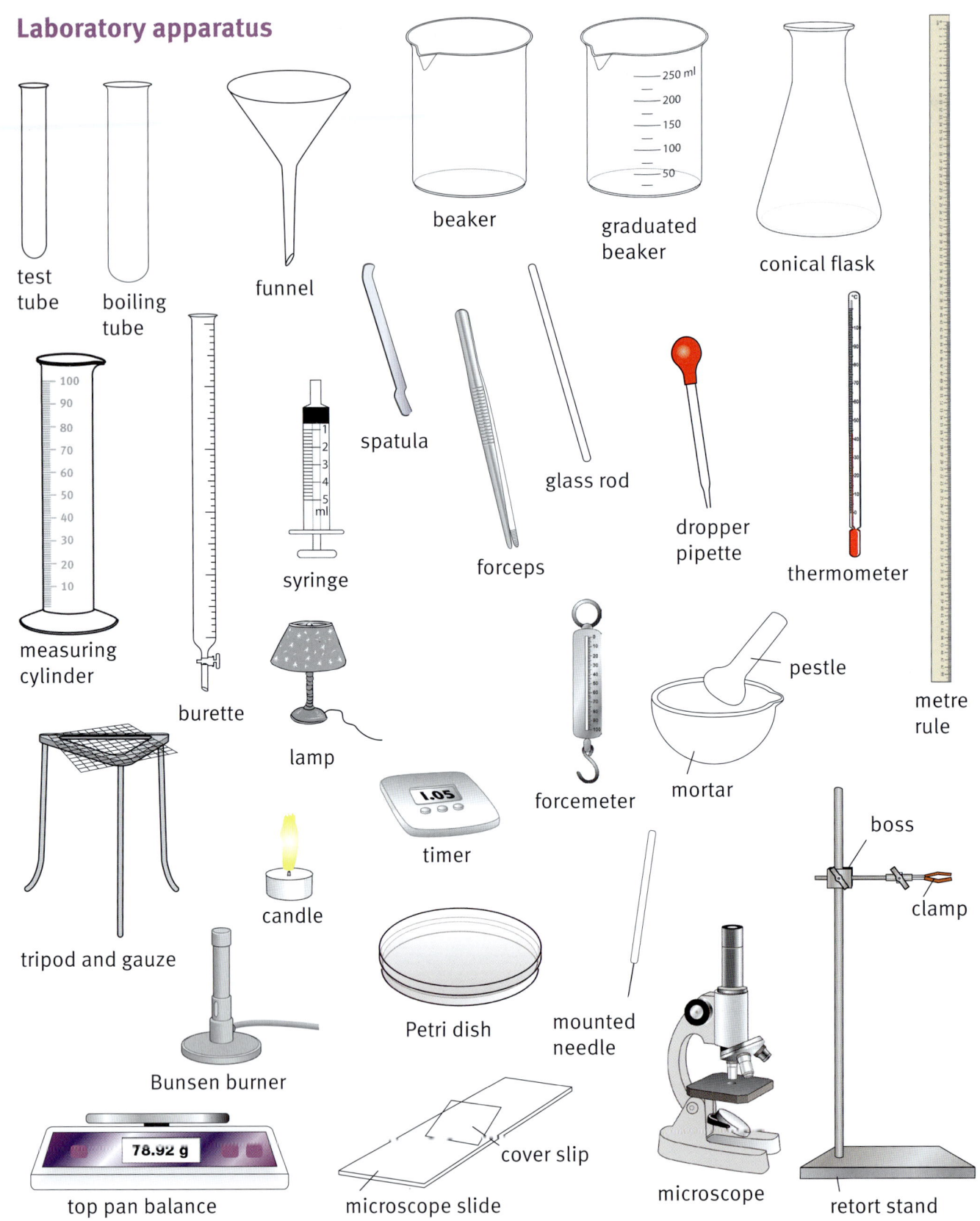

Reference

Units

We use different units for measuring different things.

For example, we use metres to measure length.

- If we want to measure very long things, we can use kilometres. A kilometre is 1000 metres.
- If we want to measure small things, we can use centimetres. There are 100 centimetres in 1 metre.
- If we want to measure very small things, we can use millimetres. There are 1000 millimetres in 1 metre.

Quantity	Unit	Abbreviation
length	metre	m
	centimetre	cm
	millimetre	mm
	kilometre	km
mass	gram	g
	kilogram	kg
force	newton	N
energy	joule	J
	kilojoule	kJ
volume	cubic centimetre	cm³
temperature	degrees Celsius	°C
time	seconds	s

How to measure a length

You use a ruler to measure a length.

Make sure you know the units the ruler is marked in.
This ruler is marked off in millimetres (mm). There are 10 mm in 1 cm.

Read the scale at the other end of the thing you are measuring.

Place the 0 mark on the ruler exactly at one end of the thing you are measuring.

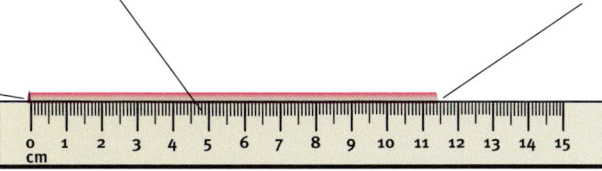

This drinking straw measures 11.4 cm. We could also write this as 114 mm.

 Reference

How to measure a temperature

Safety! Never put a laboratory thermometer into your mouth.

Measuring the temperature of the air

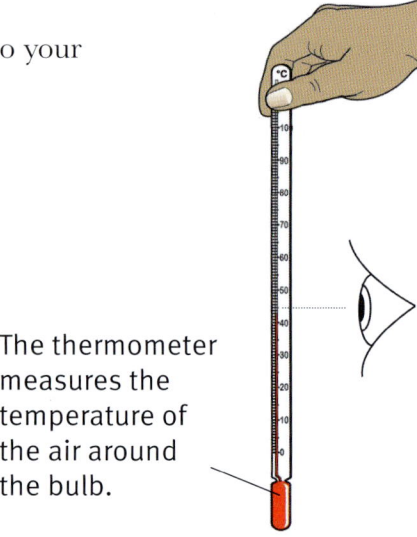

Do not hold the bulb, or the thermometer will measure the temperature of your fingers.

Put your eye level with the top of the liquid to read the temperature from the scale.

The thermometer measures the temperature of the air around the bulb.

Measuring the temperature of a liquid

Hold the thermometer at the top.

It's a good idea to stir it round gently, to make sure the liquid is mixed up and all at the same temperature.

Do not let the bulb touch the glass, or the thermometer will measure the temperature of the glass.

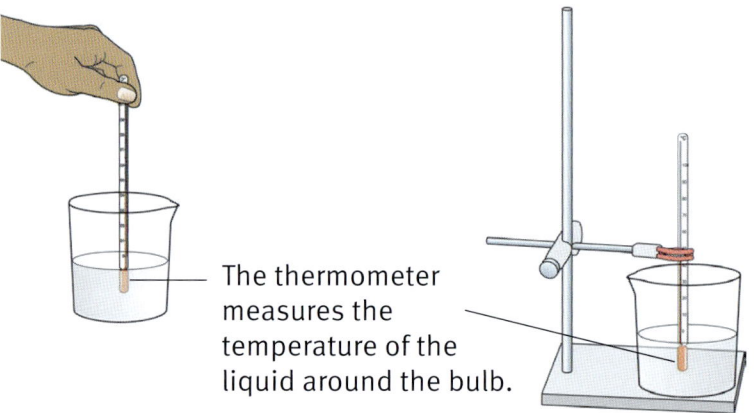

The thermometer measures the temperature of the liquid around the bulb.

How to measure a volume of liquid

The scale on apparatus for measuring a volume is shown in ml or cm^3.

ml stands for millilitres.

cm^3 stands for cubic centimetres.

1 ml is exactly the same as 1 cm^3.

Reading the scale
The top of a liquid forms a curve. The curve is called a **meniscus**.

Put your eye exactly level with the meniscus.

Note the point on the scale that the bottom of the meniscus comes to.

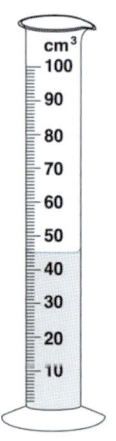
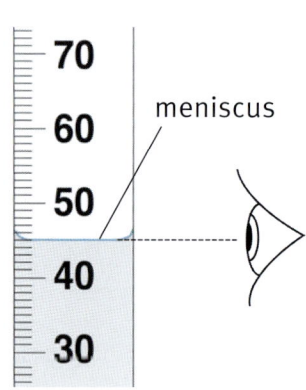

meniscus

Reference

How to construct a results table

You use a results table to record the results that you collect when you do an experiment.

The purpose of a results table is:

- to show other people your results
- to organise your results clearly, so that you can use them to draw a graph, to do a calculation or to make a conclusion.

Let's imagine that you are doing an experiment to measure how the temperature of some hot water changes as it cools. You measure the temperature of the water every five minutes for 30 minutes. Here is what your results table could look like.

Make sure that each column has a heading saying exactly what the numbers mean. (Sometimes, it might be better to have headings for the rows, rather than the columns.)

Always use a ruler to draw neat lines for the rows and columns of your table.

Time / minutes	Temperature / °C
0	76
5	64
10	54
15	46
20	41
25	36
30	34

Always include the units of your measurements in the headings.

This symbol is used to show that what comes next is the unit you have used for measuring your results.

Do not write units with your results.

 Reference

How to draw a line graph

If your results are a series of numbers, like the ones in the results table on the previous page, it's often a good idea to draw a line graph to display them. This makes it easy to see trends and patterns in the results.

- The quantity that you were in control of goes along the bottom of your graph. In this case, this is the time at which you took your readings.
- The quantity that you were measuring goes up the side of your graph. In this case, this is the temperature of the water.

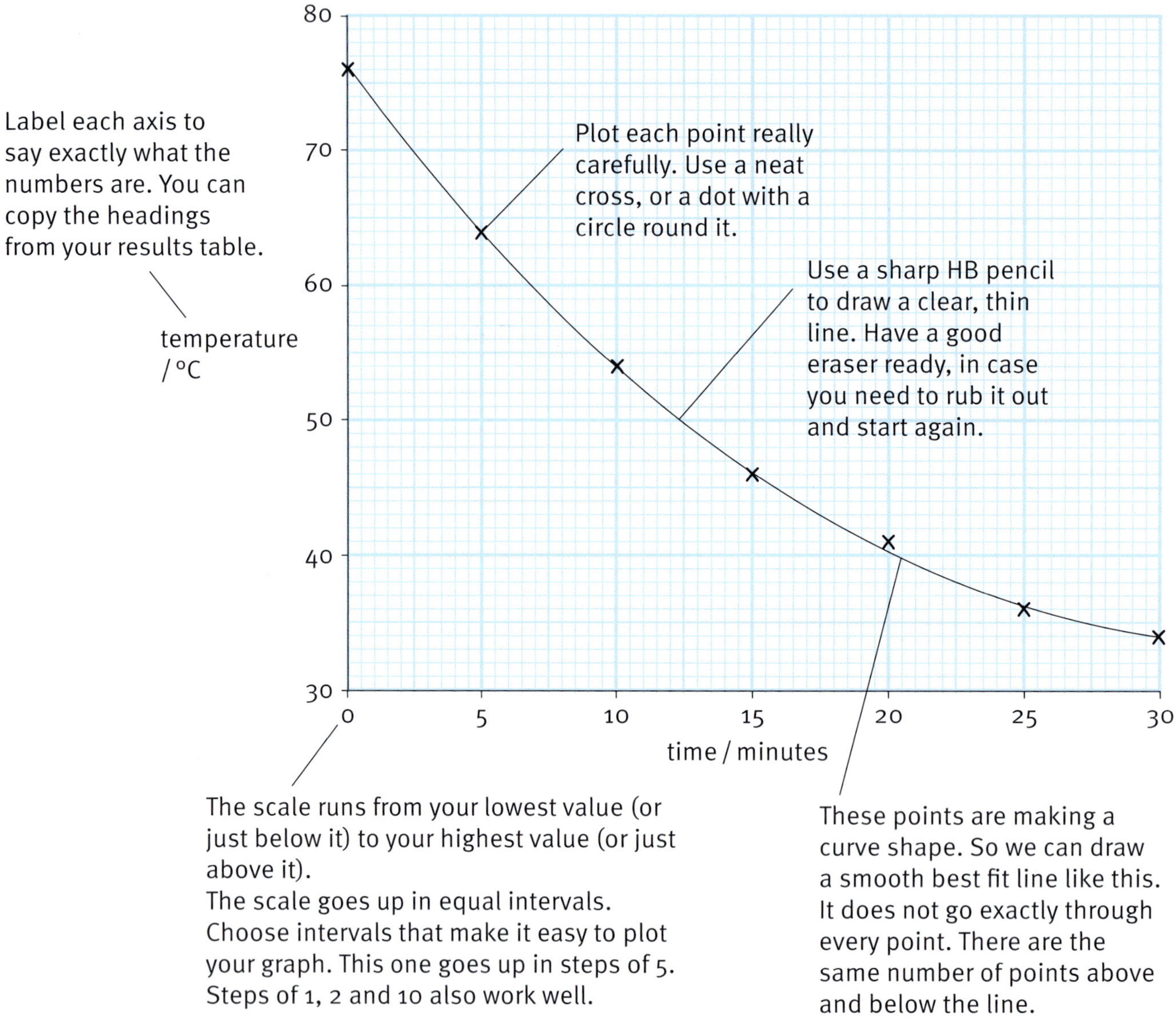

Label each axis to say exactly what the numbers are. You can copy the headings from your results table.

temperature / °C

Plot each point really carefully. Use a neat cross, or a dot with a circle round it.

Use a sharp HB pencil to draw a clear, thin line. Have a good eraser ready, in case you need to rub it out and start again.

time / minutes

The scale runs from your lowest value (or just below it) to your highest value (or just above it).
The scale goes up in equal intervals. Choose intervals that make it easy to plot your graph. This one goes up in steps of 5. Steps of 1, 2 and 10 also work well.

These points are making a curve shape. So we can draw a smooth best fit line like this. It does not go exactly through every point. There are the same number of points above and below the line.

Glossary and index

abrasion wear caused by one rock rubbing against another 117

acid rain rain with a pH much lower than normal rain 44

adaptation a feature of an organism that helps it to survive in its environment 38–39

air resistance the force of friction on an object moving through the air 138–139

algae simple plant-like organisms 22

alkali a substance that contains hydroxide particles, the chemical opposite of an acid 91

antagonistic muscles two muscles that can pull in opposite directions at a joint 15

antennae structures on the head of an arthropod that sense movement or chemicals in the environment 64

antibiotics substances that we can take to kill bacteria inside the body 28

antiseptics substances that can be used to kill micro-organisms on the skin, and surfaces such as a laboratory bench 29

asteroid a small rock in orbit around the Sun, between Mars and Jupiter 174

astronaut a person who travels into space 177

astronomer a person who studies the night sky and the objects in space 162

atmosphere the layer of air around the Earth 176

bacteria microscopic organisms whose cells do not contain a nucleus 22

balanced forces forces acting on an object which cancel each other out 138

blood vessels tubes that carry blood around the body 8

boiling changing from a liquid to gas 75

boiling point the temperature at which a liquid changes to a gas 82

brittle breaks with a snap 82, 84

cartilage a smooth material that covers the ends of bones at a joint 13

cell sap the liquid that fills the large vacuole in a plant cell 30

cell wall a layer of cellulose that surrounds a plant cell 30

cellulose the material that makes up plant cell walls 30

ceramics materials, made from clay and baked at a very high temperature 86

chemical store of energy energy stored in chemical substances 146–147

chlorophyll a green pigment (colouring) found in some plant cells, which absorbs energy from sunlight 6

clay a type of small particle found in soil 105

compressed squeezed into a smaller space 68

condensation changing from a gas to a liquid 72, 76

conductors materials that can transfer heat and/or electricity 81, 82, 84,

conservation caring for the environment 48–49

Glossary and index

constellation a pattern of stars in the night sky — 164

consumer an organism that gets its energy by eating other organisms — 41

contact force the force of one object on another when they touch — 134

continental drift the movement of the continents over the Earth's surface over millions of years — 122

contraction the way that muscles make themselves shorter — 14

core the inner part of the Earth — 122

corrosive able to dissolve or eat away other materials — 90, 91

crust the outer layer of the Earth — 104, 122

cytoplasm the jelly-like substance inside a cell — 30

decay rot; e.g. micro-organisms can cause food to decay — 24

deposition when eroded rock fragments settle — 116

digestion breaking down food into small particles that can be absorbed — 8

ductile can be drawn out into strands or wires — 80, 84

elastic energy energy stored in a stretched or squashed object — 148

electrical energy energy being transferred by electricity — 154

energy something which can be stored and which can be used in order to do things — 144–145

environment everything around an organism that affects it, and that is affected by it — 44

era a length of time in the Earth's history, measured in many millions of years — 124

erosion carrying away fragments of rock by gravity, water and wind — 116

evaporation changing from a liquid to a gas, at a temperature below boiling point — 75

exoskeleton a skeleton on the outside of the body, found in insects and other arthropods — 64

expand to get larger — 75

fibres thin strands of material — 86

filtrate the liquid that comes through a filter paper when you filter a mixture — 99

flexible able to bend easily — 86

food chain a diagram showing how energy passes from one organism to another — 40–41

force a push or a pull — 128–133

forcemeter a scientific instrument used for measuring forces — 131

fossils the remains of plants and animals from millions of years ago — 110, 118–121

freezing changing from a liquid to a solid — 72, 76

friction the force of one object on another when they slide over each other — 136–137

full Moon when the side of the Moon facing the Earth is entirely lit up — 170

fungi organisms such as toadstools and yeast — 22

Glossary and index

galaxy a cluster of billions of stars in space 174

gas matter that can spread out to fill all the space available but can be squashed into a smaller volume 68, 70

gas giants the four planets furthest from the Sun (Jupiter, Saturn, Uranus and Neptune) 167

geocentric model an incorrect picture of the solar system with the Earth at the centre 172

grains small fragments of rock 110

granite a type of igneous rock 104

gravitational potential energy energy stored in an object which has been raised upwards (also called potential energy) 149

gravity the pull of one object on another, which causes weight 134–135

habitat the place where an organism lives 38

haemoglobin a red substance found inside red blood cells, which transports oxygen 34

heat energy energy being transferred from a hot object 154

heliocentric model a picture of the solar system with the Sun at the centre 172

humus the remains and products of living things found in the soil 105, 106

hybrid an organism produced when two organisms belonging to different species breed together 54

igneous rock rock formed when ash or molten magma from inside the Earth cools and becomes solid 108

indicator a substance that changes to a different colour in acid and alkali 92

irritant a substance that will cause itching or sores to your body 90

joint a place where two bones meet 12–13

joule the unit of energy (symbol J) 159

kinetic energy energy of a moving object 152–153

lava molten rock (magma) emerging onto the Earth's surface 109

light energy energy we can see with our eyes 154

limestone a type of sedimentary rock formed from grains of calcium carbonate, from the shells of animals 111

liquid matter that has a fixed volume but takes the shape of its container 68–71

magma molten rock from below the Earth's crust 108

malleable can be easily hammered into shape 80, 84

mantle the layer of molten rock below the crust of the Earth 122

melting changing from a solid to a liquid 72, 75

melting point the temperature at which a solid changes to a liquid 82

meniscus the curve on the surface of a liquid 72

metamorphic rock a type of rock formed when other rocks are subjected to heat and pressure underground 112

meteorites fragments of rock that fall on the Earth from space 123

Glossary and index

Milky Way the galaxy in which the solar system is found   174

minerals substances that make up rock, for example mica and quartz; each mineral is made of one type of chemical   104

molten in a liquid state   108

nerves groups of long cells that carry signals from one part of the body to another   9

neutral a substance that is neither acid nor alkali, is at pH 7   92, 94

neutralisation changing an acid or alkali into a solution at pH 7   96–97

new Moon when the side of the Moon facing the Earth is entirely dark   170

newton the unit of force (symbol N)   132

newtonmeter a scientific instrument used for measuring forces (a forcemeter)   131

non-renewable energy resources energy resources that we are using up faster than they are replaced, e.g. fossil fuels   50

nucleus a part of a cell that contains the chromosomes   30

opaque light cannot pass through it   87

orbit the path of one object around another, for example, the Earth around the Sun   165

organ a part of an organism made up of different tissues, which carries out a particular function   7, 8

organ system a group of organs that carry out a particular function   8–9

organic matter material that has been made by living organisms   24

organism a living thing   7

ozone hole a reduced amount of the gas ozone in the upper atmosphere, over the Antarctic   46–47

particles very small pieces of matter that everything is made up of   69, 70–71, 75–76

period a division of time within an era   124

phase one of the stages in the changing appearance of the Moon   170

planet a large, solid object in orbit around the Sun or another star   166–167

pollution adding harmful things to the environment   44–45

porous allows water to pass through it   110–111

potential energy energy stored in an object   149

principle of conservation of energy the idea that, although energy can change from one form to another, there is always the same total amount; energy cannot disappear, or appear from nowhere   159

producer an organism that uses energy from sunlight to make food; plants are producers   41

properties the features of a material, how it behaves   80–82

protozoa microscopic animal-like organisms   22

pull a force which makes something come towards you   128

push a force which makes something move away from you   128

Glossary and index

renewable energy resources energy resources that will not run out, e.g. wind 51

rocky planets the four planets nearest the Sun (Mercury, Venus, Earth and Mars) 167

root hair cell a cell on the surface of a root that has a long extension for absorbing water and minerals 34

sand a type of large particle found in soil 105

sandstone a type of sedimentary rock formed when grains of sand were pressed together 110

sediment fragments of rocks carried in water, which are dropped when the moving water slows down 110, 116

sedimentary rock rocks formed by layers of sediment being squashed together over millions of years 110–111

solar system the Sun and all the objects which travel around it 166

solid matter that has a fixed shape 68, 71

sound energy energy we can hear with our ears 155

source an object which produces something; for example a star is a source of light 169

species a group of organisms with similar features, that can breed and produce fertile offspring 54

star a giant ball of glowing gas in space; the Sun is a star 168

steam water vapour produced when water boils 72

streamlined describes the shape of an object that has low air resistance 139

stretch to pull something so that it becomes longer 128

synovial fluid a thick fluid that lubricates joints 13

synthetic made by humans, not naturally occurring 86

tectonic plates very large pieces of the Earth's crust that move about very slowly 122

telescope a scientific instrument which uses lenses or mirrors to help us see distant objects 166

tendons strong cords that join muscles to bones 14

theories ideas to explain evidence 69

thermal energy energy stored in a hot object

tissue a group of similar cells that work together to carry out a particular function 35

toxins poisons 28

translucent light can pass through it but you cannot see an object through it 86

transparent light can pass through it and you can see through it easily 86

turn to make something move around or change direction 128

ultraviolet light light that we cannot see, but that can damage skin and eyes 46

Universal Indicator a mixture of different indicators that gives a range of colours in solutions of different pH 94

Universe all the matter and energy that exist 174–175

# Glossary and index

vacuole a liquid-filled space inside a cell   30

variables in an investigation, something that can change   100

variation differences between the individuals belonging to the same species   56–57

vibrate move backwards and forwards repeatedly   70

virus a tiny particle, not made of cells, that can only reproduce inside living cells   28

volume the amount of space taken up by a solid, liquid or gas   68, 72

water vapour water in the form of a gas   72

weathering wear on rocks caused by rain, wind, frost and temperature changes   114–115

weight the force on an object caused by another object's gravity   134–135

Acknowledgements

The authors and publisher are grateful for the permissions granted to reproduce copyright materials. While every effort has been made, it has not always been possible to identify the sources of all the materials used, or to trace all the copyright holders. If any omissions are brought to our notice, we will be happy to include the appropriate acknowledgements on reprinting.

Cover image: Steve Bloom/Alamy; pp. 6, 47t, 47m, 47b, 166bl, 177b NASA.gov; p. 10 Edward Kinsman/SPL; p. 14 ImageState/Alamy; pp. 16t, 176t RIA Novosti/Alamy; p. 16b Sean Bagshaw/SPL; p. 17 University of Durham/Simon Fraser/SPL; p. 20 Steve Bloom Images/Alamy; p. 21t Oleksiy Maksymenko/Alamy; p. 21b David Bowman/Alamy; p. 22t Medical-on-Line/Alamy; p. 22m SPL/Alamy; p. 22b Laguna Design/SPL; p. 23 Guntars Grebezs/iStockphoto; pp. 24, 32t, 48, 56tr, 57, 59, 61, 67bl, 67bm, 67br, 87t, 98t, 130 Geoff Jones; p. 25 Image Source/Alamy; p. 26 Cephas Picture Library/Alamy; p. 27 Simon Belcher/Alamy; p. 28t A. Crump, TDR, WHO, SPL; p. 28b Ray Wilson/Alamy; p. 29 North Wind Pictures/Alamy; pp. 30, 87b, 148t Eleanor Jones; pp. 32b, 109m E. R. Degginger/Alamy; p. 34 Dr Jeremy Burgess/SPL; p. 38 Juniors Bildarchiv/Alamy; p. 39 Steve Bloom Images/Alamy; p. 40 Karl H. Switak/SPL; p. 41 Juniors Bildarchiv/Oxford Scientific Press; p. 42t DPK-Photo/Alamy; p. 42m Eye Ubiquitous/Alamy; pp. 42b, 49t Nigel Cattlin/Alamy; p. 43t Dr P. Marazzi/SPL; p. 43b Tony Camacho/SPL; p. 44t John Brown/Alamy; p. 44b David Dorey – India Collection/Alamy; p. 45 BrazilPhotos.com/Alamy; p. 46 Nick Hanna/Alamy; p. 49b Paula Solloway/Alamy; p. 54t Aterra Picture Library/Alamy; p. 54m Bill Brooks/Alamy; p. 54b Boaz Rottem/Alamy; p. 55 Cornforth Images/Alamy; p. 56tl Carolyn A. Mckeone/SPL; p. 56b Blend Images/Alamy; p.67tl Andrew Walmsley/Naturepl; p. 67tr Andrew Walmsley/Alamy; pp. 69, 94 Gustoimages/SPL; p. 80tl Images of Africa Photobank/Alamy; p. 80tr Penny Tweedie/Alamy; p. 80ml LOOK Die Bildagentur der Fotografen GmbH/Alamy; p. 80mr Jeff J Daly/Alamy; p. 80bl Sally McCrae Kuyper/SPL; p. 80br James Holmes/SPL; pp. 82l, 84r, 83l, 91, 98m, 111r, 147t Andrew Lambert Photography/SPL; p. 82ml Photostock-Israel/SPL; p. 82mr Chris Martin-Bahr/SPL; p. 83r TEK Image/SPL; p. 84 Alain Machet (3)/Alamy; p. 86 Ted Foxx/Alamy; p. 90 Sciencephotos/Alamy; p. 97 Martyn F. Chillmaid/SPL; p. 98b Claire Deprez/Reporters/SPL; p. 102 GeoPic/Alamy; p. 104l Imagebroker/Alamy; pp. 104tm, 112mr, 112bl, 112br, 114bl, 114br Geoscience Features Picture Library; p. 104r Michael St. Maur Sheil/Corbis; p. 105 Blickwinkel/Alamy; p. 106 Dan Roitner/Alamy; p. 107 Fire Pig Images/Alamy; p. 108t Sciencesphotos/Alamy; p. 108b Susan E Degginger; p. 109t The Natural History Museum/Alamy; p. 110 Phil Degginger/Alamy; p. 111l David Cantrille/Alamy; p. 112t Arco Images GmbH/Images; p. 112ml George Bernard/SPL; p. 113l G. Brad Lewis/SPL; p. 113r Tom Bean/Alamy; p. 114t Martin Bond/SPL; p. 115t John Kellerman/Alamy; p. 115bl Richard Broadwell/Alamy; p. 115br Geogphotos Film/Alamy; p. 116t Wildscape/Alamy; p. 116mt Nagelestock.com/Alamy, p. 116mb Westend61 GmbH/Alamy; p. 115b Michael Bussell/Corbis; p. 117 Peter Stone/Alamy; p. 118t Carver Mostardi/Alamy; p. 118b Reimar 5/Alamy; pp. 119l, 119r Sabena Jane Blackbird/Alamy; p. 119m Red Square Photography/Alamy; p. 121 Natural Visions/Alamy; p. 123 Prisma Bildagentur AG/Alamy; p. 124 Ludek Pesek/SPL; p. 128 Robert Harding Picture Library Ltd/Alamy; p. 135 NASA Charles M. Duke Jr.; p. 138t Forget Patrick/Sagaphoto.com/Alamy; p. 138b Nicholas Bergkessel, Jr./SPL; p. 139t Wolstenholme Images/Alamy; p. 139b Ria Novosti/SPL; 140 Erich Schrempp/SPL; p. 144t Juice Images/Alamy; p. 144b dbimages/Alamy; p. 145 Robert Estall Photo Agency/Alamy; p. 146 Chris Pearsall/Alamy; p. 147m Charles D. Winters/SPL; p. 147b Silvere Teutsch/Eurelios/SPL; p. 148b Blend Images/Alamy; p. 149 Barry Mason/Alamy; p. 150 Tony McConnell/SPL; p. 151 J Marshall – Tribaleye Images/Alamy; p. 154t Jeremy Horner/Corbis; p. 154b D. Hurst/Alamy; p. 155 Redsnapper/Alamy; p. 156 David R. Frazier/SPL; p. 158 Joseph Nettis/SPL; p. 159 World History Archive/Alamy; p. 162 Mike Harrington/Alamy; p. 164 David Nunuk/SPL; pp. 166tl, 166mtr US Geological Survey/SPL; pp. 166tr, 166mbl, 168 NASA/SPL; p. 166mtl MDA Information Systems/SPL; 166mbr Detlev Van Ravenswaay/SPL; 116br JPL/NASA/SPL; p. 170 John Sanford/SPL; p. 172t Royal Astronomical Society/SPL; p. 172b North Wind Picture Archives/Alamy; p. 173 SPL; pp. 174t, 176b Photri Images/Alamy; p. 173m Lynette Cook/SPL; p. 173b Harvard College Observatory/SPL; p. 175 Emilio Segre Visual Archives/American Institute of Physics/SPL; p. 177t Dennis Hallinan/Alamy.

SPL = Science Photo Library, l = left, r = right, t = top, b = bottom, m = middle

Typesetting and illustration by Greenhill Wood Studios www.greenhillwoodstudios.com

The publisher would like to thank Beverly Nash for reviewing the content.